Lucy Breckinridge of Grove Hill

A tintype taken at Grove Hill in 1858. Standing, left to right: Eliza Breckinridge, Lucy Breckinridge, Kate Oden, Emma Breckinridge; seated, left to right: Miss Oden (tutor) and Jennie Whittle.

Lucy Breckinridge

of
L Grove Hill B

The Journal of a Virginia Girl

1862-1864

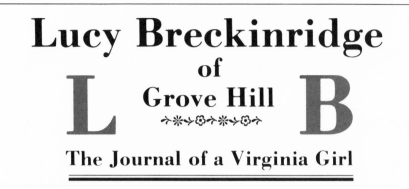

Edited by Mary D. Robertson

The Kent State University Press

Parts of this journal appeared in *Civil War History*, Vol. 23, No. 1 (March 1977)

Copyright © 1979 by The Kent State University Press, Kent, Ohio 44242
First paperback edition 1981. Second printing 1988
All rights reserved
Library of Congress Catalog Card Number 79-88609
ISBN: 87338-234-X
ISBN: 87338-266-8 (pbk)
Designed by Robert Szabo
Manufactured in the United States of America

Library of Congress Cataloging in Publication Data

Breckinridge, Lucy, b. 1865
    Lucy Breckinridge of Grove Hill.

    Bibliography: p.
    Includes index.
    1. Breckinridge, Lucy, b. 1865. 2. Grove Hill,
Va. 3. Plantation life—Virginia—Sources.
4.Botetourt Co., Va.—Biography. 5. Virginia—
History—Civil War, 1861-1865—Sources.
I. Robertson, Mary D. II. Title.
F234.G816B733   975.5'83   [B]   79-88609
ISBN: 0-87338-234-X
ISBN: 0-87338-266-8 (pbk)

To
Mason, Mary Lynn,
Bill, Susan,
and All
the Breckinridge Progeny

Contents

1863

1864

Foreword

A reading of recent monographs on the history of the South and of Southern women in particular should disabuse us of the notion that the "Southern Lady" was much more than a fantasy similar to the romanticized idea of womanhood that abetted their subjugation. In addition, the recent, and not so recent, publication of diaries, letters, and memoirs of Southern women leads us inevitably to the conclusion that within the bonds established for them, they often were perceptive analysts of their society. They understood that a pedestal was and was meant to be a prison.

Lucy Breckinridge was a Southern lady, a daughter of an old-line Virginia family, and at first glance almost stereotypical. But upon reading her journal of the Civil War years we find that she understood very well that her lot, as a woman, was less than perfect. Passages in her journal reveal a sensitive, intelligent, and, perhaps necessarily, pessimistic young woman. She loved her family, her brothers in the Confederate army, her parents, sisters, cousins, and servants. And she despised the war even if she might have justified it.

A careful reading of her journal reveals much more. In spite of her strongly held family feelings, and in spite of her sense of place, she understood and recorded the state that women even of her social station endured.

At a later date, or had she lived in a different environment, she might have been a feminist, a crusader for the rights of women. She was not part of a political movement, but a lonely voice. Had she lived longer perhaps she would have recognized in other women the same misgivings and resentments. It may be a commentary on her time to note that she confided only, or mainly, in her diary.

Indeed, she did not seem to see the place of women as a matter of social or political arrangements. Rather, it was a matter of innate differences, of natural differences between men and women. Of course, it is a rare person who at an early age recognizes that social systems produce "innate differences."

We can only surmise the resentment she may have harbored over the fact that she was expected to defer to men—father, brothers, fiancé and husband, or even family friends—who may or may not have been her equal, especially in matters of the mind. She wanted to love her husband but resigned herself (perhaps feared) that given the course of events, he would not love her in the same manner or with the same depth. This was not the meanderings of a romantic girl; it was the pessimistic conclusion of an intelligent woman who understood her society. She did not hate men, they simply disappointed her. The disappointment was not selfish, and her conclusions were not applied universally. She recognized that her brother grieved at the death of his young wife and that her father held her mother in the highest regard. But her general views were not altered by such recognition. Her lot, and that of women like her, was one of denial. Given the chance she knew that she could be a scholar, a manager, even a soldier. Her frustration is almost palpable in passage after passage.

We might guess that because of her tragic, early death (itself a melancholy commentary on her times) that her frustration did not become bitterness. Within the bounds imposed upon her she had resolved to better herself, to improve her mind, and not least to become a model wife and mother. She would marry her lieutenant, her Tommy, and would address herself to his well being. Call it duty, call it resignation—we can only admire Lucy Breckinridge.

We can also admire Mary Robertson's sensitive and scholarly editing of this journal. And we can sympathize with Ms. Robertson's open and refreshing respect for her subject. As a historical source, the journal compares favorably with other, more famous, collections such as *Diary from Dixie* and *Children of Pride*. It is also a touching portrait of a young woman beset by doubts about herself, doubts that are universal in application. It may seem almost an intrusion to read these pages, but we can excuse ourselves on the grounds that as we grow to understand Lucy Breckinridge, we come to understand better ourselves and our history.

John T. Hubbell

Preface

Lucy Gilmer Breckinridge of Grove Hill was only eighteen years old when the war began. Before this tragic conflict ended, five Breckinridge brothers had joined the Confederate forces in defense of Virginia. Time passed slowly for the Breckinridge women who remained at home to watch and wait. Lucy began keeping a journal in the summer of 1862 to assuage the boredom of wartime when there were "no visitors to receive and no visits to pay, no materials to work upon and no inclination to read anything but the Bible and the newspapers." Lucy's journal is not merely a chronicle of the crucial events of the war, but is also an intimate and trenchant critique of Southern society as viewed by an intelligent, introspective young woman. As a spectator of society, Lucy often exhibited an amazingly detached objectivity which permitted her to transcend the limits of her own era, giving the journal a timeless quality. At other times Lucy's percipience was limited by her own role as a participant in her society. It is this artfully written amalgam of *insightful* wisdom and child-like naïveté that embues Lucy's journal with a special quality above and beyond its value as an historical work.

The original manuscript of the *Journal,* now in my possession, was written in an old ledger book, its inner covers adorned with favorite poems, sayings and special happenings, and inscribed "Lucy G. Breckinridge, Grove Hill, August 11th, 1862." Although its pages are brittle and yellowed and the ink faded to a pale brown, the manuscript is remarkably well preserved. The journal entries, written in Lucy's fine hand, are, for the most part, amazingly legible.

The task of transcribing, researching, and annotating the journal of this remarkable young woman has been a total fascination for me over the past four years. I must confess to an occasional loss of scholarly objectivity as I became privy to Lucy's innermost thoughts and feelings about herself, her family and loved ones; her doubts and apprehensions about the "cruel war," love, marriage, religion, and her own role as a woman. More than once I fancied myself her "blue-eyed fidus Achates"! I was deeply moved by Lucy's expressions of joy and sadness; I empathized with her feelings of self-doubt and self-reproach; shared her frustrations as an intelligent woman in a male-dominated society in which marriage represented a severe curtailment of her freedom; applauded her strength and courage in the face of tragedy and danger; admired her wit and culture; and experienced an acute sense of loss upon learning of her death.

Lucy's journal has been reproduced with as few alterations as possible in order to retain the historical flavor and authenticity of the original manuscript. In almost every instance, Lucy's spelling, capitalization, use of dashes, incomplete sentences, and punctuation have been followed. The words she underlined for emphasis have been italicized, and her liberal use of exclamation marks has been faithfully reproduced. Minor changes to correct errors in punctuation, spelling, and dates have been made in the original text only when deemed necessary for the sake of clarity. To make the original manuscript more readable, I have divided the journal into chapters for each of the three years, and selected chapter titles in keeping with the mood of the author and the spirit of the times. Notes regarding persons, places, literary works, and military events have been provided for the sake of explication and to present the journal in its historical setting.

Publication of this edited work represents the fulfillment of a promise made to my husband, Mason Gordon Robertson, when, following the death of his parents, he rescued several cartons of family papers from consignment to the trash heap. Among the many family letters and documents was the Civil War journal of his great-great-aunt, Lucy Gilmer Breckinridge.

Some forty years ago my husband's father, William Joseph Robertson, a journalist-scholar, began work on the journal. Although he never completed his task, Mr. Robertson transcribed and annotated the greater part of the first year's entries. Numerous copies of his work have been disseminated among the Breckinridge progeny. The genealogical notes of "Judge" Robertson have been extremely helpful to me in identifying many individuals mentioned in the first year of Lucy's journal.

It would be impossible to mention here all of the many individuals who have contributed to the completion of this book. My research efforts were made easier by the assistance of the staff members at the following institutions and organizations: the Library at Duke University; the Library at the University of Virginia; the Library at Virginia Military Institute; the Library at Hollins College; the Library of Congress; the National Archives; the Botetourt County Court House; the Roanoke Valley Historical Society; the Roanoke Public Library; the Library at Armstrong State College, with special thanks to Susie Chirbis, David Evans, and Ruth Swinson; the Savannah Public Library, especially Catherine Nathan of the Reference Department; and Joyce Pelkemeyer, Assistant Librarian at the Nancy Carol Roberts Memorial Library in Brenham, Texas, who helped me with research regarding the Bassett family.

I am very appreciative of the patience and support of my colleagues in the History and Political Science Department at Armstrong State College over the past five years, especially for the encouragement of my department chairman, Dr. Roger K. Warlick, and for the friendship, advice and counsel of Dr. Janet D. Stone, Dr. Jimmie F. Gross, and Dr. Robert L. Patterson; and for the kindness of Dr. John D. Duncan for making available to me books from his personal library. To Diane Wagner, department secretary, and dear friend, I am indebted for favors too numerous to mention.

Former students, Christine Britt, Beth Ford, and my daughter, Susan Robertson, contributed time and energy above and beyond the call of research assistants in helping to complete the manuscript. To Barbara Hardwig, who took the time to befriend a total stranger one snowy Sunday in Salem, Virginia, go my heartfelt thanks. I am also indebted to Mrs. Katherine Hutcheson of Savannah, Georgia, for sharing with me her reminiscences of Fincastle, Virginia.

Many Breckinridge family members have been of immeasurable assistance to me in my research efforts. I wish to thank particularly Jean Staples Showalter for sharing with me over the years her knowledge, energy, and ideas. Jan and George St. John have been most helpful in providing valuable contacts, identifying photographs, and sharing family papers. I am also indebted to Jim Robertson, Lindsay Robertson, Lomax Breckinridge, Miss Anne Breckinridge, Anne Larson, and Mrs. Jane Bryan for their aid.

I am greatly indebted to Dr. John T. Hubbell, Editor of *Civil War History*, for his consistent interest in my work, his encouragement, advice, and counsel over a period of several years.

To my dear family I owe a great debt of gratitude for cheerfully sharing our home with Lucy for the past five years. I wish to thank my husband, Mason, without whom this book would never have been conceived, for his sense of history and unflagging support of my research; my daughter, Mary Lynn, for her pride in and encouragement of my work; my son, Bill, an author in his own right, for helping me think through some of the rough spots; and my daughter, Susan, my scribe, research assistant and traveling companion.

Prologue

At the southernmost part of the Great Valley of Virginia lies the quiet, old village of Fincastle, seat of Botetourt County. The history of Botetourt dates back more than two hundred years when, in 1770, Augusta County was subdivided to create a new county. This offspring was named in honor of the colonial governor of Virginia, Norborne Berkeley, Lord Botetourt, and in 1772, its county seat was named after Governor Dunmore's son, Viscount Fincastle.

In its early days, Botetourt County spread over a vast area that stretched from the crests of the Blue Ridge and Allegheny Mountains westward to the Mississippi River, and included Kentucky, parts of Ohio, Indiana, Illinois, and Wisconsin. Prior to the Revolutionary War, Botetourt had the distinction of being the only county in the Mississippi Valley, and Fincastle became a gateway for the expeditions into the southwestern wilderness. In 1772 Fincastle County was carved out of Botetourt, and a further subdivision in 1777 gave rise to Greenbrier County. During the Revolutionary War, Fincastle County was subdivided into Kentucky, Montgomery, and Washington counties.[1] By the 1830s the frontier village of Fincastle had become a bustling, prosperous town with a newspaper, numerous business and industrial enterprises, established churches, and schools. The lands adjacent to Fincastle were dotted with several landed estates and a number of small farms.

1. Robert Douthat Stoner, *A Seed-Bed of the Republic*, p. 40.

'Lucy Gilmer Breckinridge's ancestral roots were deeply embedded in the fertile hills and valleys that surrounded the town of Fincastle. The Breckinridge family history is closely tied to the history of Botetourt. Lucy's great-grandfather, Robert Breckinridge, commissioned by George III in 1769 as one of Botetourt's first colonial justices, held the first session of court in his home. Lucy's grandfather, James, third son of Robert Breckinridge and Letitia Preston, became Deputy Clerk of the court at age nineteen, following service in the Revolutionary War under the commands of his uncle, Colonel William Preston of "Greenfield" and General Nathanael Greene. Young James Breckinridge pursued his academic studies at Washington College (now Washington and Lee University), and graduated from William and Mary College in 1785. He studied law under one of the great legal minds of his day, George Wythe, who numbered among his students such political leaders as Thomas Jefferson and John Marshall. Shortly after completion of his legal training, Breckinridge was admitted to the bar and established a law office in the town of Fincastle.[2]

James Breckinridge's political career was launched in 1789 when he was elected a member of the Virginia House of Delegates, a post he held intermittently for thirteen sessions. Judge Thomas D. Houston in 1873 described him as "the noblest Roman of them all. At the local bar, he had no equal, as a local politician, no superior." This frontier patriot and statesman served, also, in the Eleventh United States Congress and three succeeding Congresses (4 March 1809 to 3 March 1817).[3] His term of office was interrupted temporarily when he responded to a call to serve in the War of 1812 as a brigadier general.

Although General Breckinridge's political affiliation was with the Federalist party, he was a friend and associate of Thomas Jefferson. It was Thomas Jefferson who sent plans to General Breckinridge in 1818 for the construction of the second Botetourt County Court House. It was James Breckinridge who

2. General Breckinridge's law office, located in the Court House Complex in Fincastle, Virginia, was restored in 1972 by the General James Breckinridge Chapter of the DAR.

3. *Biographical Dictionary of the American Congress 1774-1961*, p. 591.

gave legislative support to Jefferson's plans for establishing the University of Virginia. He served on the commission to select the building site for the University and later on its first Board of Visitors. It is also interesting to note that Thomas Jefferson commissioned Francis Walker Gilmer, Lucy Gilmer Breckinridge's maternal great-uncle, to recruit the first faculty for the new university.[4]

As Botetourt prospered, so did the Breckinridge family fortunes. James Breckinridge had, by the nineteenth century, become the county's most active, influential, and prominent citizen. He was eminently successful as a land speculator and by 1804 his land holdings included some 4,000 acres. James Breckinridge married Anne Selden of Elizabeth City County, Virginia, in 1791, and shortly thereafter began construction of the elegant family home, Grove Hill. The site chosen for the Breckinridge manor house was a grassy knoll overlooking the fertile hills and valleys of the surrounding countryside, with a magnificent view of the distant mountains. Built in the architecturally fashionable Federal style of the period, Grove Hill, with its high ceilings, broad "passages" or halls, elegantly furnished rooms (twenty-six in number, most of which were heated by fireplaces), and handsome, Flemish-bonded brick exterior, was considered the most impressive home in the environs of Fincastle. Located along the route to the popular springs of Virginia, Grove Hill offered gracious hospitality to many of Virginia's most distinguished families. It was not uncommon for the Breckinridge family to entertain overnight as many as fifty people at Grove Hill. Among its most illustrious visitors were Thomas Jefferson, James Madison, Patrick Henry, James Monroe, and Edmund Randolph.

In 1804 James Breckinridge petitioned the Botetourt County Court for permission to build a dam on Catawba Creek in order to provide power for a grist mill. Catawba Mill, built largely by slave labor, and later run by slaves, operated successfully for many years in the manufacture of corn meal and graham flour.

---

4. Among the documents found with Lucy's journal were Jefferson and Gilmer papers pertaining to the founding of the University of Virginia. These papers were given by the family to the University, and have been placed in the Jefferson Collection.

The Breckinridges were without a doubt among Botetourt's most affluent and respected citizens.

Lucy's father, Cary, was the eldest son of General Breckinridge and Anne Selden. In 1831, shortly after Cary's marriage to Emma Walker Gilmer of Bedford County, Virginia, General Breckinridge began construction of Catawba, a home for the young couple modeled after Grove Hill. It was at Catawba, located a mile and a half southwest of Grove Hill on Catawba Mountain, that six of Cary Breckinridge and Emma Walker Gilmer's children were born (the eldest and the two youngest were born at Grove Hill).

When General Breckinridge died in 1833, a codicil to his will, dated 10 May 1833, left "the land on which I live" to his two surviving sons, Cary and John. John, the younger brother, received the lower part and Cary, the upper part. Following the death of his mother in 1843 and the death of his brother in 1844, Cary moved his young family into Grove Hill. It was here that Lucy Gilmer Breckinridge lived all but one year of her life, and here that she commenced keeping a journal in 1862.

Lucy's father, Cary Breckinridge, a large, taciturn man, received his education at William and Mary College, was made a Justice of Botetourt County in 1822; and in 1849 was appointed county sheriff by a commission from the Governor. A reserved, private man, Lucy's father devoted his energies to management of the Grove Hill estate rather than to the pursuit of a more public role as a lawyer and politician.

The "golden decade" of the 1850s was a profitable one for Grove Hill. The Breckinridge lands produced tobacco, corn, and other vegetables and fruits, and the livestock provided meat, eggs, and other necessities for family consumption. Catawba Mill continued to operate successfully in the manufacture of meal and flour as it served the needs of Grove Hill and the area farms. By the middle of the nineteenth century, the total slave population of Virginia was 472,528. According to the census schedule Botetourt County had 3,737 slaves. Cary Breckinridge was the second largest slaveholder with 131 slaves, and only four farmers in the county had more than 50 slaves.[5]

5. From the 1850 Slave Census, Botetourt County, Virginia, taken on 15 September 1850. A decade later, Cary Breckinridge was the largest slaveholder in the county with a total of 149 slaves.

Management of the large estate consumed the greatest part of Cary Breckinridge's time and interest, and by 1862, according to county court house records, the total value of Grove Hill including lands and buildings was listed at $28,314 and Catawba Mill at $33,270.

Cary Breckinridge's preoccupation with the farm and the mill placed the responsibility for the management of the domestic economy of Grove Hill squarely on the shoulders of his wife, Emma Walker, eleven years his junior. She was, indeed, "mistress, manager, doctor, nurse, counsellor, seamstress, teacher, housekeeper, slave, all at once."[6] Not only was she required everywhere, but her presence also permeated every aspect of life at Grove Hill. Emma Walker is described in Letitia (Letty) Burwell's *A Girl's Life in Virginia Before the War*, as possessing "A cultivated mind, bright conversational powers, and gentle temper, with a force of character which enabled her judiciously to direct the affairs of her household, as well as the training and education of her children."[7]

Journal references to Lucy's father are infrequent and distant. He is characterized as a man of stern mold, a typical Southern patriarch of declining years. It is Lucy's mother who emerges from the pages of the journal as the mainstay of the Breckinridge family. Lucy's references to her mother are warm, loving, and embued with respect and admiration: "We miss Ma so much. The house seems so quiet and desolate when she is away. There never was such a sweet, loving Mamma as ours."

The mistress of Grove Hill was not only the keystone of the domestic economy but also of the entire Breckinridge clan. She maintained Grove Hill's tradition of culture and hospitality during the exigencies of war. Grove Hill became a haven for distant friends and relatives, Confederate officers, visiting ministers, and wounded soldiers, as well as a manufactory for bandages and clothing for the Confederate army. It was Emma Walker's quiet strength that directed and sustained the Breckinridge family throughout the tragic war years.

It was not until 17 April 1861, following the firing on Fort Sumter, South Carolina, and President Lincoln's call for troops, that the Virginia Convention passed a secession ordi-

6. Thomas Nelson Page, *The Old South, Essays Social & Political*, pp. 154–55.
7. Letitia Burwell, *A Girl's Life in Virginia Before the War*, p. 84.

nance. Lucy's oldest brother, Peachy Gilmer, had run as a candidate in the election of 4 February 1861 for delegates to the state convention. In a campaign statement to the voters of Botetourt and Craig counties, Gilmer had questioned whether slavery was worth the price of Union, and suggested that "he who raises his hand against the Constitution of the United States which he is sworn to defend, will not be a reliable man even in a slave confederacy." Gilmer ended his lengthy statement with a moving appeal for Union: " . . . let us gather as a band of brothers, and raising high our 'Star Spangled Banner' so that naught from the devouring element may sully its brightness, cry now and forever, not only Union is strength, but Union is ours!" Gilmer was not elected to the convention, but shortly after Virginia seceded he and three of his brothers responded to the call for troops and enlisted in the Confederate army. Gilmer entered the war not as a secessionist but as a unionist fighting to protect the rights of his mother state.

The only men in the family to remain at Grove Hill were Lucy's father, age 65, and younger brother, George, age 14. Cary Breckinridge, although too old to serve, played a significant role in the war by financing and equipping a company of Confederate cavalry. George, feeling his honor was at stake, finally persuaded his parents to permit him to join the army during the last year of the war.

Grove Hill, located southwest of the major military operations of the Valley campaign, survived the war years relatively unscathed. Life for those remaining at home was, for the most part, peaceful, marred only by the inexorable anxieties and tragedies of wartime. For the women at Grove Hill the days were spent sewing clothing, making bandages, caring for the sick and wounded, reading, praying, and anxiously awaiting news of their loved ones.

Lucy's journal represents an uninhibited and unique perception of Southern plantation society in its terminal years. Unlike Mary Chesnut, Kate Stone, and Eliza Frances Andrews, Lucy made no revisions of her journal entries. Eliza Frances Andrews, editing her diary fifty years later, admittedly had mutilated the manuscript in some places to delete entries "considered too personal for other eyes than her own."[8]

The highly personal nature of Lucy's entries affords the reader a candid view of Southern society. Her journal became her confidante, the receptacle of her most intimate thoughts and feelings about her world and her place in it. Lucy's journal, therefore, is not merely a chronicle of events, but, rather, a stereoscopic picture of Southern society as viewed by a perceptive, highly literate daughter of the landed gentry during a momentous period of history.

The portrait of Lucy that emerges from the pages of her journal is that of an attractive, cultured, witty, strong-willed, courageous, and sometimes capricious young woman struggling to understand herself, her world, and her God. Her bright and inquisitive mind, fed by an insatiable literary appetite, grappled with such diverse subjects as the war, slavery, religion, politics, love, and marriage.

Although conditioned by the conservatism of the patriarchal, slave society of the South into which she was born, Lucy often expressed ambivalent feelings regarding the traditional male-female roles. "It is woman's nature to love in a submissive, trusting way," she wrote on one occasion, "but it is better and safer to rely altogether upon themselves—poor creatures! God help them!"

The disclamatory tone of many of Lucy's commentaries regarding woman's role might, in a different era, have placed her in the front ranks of the woman's movement. Lucy's unorthodox thoughts and feelings, however, found expression only on the pages of her journal. Perhaps because she considered some of her entries "too personal for other eyes than her own," Lucy planned to destroy her journal shortly after her marriage. Fate contravened, however, and the "old journal survived to tell its story to future generations yet unborn."

---

8. Spencer Bidwell King, Jr., ed., *The War-Time Journal of a Georgia Girl, Eliza Frances Andrews*, p. 5.

Principal Characters Mentioned
in
the Journal

The Breckinridge Family:

Captain Cary Breckinridge (*"PAPA"*)
> owner of Grove Hill, was the father of Lucy Gilmer
> Breckinridge.

Emma Walker Gilmer Breckinridge (*"MAMMA"*)
> wife of Cary Breckinridge, was the mother of Lucy
> Gilmer Breckinridge.

Their Children:

Mary Ann Breckinridge (*"SISTER"*)
> married *Dr. James Lewis Woodville* (Brother Lewis)
> and was the mother of *"Little" Emma,*
> *Jimmy, Cary, Mary,* and *Fanny.*

Peachy Gilmer Breckinridge (*BROTHER GILMER*)
> married *Julia Anthony* (Sister Julia), of
> Lynchburg, Virginia, and had two children,
> *"Nannie"* and *"Little" Johnny.*

James Breckinridge (*BROTHER JAMES*)
> married *Fanny Burwell* (Fan) of Liberty (Bedford
> City), Virginia.

Cary Breckinridge (*THE MAJOR*)
> married *Virginia Caldwell* (Jennie), of
> Greenbrier County, Virginia, in 1866.

Eliza Breckinridge
> remained unmarried and lived on at Grove
> Hill after the war.

Lucy Gilmer Breckinridge
> author of the *Journal*, married *Thomas
> Jefferson Bassett* ("Tommy") in 1865.

John Breckinridge (*JOHNNY*)
> died in 1862, at the age of 17, in the Battle of
> Seven Pines.

Emma Jane Breckinridge (*"BIG" EMMA*)
> youngest of the Breckinridge sisters, remained
> unmarried, and lived on at Grove Hill after the war.

George Breckinridge
> youngest of the Breckinridge brothers, was
> only fifteen when Lucy began keeping her *Journal*.
> He married twice, first Anne Hamner and
> then Letitia Maurin St. Martin.

Relatives and Friends:

Robert J. Breckinridge, Jr. (*COUSIN ROBERT*)
> of Lexington, Kentucky, was a Colonel in
> the Confederate army and a member of the
> Confederate Congress. He married *Kate Morrison*
> (Cousin Kate), and had a son, *"Little Robbie."*

Fannie Burwell (*MISS FANNIE*)
> of Liberty (Bedford City), Virginia, was an aunt
> of James Breckinridge's wife, Fan.

Jordan Anthony
> an uncle of Gilmer's wife, Julia, was president
> of a small bank in Buchanan, Virginia. His home,
> The Bank, is frequently mentioned in the
> *Journal*.

Deborah Couch (*MISS DEBORAH*)
> a close friend of Jordan Anthony's for forty
> years, was a frequent visitor at The Bank, and
> at Grove Hill.

Lulie Meredith
> The wife of Dr. Samuel Meredith, and daughter
> of Henry Bowyer and his first wife, Sarah
> Preston, former mistress of East Greenfield.

Mrs. Thomas M. Bowyer (*KATE*)
> formerly Catherine Burwell of Liberty (Bedford
> City), Virginia, married Lulie's brother and
> was current mistress of East Greenfield.

Mr. and Mrs. William M. Burwell
> of Avenel, Bedford County, Virginia, were
> the parents of James Breckinridge's wife,
> Fan. *Rosa* and *Letty Burwell* were Fan's sisters.

Elizabeth Breckinridge Watts (*AUNT WATTS*)
> Captain Cary Breckinridge's sister, was married
> to General Edward Watts of Oaklands,
> Roanoke County, Virginia.

Peachy Harmer Gilmer (*UNCLE HARMER*)
> of Soldier's Joy, Nelson County, Virginia,
> was the brother of Lucy's mother, and was married
> to *Isabel Walker* (Aunt Belle). They were
> the parents of *Walker*.

Mrs. H. M. Bowyer (*AUNT MATILDA*)
> was Captain Cary Breckinridge's sister,
> and was married to *H. M. Bowyer* (Uncle Bowyer)
> of Fincastle, Virginia.

Captain David Gardiner Houston ("*CAPT. H.*")
> a native of Botetourt County, was a childhood
> acquaintance of Lucy Breckinridge, and was
> briefly engaged to Lucy during 1862.

Dr. George Woodbridge
> rector of Monumental Church in Richmond,
> Virginia, was a great-grandson of Jonathan
> Edwards, the famous theologian and philospher.
> Dr. Woodbridge's son was Jonathan Edwards
> Woodbridge, the "*Eddie*" mentioned in the
> *Journal*.

Annie and Mary Wilmer
> were the daughters of *Rev. George T. Wilmer*
> (Uncle Wilmer) and Lucy's maternal aunt,
> Peachy. The *Aunt Marianna* mentioned in
> the *Journal* was his second wife.

Sallie Grattan
> of Richmond, Virginia, was Lucy's cousin
> and close friend.

Mr. Breckinridge Cabell, his daughters,
the Misses **Marian, Betty, Sallie,** and **Kate,**

10

and his son, **John J. Cabell**
> lived at Foston, a small home on the Grove
> Hill lands.

Grove Hill Servants:

Uncle Phil
Joe
Jim
Susan
Virginia
Matilda
Strother
Dolly
Nelson
Joshua

Dr. George Gilmer 1742-1796	Thomas Gilmer 1772-1791	Lucy Gilmer 1774 died in infancy	Mildred Gilmer 1773-1799	Dr. Georg Gilmer 1778-183
M.				
Lucy Walker 1751-1800			Hon. William Wirt	Elizabeth Hudson

		William Wirt Gilmer 1804-?	George Henry Gilmer 1810-?	Emma Wal Gilmer 1807-189
			M.	M.
			Jane Preston	Cary Breckinri 1796-186

Emma Woodville
James L. Woodville
Cary B. Woodville
Mary L. Woodville
Fanny B. Woodville
Oliver B. Woodville

Mary Ann Breckinridge 1831-1883	Peachy Gilmer Breckinridge 1835-1864	James Breckinridge 1837-1865	Cary Breckinric 1839-191
M.	M.	M.	M.
James Lewis Woodville	Julia Anthony	Fanny Burwell	Virginia Caldwel

Ann Anthony Breckinridge
M.
Judge William Gordon Robertson
John Gilmer Breckinridge

Col. Robert Breckinridge died 1772	William Breckinridge	Preston Breckinridge	Gen. James Breckinridge 1763-1833	Elizabeth Breckinric
M.	M.	M.	M.	M.
Letitia Preston	Miss Gilham	Elizabeth Trigg	Anne Selden died 1843	Col. Samuel Mer

		Elizabeth Breckinridge 1784-1862	Letitia Breckinridge	Mary An Breckinric
		M.	M.	
		Gen. Edward Watts 1779-1859	Col. Robert Gamble	

Emma Watts
Col. George Carr
Henrietta Watts
Robertson (2nd)
Judge William Joseph
Dr. George Morris (1st)
Alice Watts
Dr. Francis Sorrell (2nd)
Dr. Landon Rives (1st)
Letitia Watts
Edward Watts
Thomas S. Preston
Elizabeth Watts
G. P. Holcombe
M.
Anne Selden Watts
M.
Col. William Watts
James B. Gamble
M.
Mary S. Watts
James Watts

chy Ridgeway **Gilmer** *1779-1836*	Dr. John Gilmer *1782-1835*	James Blair Gilmer *1784-1810*	Lucy Gilmer *1785-?*	Harmer Gilmer *1787-1812*	Francis Walker Gilmer *1790-1826*	Susan Gilmer *1793-1817*
M.	M.					M.
Mary House *died 1854*	Sarah Gilmer					Zachariah Shackelford

ancis Walker Gilmer *1816-1845*	Lucy Walker Gilmer *1821-1845*	John Gilmer *1821-?*	Mary Peachy Gilmer *1829-1850*	Peachy Harmer Gilmer *1813-1872*
		M.	M.	M.
		Elizabeth Patton	Dr. George Wilmer	Isabelle Walker

❧❈❧✿❧❈❧

Eliza Watts Breckinridge *1841-1928*	**Lucy Gilmer Breckinridge** *1843-1865*	John Harmer Breckinridge *1844-1862*	Emma Jane Breckinridge *1845-1892*	George William Breckinridge *1847-1911*
	M.			M.
	Thomas Jefferson Bassett			Anne Hammer (1st) Letitia Maurin St. Martin (2nd)

Jane Breckinridge	John Breckinridge
	M.
	Mary Hopkins Cabell

Matilda Breckinridge	James Breckinridge	John S. Breckinridge	Robert Breckinridge	**Cary Breckinridge** *1796-1867*
M.			M.	M.
. M. Bowyer			Mary C. Meredith	**Emma Walker Gilmer** *1807-1893*

1862

1

A Whimsical Chronicler

Grove Hill, August 11th, 1862
I am going to keep an Acta Diurna, no, that would not be an
appropriate name—I think I shall write in the epistolary style,
telling all the events of the day, my thoughts, feelings, etc. It
will be good employment these war times, when we have no
visitors to receive and no visits to pay, no materials to work
upon and no inclination to read anything but the Bible and the
newspapers. Well, the question presents itself; what sort of
friend shall I choose? A discreet female of advanced age? A
respectable maiden aunt? A young and intimate school mate?
Or an old and attached governess or tutor? It is a hard question
to decide. Upon reflection, I think I shall select a female, rather
older than myself and a great deal smarter, but whose sweet and
gentle disposition shall call forth all my confidence, an expression of all my feelings and doubts, etc., and whose deep and
loving interest in my family shall induce me to write anything
which concerns them. I never had such a friend and I shall love
her so much. So, my dear, kind, blue-eyed friend, my fidus
Achates, here comes my first letter, dated—

Monday, August 11th, 1862
I have not written to you for so long, sweet friend, that I shall
very frequently have to resort to the past. You have not seen
nor heard from us for five years?—that is shocking. The
earliest and most delightful associations I have are connected
with your name, Harriet Randolph. You are named after an old

and valued friend of my mother's, one of the noblest and most beautiful characters I ever heard of, whose life seems more like some sad romance than anything else, and you are *my* friend Harriet, talented and good, as was my mother's.

So, it has been five years since you were at Grove Hill! A great many changes have taken place since then. There have been two marriages in the family and ever so many babies. But, as I am going to write you every day now, I shall let my recitations concerning the family be gradual.

On this day we are very much scattered. Mamma and George are over at Glencary helping Sister to make arrangements to come over here to stay during the war. Brother Lewis is surgeon and away from home constantly, so that the farm has been under Mr. Mahan's direction, but he has not proved a faithful steward. He entertains deserters at the expense of Brother Lewis' flocks of sheep, etc., and steals things generally. I am glad that Sister is coming over here to live. That she has a very sweet little home is true, but there never was a wilder and more desolate country. The three eldest children are here, and very sweet, interesting little things they are. Though Jimmy is *my* boy, I think Cary is my pet; he talks so sweetly and indistinctly.

We always feel very desolate without Mamma, but tried to amuse ourselves with some books Sister sent over.

We went to the Episcopal Church yesterday, expecting to hear a poor sermon from Mr. McGuire,[1] and were delightfully surprised when our old tutor, Mr. F. Martin, walked into the pulpit—not that he is a very interesting preacher, *au contraire*, but anything is better than Mr. McGuire. We are not satisfied with Mr. McGuire. He is not an Episcopalian at all. Yesterday, he administered communion and left out all of the morning service. Mr. Martin remonstrated with him about it, but his excuse was that the service was so long that the Presbyterians

---

1. The Reverend Mr. William McGuire was rector of the Episcopal Church in Fincastle.

and Methodists get tired. I wish he would read the service and omit his sermon!

On Sunday, he preached a sermon on the subject, "Too late for repentance," and compared a man's putting off religion to a traveler. These are his words: "The traveler arises late in the morning. He reaches the station. Just as he arrives there, he hears the whistle, 'Toot! toot!' and the cars have left him! He runs after them (a long and impressive pause) but they are too fast for him! My friends, (leaning over the pulpit, stretching and winking his bright, blue eyes, and pointing that long, terrible first finger to the congregation) my friends, he is— *TOO—late!!*"

I need scarcely tell you that he is killing out the church here completely—poor man, he has broken up every congregation he ever had anything to do with. After church we went up to speak to Mr. Martin and begged him to come out to see us, which he promised to do that evening. So, after dinner, he arrived and we enjoyed his visit very much. Brother Gilmer and himself got to discussing the doctrines of the different churches. I always drink in anything doctrinal very eagerly. He spoke of predestination, but I have never met anyone yet who could throw any light on that subject. I am sorry I ever thought of it, it puzzles me so.

Then Brother Gilmer spoke of a Carmelitish doctrine. Some man in Tennessee told him about it. He argues that the thief who was crucified with Jesus was not saved. His arguments are these: If the thief was saved it is one of the most important events mentioned in the New Testament, and it is very singular that Luke was the only one of the Evangelists who gives that version of it. The others say that the thieves reviled Him, and if Luke's account is true the sentence may be differently construed from the way it is generally received. The soldiers mocking Jesus, called Him, "King of the Jews," so the thief might have mocked when he said, "Lord, remember me when thou comest into thy Kingdom," and Jesus said, "Today shalt thou sup with me in Paradise." The man argues that Jesus slept in the grave three days and Paradise means a "hidden place," so that Jesus did not mean Heaven, but the grave. The argument is too weak to take the trouble to confute.

Mr. Martin left soon after breakfast this morning. I amused myself during the day reading, *Alone*,[2] quite an interesting novel, but not very well written. Late in the evening Miss Fannie Burwell, who has been with us for the last three weeks, Eliza, Emma, the three children and myself walked to the garden and from there to the stable. I went in to see Little Dorrit, who in spite of my neglect, knows and loves me still. She tried very hard to talk to me, bless her little heart. When we came back to the house we found Cousin George Carr here. We had gone out walking in our dressing wrappers; and to show how cunning girls are, Eliza and Miss Fannie slipped upstairs and dressed, then put on their hats and walked in at the front door as if they had just returned from walking. We sat up quite late discussing the war, generals, etc., and then Monday ended.

Tuesday, August 12th, 1862

Cousin Carr left this morning to go to the Sweet Springs[3] for his health. The day was a very quiet one. We all read most of the time. Papa came home after dinner, bringing the papers, containing the news of a victory over Pope's army near Gordonsville,[4] 400 prisoners captured. How I wish we could get hold of Pope. Since he issued those cruel bulls[5] of his, I have

2. A novel by Marion Harland (pen name of Mary Virginia Terhune, 1830–1922), published in 1854.
3. Grove Hill was located along the main route to "the Springs" of western Virginia: the Sweet, the Warm, the Hot, the White Sulphur, the Salt Sulphur, and the Red Sulphur. These fashionable spas were noted for the medicinal effects of their waters which were heavily laced with natural minerals. Perceval Reniers, *The Springs of Virginia*, pp. 25–32.
4. Confederate losses in the battle of Cedar Run, 9 August 1862, under the command of General Thomas J. "Stonewall" Jackson, were 1,314. Union losses in this encounter, under the command of General John Pope, were 2,393. The Confederate forces captured 400 prisioners, a 12-pounder gun, and gathered 5,300 small arms from the battlefield. Clement A. Evans, ed., *Confederate Military History*, 3, p. 312 (hereafter cited as *CMH*).
5. This undoubtedly is a reference to General Pope's order requiring his troops to subsist upon the land. In a report to Brigadier General G. W. Cullum at Army Headquarters in Washington, D.C. on 27 January 1863, Major General John Pope

felt a peculiar spite for him. We went to walk late in the evening, met some cows and a skeedaddle ensued. After supper Brother Gilmer and Miss Fannie played chess. Miss Fannie beat him every game. Brother Gilmer indulged his taste for saying original things by advising us not to marry for love. He says that no one knows the person they marry until *it is too late;* that gentlemen are actors and hide their real feelings and characters. The reasons he urged for not marrying for love are that if we do it we are sure to be bitterly disappointed. We find after marriage that the gentleman is not at all what we expected, and if we love him we cannot but feel that very bitterly, whereas, if we only liked him and were disappointed, it would not touch our hearts at all. Very few people can expect happiness after they are married; but then they ought to love each other enough to be willing to make many sacrifices and excuse many faults. From observation, my theory is that wives generally love their husbands more than their lovers. The wife's love grows, becomes deeper, more patient and fonder than ever the girl's could be, while the husband's almost invariably cools down into a sort of patronizing friendship. If they care for their wives at all it is only as a sort of servant, a being made to attend to their comforts and to keep the children out of the way. It is very inconsistent of Brother Gilmer to give us such advice. If ever a couple did marry for love, it was Brother Gilmer and Sister Julia. And he is one of the few husbands I ever saw who I think does and always will love his wife as much as she does him. Seeing their happiness in each other is almost enough to reconcile anyone to matrimony.

Eliza and Miss Fannie have been arguing one question for three weeks. Eliza generally gets the better of it. Miss Fannie maintains that men are in every way superior to women, while

makes reference to this order and its repercussions: "The order requiring the troops to subsist upon the country in which their operations were conducted has, with a willful disregard of its terms, been construed, greatly to my discredit, as authorizing indiscriminate robbery and plunder; yet the terms of this order are so specific as to the manner and by whom all property or subsistence needed for the use of the army should be seized, and the order is so common in the history of warfare, that I have been amazed that it could have been so misinterpreted and misunderstood." *The War of the Rebellion*, I, 12, pt. 2, p. 23 (hereafter cited as *O.R.*).

Eliza argues warmly in defense of woman. I am neutral and listen to their discussions with great interest. Eliza brings forward so many instances where the woman is the superior or equal that she nearly always vanquishes her opponent. Sometimes they forget the argument and commence talking of their acquaintances, and Miss Fannie will say, "What a pity Miss Blank married Mr. Blank. She has to support the family." Then Eliza exclaims, "Another instance, Miss Fannie, of woman's superiority!" And where Miss Fannie can mention only one instance of the husband's superiority, Eliza can bring forward ten where the wife is the laborer, the head of the family, the gentle and good angel of the household. I rather incline to the opinion that women are purer and better than men, but, then, they are so guarded from evil and temptation, while men are exposed to every temptation to wickedness, and have so many disadvantages to struggle with; and (I think) they have not the moral courage that women have. When a man is good he is certainly the noblest work of God.

One part of the question they argue, I can entertain no doubt upon, viz., which has the most trouble and suffering. A woman's life after she is married, unless there is an immense amount of love, is nothing but suffering and hard work. I never saw a wife and mother who could spend a day of unalloyed happiness and ease. The children are constantly getting hurt, and crying and tearing their dresses, thereby keeping "Mamma" miserable and busy. And then "husband" is cross, and all of her patience and gentleness is necessary to prevent a quarrel. Bless the little babies, though, the trouble they give is almost pleasure. "Mamma" can be quite happy and contented, even with an ill-natured husband, if the "baby" will only sleep well and not have the colic. I wish I was a man! I would make my wife so happy. She should never repent having married me.

Wednesday, August 13th, 1862
I was very sick last night and did not go down to breakfast this morning. Little Emma sat with me several hours. She is a very smart and peculiar child. After she left me I sat in the room over the parlor knitting, looking as old and grave as if I really

had on spectacles and a cap. Knitting will make anyone think so fast and such silly things. I thought of things that Fan and I used to talk of when she was here. Fan says she's glad she lives in war times, that it makes her feel like a heroine; that some of these days she will call little Augusta, Walter and Marguerita, etc., around her chair and tell them how she and Papa were married during the Revolution, and how, after five weeks of bliss he went back to the Army and how she cried and thought she could not live unless Papa came back, etc., etc. And then she amused herself telling me what I would tell my little Emma, Cary, Johnny, Peachy G., etc., etc, about my romantic courtship—how my lover went into the Army and I did not see him for ten months, and how one Sunday (the 29th of December), I went to church feeling very sad, and how when I looked up I saw a face there that I knew and loved so well; and how my heart seemed to be still and frozen, and then the rush of joy and the determination that no one should see how glad I was. And after church I avoided looking where he was, and how two days afterwards I met him at a party at Mr. Miller's and we played indifference for a while, and then we got more, ahem! interested and he asked me something, which I did not want to answer, and joked about until he was going, and then I could not help it, and answered as he wanted me to. And then I would tell how a few days afterwards he went to Manassas and I went to Richmond and we wrote to each other, and then how he went down to Yorktown, and how soon afterwards we heard of the battle of Williamsburg, and how when the papers came, giving an account of that battle, Mamma took them to read out, and saw a list of the killed and wounded in the Eleventh Virginia Regiment, and how she looked for Company D, and Papa told her to read the list, and she, looking very pale and distressed, said she could not, and how I got up, very calm and quiet and went upstairs and sat down almost unconscious of anything, with that cold shuddering about my heart, and how soon after Eliza came in and told me it was a mistake, and that he was not killed, and how I, for the first time, shed tears and was so very thankful. And how when I looked at the paper I found that the mistake was a very natural one, as the list was put thus: "Company D., Captain H. killed, E. James," etc. And then how

I shall proceed to tell how on the 31st of May he was wounded and how they all said it was a slight wound, and I never felt uneasy, and how about two weeks afterwards George came home from Fincastle and said he had heard he was not expected to live. And the next day we heard that he was probably dead and then,—but I won't tell of those hours of wicked despair! I will tell how when I opened my Bible that night, my eyes rested on the scene of Christ's agony in Gethsemane, when he prayed, saying, "Father, if Thou be willing remove this cup from me; nevertheless, not my will but Thine be done." Then, how a feeling of hope and comfort came over me, and I used that same prayer, and God in His infinite mercy heard me. And then I'll tell of one Sunday, the 3rd of August, that I went to the Presbyterian church, and without any cause at all, I felt very miserable about him, and I thought I never had loved him so much; and after church, if anyone spoke to me I trembled, fearing to hear some bad news, and how after we came home, Cary said that a man from Rockbridge said that Captain H.'s father said that he could not possibly recover, and that I felt as if I should never see him again; and how two days after I was sitting in my room alone, feeling very miserable when Emma brought me a letter from him. Oh, joy unspeakable! How ridiculous all of that will sound to me fifteen years hence, when I am a fat, rosy-cheeked, old matron of 34. But I am not sentimental. Fan did not say any of that. She drew a fancy picture, and I drew a foolish one.

My thoughts of Wednesday are taking up too much room. I must return to the events. Eliza and Miss Fannie went over to Greenfield to see Lulie. They found her still quite sick. They report little Virginia quite pretty. I think Henry's death will make Lulie more tender and gentle with her little girl. Late in the evening, Brother Gilmer returned from Fincastle, bringing Colonel Tom Swann[6] with him; and soon after Eliza and Miss Fannie came. We sat on the porch until a late hour, enjoying Colonel Swann's charming conversation. He is so handsome

6. Lieutenant Colonel Thomas B. Swann commanded a battalion of Virginia cavalry in Lieutenant Colonel Vincent A. Witcher's Brigade under the Department of Western Virginia. *O.R.*, I, 49, p. 1022; *CMH*, 2, pp. 103-4.

and agreeable that we all fell quite in love with him. I think he thought I was a married lady for several hours. I wore a shawl as it was a cool evening, and that will account for it. Eliza and Miss Fannie were more enthusiastic about him than I was. They seemed to think all men geese when compared to this Swann. Colonel Swann and Brother Gilmer talked politics and I learned a great deal that I never knew before, for instance, that Calhoun [John C.] was not a secessionist, but a revolutionist—just what Papa is! Then he and Brother Gilmer talked about Swedenborg's doctrines, and he explained some of his theories.[7] They are certainly very beautiful and attractive. I think the Colonel talks as if he was an Episcopalian, but he seems to be very much under the influence of Mr. Cralle and Judge McComas, two celebrated followers of Swedenborg.

Thursday, August 14th, 1862

Brother Gilmer and Colonel Swann left this morning to go to Covington. Not, however, before the Colonel had confirmed and strengthened the good opinion already formed of his talents, etc., by the ladies of Grove Hill. We spent the day watching for George, and Mamma, who arrived late in the evening. The house is much brighter now.

Friday, August 15th, 1862

We have been busy fixing today to go to Buchanan tomorrow. I wrote a letter to Fan, and soon after sending it, Jim came home from the army bringing a note from Miss Letty Burwell, telling Mamma that Fan has typhoid fever. Poor little thing, I wish I could help to nurse her. The house is so busy that I have not had time to read much today. I read some in Michelet's book on "Woman."[8] I do not like that kind of reading. It scares me of myself, and makes me rebel against my lot.

---

7. A religious movement which stemmed from the religious thought of Emmanuel Swedenborg (1688–1771). Swedenborgianism, with its optimism and comprehensiveness coupled with expressions of freedom and promise, experienced considerable popularity in America during the antebellum half-century. Sydney E. Ahlstrom, *A Religious History of the American People*, pp. 483–88.

8. *La Femme* (1860) was written by the French author-historian, Jules Michelet (1798–1874).

Saturday, August 23rd, 1862

Miss Fannie, Eliza and myself went to Buchanan on the 16th
and had a charming time. We got acquainted with Colonel
Edmund Pendleton[9] of New Orleans and his family. The Colonel
was just released from Fort Warren, and gave us very
interesting accounts of his travels. He is strikingly like
Captain Houston, but very smart and agreeable.

I sent all of Jennie Whittle's letters back to her, with a very
kind and polite note, requesting the same favor of her. She
wrote me a very touching note, and sent two or three of my
letters and a ring I gave her. She is so insincere and dishonest
that it is impossible to know how to manage with her. God
deliver me from such people for the rest of my life! On
Wednesday, the 20th, Eliza and I returned to Grove Hill. When
we arrived we were surprised to find Captain H. here, still quite
lame, but looking remarkably well and handsome. Thursday I
spent the day making mint juleps for Mr. H. and enjoyed it very
much. He left in the evening and we missed him sadly. Eliza,
under Captain H.'s superintendence, fired a pistol for the first
time. He admired my shooting very much. This has been a
happy day, sitting in the hall, talking of old times with Captain
H. We explained so many of our little misunderstandings. He
took the ring I gave Jennie. I am afraid it is fated and something
mournful will occur.

I came upstairs soon after he left and retired. Friday I was sick
all day. George laid down by me all the morning and tried by
telling bad anecdotes to solve a question which has long puzzled
him, viz, whether I can blush or not. He succeeded at last, and
then amused himself laughing at my "soft, little arms," and
then when he saw that I was pleased at his thinking they were
small, declared they were "so big that they were almost legs."
Boys are funny things!

9. Edmund Pendleton, a Virginia-born attorney, commanded Starke's Brigade of
the 15th Louisiana Infantry when captured 28 June 1862 during the Seven Days
campaign. He was released from prison on 5 August 1862 and shortly thereafter
rejoined his regiment, serving as commander until his parole at Appomattox on 9
April 1865. Andrew B. Booth, *Records of Louisiana Confederate Soldiers and Louisiana
Confederate Commands*, III, p. 101.

Today Brother Gilmer brought Miss Fannie home. We were delighted to see her, but I made her jealous by telling her of the compliments that Colonel Swann paid my brilliant and intellectual(?) eyes. George took a fox hunt; a thing of such rare occurrence deserves mention. He started a "red" and had a "bully chase." Music and Hector led the pack. Old Prompter started the fox, although his hind leg was almost off, and ran half the chase on three legs. George is thinking a great deal of matrimony, but declares he will never marry a Smith or Jones. He has a decided preference for Gwathmeys!

Ma, Sister, Little Emma and Mary went on Thursday morning to Liberty to see Fan who continues sick. I have been mad all day with Jennie Miller for telling Mr. McCue of a conversation she overheard at her house between myself and Captain H. It was a dishonorable thing, and she had better warn her friends of her too acute hearing. Of course, she has told everyone! I'll remember!

27

2

Grievous News

Sunday, August 24th, 1862

It rained so steadily today that we could not go to church. I sat all the morning in the library with George talking about "reds" and marriages. He said very earnestly, "Well, Luce, take my advice and do not get married until the war is over. There are many reasons why you should not; for instance, you might be a widow in a short time." Then, after thinking a few minutes, it seemed to strike him that it would not be such a bad thing to be a pretty young widow. He has an idea that I am engaged, and seems to take a great deal more interest in me; treats me with marked respect and unwonted tenderness. He is a funny boy and a very sweet one. I never loved him so much before, because all my special love was given to John. He and I were so nearly the same age, and never were separated in any way until the last two or three years. I loved him better than anyone on earth. Though we were playmates from our babyhood, I do not remember ever having been angry with John. I was more intimate with him and stayed with him more than I did with Eliza. We never formed a plan for the future in which we were not connected. Everything seems changed to me since he died. He was the noblest and best of us all, and all his life had been the favorite with his brothers and sisters. "God takes our dearest even so; the reason why we cannot know; helpless he leaves us crushed with woe."

Eliza and Emma went over to the graveyard and put up a white cross with John's name on it and the date of the Battle of Seven

Pines [1862] with the inscription, "He hath entered into peace," and put garlands of ivy on it. It is only a temporary mark for the grave. All of his brothers and sisters wish to raise a monument to his memory, the first of our band who has been taken from us. What a sad summer this has been. John came home on Saturday, the 17th of May, and we were so happy the ten days he stayed at home. We tried to vanish all sadness from our minds and make him happy, but it is singular that we all felt that it was his last visit. On the 27th of May, he left. He was not strong and well, and we begged him to stay, but he said he thought there would be a battle in a few days and it was his duty to be there. And when he saw how sad Ma looked, he said he would come home again after the battle, and stay longer. Five days after he left he was mortally wounded. Late on Monday night as Eliza and I lay awake talking, we heard a strange footstep in the passage, and then a scream of agony, and in a few minutes Ma came upstairs almost fainting, and handed us a dispatch from Mr. Gwathmey. Ma intended starting to Richmond the next day, but fortunately was too ill to travel. But on Wednesday, she went to Bonsacks and was detained there by a slide on the railroad, and the next day George told her she must come home, and handed her the dispatch, dated Tuesday, 3rd of June, telling us that our noble boy was dead. On Sunday the 8th, he was buried.[1]

Those days of intense agony seem more like some dark dream. Our friends were so kind to us then. I shall never cease to

1. Peachy Gilmer Breckinridge in a letter to his wife, Julia Anthony Breckinridge, 21 June 1862, writes of his brother John's mortal wound, received in the Battle of Seven Pines: " . . . There were two men from my old company on the cars who wanted to go to Mayo's Hospital to leave a bundle. I went to show them the way and found Lt. Kelly there. He said he saw John when he was shot—they were lying down and John had loaded and was on his knees putting on a cap when he saw him fall on his face and remain motionless without speaking. He went to him and saw that the ball had come out at his back. He then ordered two men to remove him and after awhile seeing that it had not been done, he asked the reason and was told that John refused to be moved . . . he ordered the men back and told them to carry him off anyhow and it was done . . . Someone told me that Gen. Longstreet offered a distinction to any soldier or officer recommended by the Col. after a battle and that Col. Allen recommended John after the battle of Williamsburg." Breckinridge-Preston Papers, Roanoke Valley Historical Society; microfilm, Alderman Library, University of Virginia, Charlottesville,Virginia.

remember Mr. and Mrs. George Gwathmey with the warmest gratitude. They did all that the kindest and gentlest friends could do for Johnny, and wrote us such sweet, comforting letters about him.

Monday, August 25th, 1862

Brother Gilmer and George went to Bonsacks; Brother Gilmer on his way to Wytheville. Miss Fannie made me a white tarleton van dyke. Emma went to Buchanan. I do miss her so much. She and I are very confidential. I was so busy thinking that I could not read any all day. I wanted to see Mr. H. so much. After dinner we three females went to Fincastle. We went to see the Millers. Mr. Miller tried to accuse me of being a coquette. I felt mad when I looked at Jennie and remembered what she told Mr. McCue, but girls will tell everything they hear. I'll take care never to tell *her* anything. We went to see Mrs. Logan, who is very kind and gave us some plums. She quarreled a little bit about Miss Fannie staying with us so long. We then went to see Mrs. Meredith, who was in a remarkable good humor, and also gave us some plums.

We got a letter from Mamma telling us that Fan had been extremely ill, but was recovering. Eliza got a letter from Cary. He seems to be having quite a pleasant time, camped near Gordonsville, in daily expectation of battle. Dr. Meredith has been assigned to the Second Cavalry again,[2] for which I am very thankful. He is a good surgeon and a kind friend of ours. Jimmy and Cary have been very good today. Cary says he wished Capt. Houston would come again. At the mention of the Captain's name a vision of peaches and apples float before Cary's mind. When I refused several times the other day to let him have an apple, Captain Houston would tell him in the most imperative manner to take one, which quite won Cary's heart.

2. Samuel Meredith served as assistant surgeon in both the 2nd and the 5th Virginia Cavalry Regiments as well as in the military hospitals in Richmond. He died in service. H. B. McClellan, *Life and Campaigns of J. E. B. Stuart*, pp. 423, 428; Wyndham B. Blanton, *Medicine in Virginia in the Nineteenth Century*, p. 410.

Tuesday, August 26th, 1862

We were surprised this morning to find that Brother Gilmer and George had returned during the night. Brother Gilmer met Colonel Swann at the depot, and returned to Fincastle with him. They went over to Covington together today. George called at "Oaklands" and brought news of Cousin Anne Holcombe's addition to her family, a little son, named Cary Breckinridge, after Papa. Cousin Anne is becoming quite prolific. I expect Cousin James' *quires will be full yet.* Poor women! Why did God curse them so much harder than men. I am sure there was no more sin in being tempted by a wily serpent, a fallen angel, than by a pretty woman. So Eve did not show more weakness than Adam. I read a novel today by Anthony Trollope called *The Bertrams.* It is quite good.

George brought in the mail at dinner time. I got a letter from Sister saying that our dear little Fan is no better. I wish I could go to help nurse her. I promised her when she was here that if she ever was sick I would go to her. She wished for my hands, Sister says. She used to love for me to pet her; but I think it was a sort of association of ideas. My hands were Brother James' sister's hands. I never felt so sad parting with anyone as I did when we told Fan goodbye at the Big Lick depot,[3] and watched her little figure with the grey bonnet, walking down to the lady's car all alone. She and I learned to love each other so much. We used to sleep together and little sleep did we accomplish. It was generally about 3 o'clock when we stopped talking every night.

Aunt Matilda and Letty came out to see us this evening. Aunt M. looks very sad since poor Cousin Edward's death. Letty says that Mr. Glasgow and Miss Verser are to be married. God help poor, little Maggie and the rest of Mr. Glasgow's children! It is very cruel of Mr. Grasty to maneuver so to get them such a stepmother. She is the most disagreeable looking woman I ever saw, but Mr. Glasgow deserves a bad second wife for forgetting so good a first.

3. The town of Big Lick was rechartered in 1884 and named Roanoke.

Wednesday, August 27th, 1862

This has been one of the saddest days of my life. I felt all day a
fear that we should hear bad news from our darling, little sister,
and at dinner time Pa brought us a letter from Mamma telling
us that at half past 3 on Tuesday Fan died. Poor Brother James!
His married life has been a sad one. He and Fan have been
married six months, and have only been together six weeks. She
did love him so devotedly, gentle, pure, little Fan. I never
expected to love her as fondly as I did. I wish so much that I
could have seen her. I felt that when I parted with her we
should never meet again, and she seemed to feel so sad, too. All
the way from "Oaklands" to the Lick we did not speak a word,
but sat looking at each other mournfully. She and Johnny are
together, now.

We received a letter from Cousin Kate Breckinridge saying that
she would be here on Monday. We feel so little like having
strangers with us now. I got a letter from Captain Houston,
which I answered this evening. Eliza and Miss Fannie have both
been sick today. We miss Ma so much. The house seems so
quiet and desolate when she is away. There never was such a
sweet, loving Mamma as ours. I wish I could be more industrious and useful for her sake. She can't help thinking that I am a
good-for-nothing, lazy girl, and my good qualities, if I have any,
are so hidden by the bad ones that I am afraid Ma has nothing to
comfort her about me. But the other children are so good and
noble that if ever a mother did have cause to be proud and
thankful, Ma has. Eliza made a beautiful wreath this evening to
put on the cross by Johnny's grave. I wish Fan's grave was near
us. I should love to put flowers on it. It would seem appropriate
to decorate her resting place with flowers. It seems hard to
realize that we shall never see our little pet again. We all made a
pet of her, the smallest of the family.

Thursday, August 28th, 1862

Miss Fannie, George and I took a delightful ride on horseback. I
rode Little Dorrit to Foston and Miss Fannie rode Selim, who
trotted so hard that I insisted upon her riding Little Dorrit, and
I tried the little trotter who paced with me and galloped. George

32

paid me the compliment to say that he believed I could manage
any horse. George has named his fine, black colt after the
gallant Ashby.[4] About 1 o'clock Eliza and Miss Fannie went to
town; Miss Fannie to stay the rest of the week at Mrs. Logan's;
Eliza to bring Mamma back. Ma told us a great deal about poor
Fan's illness and death. I had hoped that she had suffered no
pain, but Mamma says that from Sunday until Tuesday she
suffered great agony.

In the evening, Ma, Eliza, and I walked over to the graveyard.
John's grave is turfed, and there are fresh flowers and garlands
on it and the cross. It is the sweetest grave I ever saw. It looks
as if he were loved and remembered. Ma said something to me
about my affairs which distressed me very much. She never has
seemed to be satisfied with me since last March. She does not
seem to love me as she used to, and her love to me is more
precious than anyone else's. When we came home I went into
the parlor and took a good cry, and gallantly determined to
break off that engagement [to Captain Houston], because I
know Papa and Mamma would never like it. I said something of
the kind to George who takes great interest in it, and he advised
me not to do it, and said it would distress him very much for me
to die of a broken heart, or to spend the rest of my life writing
love novels; but, truly, I do feel terribly perplexed and
distressed. It would be such a comfort to be able to talk to him
about it, but I can't. Eliza is so sweet and kind to me, God bless
her. George and I sat in the porch talking until bedtime. And so
ends Thursday.

Friday, August 29th, 1862

This morning after breakfast all of us walked over to the
graveyard to have the pine thickets cleared out so that we could
see it from the house. Mamma, Eliza, and I sat on a pile of pines
and talked a long while. Ma seemed to be sorry for me and was
very kind and gentle about that engagement. Pa has no

4. Brigadier General Turner Ashby, a brave and spirited officer, commanded
Jackson's cavalry in the Shenandoah Valley. He died on 6 June 1862, while leading a
charge in an engagement near Harrisonburg. *CMH*, pp. 577–79.

suspicion of the state of things, and Ma thinks that he would not be pleased. Oh dear, it is a miserable thing! He ought to love me a great deal. I do not think, myself, that we shall be very happy after we are married, and I am not at all anxious to hurry that event. I do tremble at the idea of ever being married, but I do not expect to be more sensible and stronger than other women. And I love him enough to risk my happiness for his sake. I miss dear, old Emma so much. I can't let her stay at the Bank much longer. She is a splendid girl. After dinner we got a letter from Emma. She seems to be having a dull time, and says that not a girl has been to see her. She says Nannie is becoming sweeter and smarter daily. She was showing the little thing some pictures the other day and came to one that Nannie thought particularly pretty. Clapping her little hands, she exclaimed, "My soul and body, hos b'uful!" That's very smart for a little girl who is not quite two years old.

I read and talked to Mamma all the evening. Ma sat up in our room, a great treat to us always. After supper Eliza and George and I sat in the porch for a good while. Then Ma had prayer and we came downstairs. Eliza wrote four letters, and I laid down and meditated very sadly about Fan.

3

Victories at Manassas

Saturday, August 30th, 1862

This morning directly after breakfast we went to Fincastle to do some shopping. We went to Mr. Miller's new store and among other articles purchased three calicoes at $1.50 a yard. We went to Mr. Logan's and saw Miss Fannie Burwell. After dinner we all walked over to the graveyard. It is a bright, beautiful place now. I finished *The Bertrams.* It is a very interesting book to me as the characters remind me of people that I know, and it is very well written. We had good news from General Jackson—another victory, 8,000 prisoners captured, and 2,000 negroes [*sic*] who had been stolen by Pope's army.[1]

Sunday, August 31st, 1862

It rained so steadily today that we could not go to church. We all spent a very quiet day reading. In the afternoon we all walked down to the garden. George told us of a conversation he overheard between Uncle Phil and some of the young servant men, *Uncle Phil telling* the direction they must take when they wish to run off to join the Yankees. We always treated him like a *friend* rather than a servant, and his ingratitude is more disgusting than it would be in the others. Slavery is a

1. Campaign of the Second Manassas. A reference to the capture of two trains of cars, 8 guns, 72 horses, equipment, ammunition, a large supply of commissary and quartermaster's stores in addition to prisoners and Negroes, in action at Bristoe Station and Manassas Junction on 26 August 1862. According to General Jackson's report, however, 200 Negroes were recovered, not 2,000. *O.R.*, I, 12, pt. 2, p. 643.

troublesome institution and I wish for the sake of the *masters* that it could be abolished in Virginia.

Tonight we all amused ourselves reading over the old *Churchmans*. Ma gave me a long article on *marriage*.

Monday, Sept. 1st, 1862

Eliza went to town this morning and brought Miss Fannie home with her. We expected Cousin Kate Breckinridge and sent for her, but she did not come. We heard today that Lulie is very sick and Eliza and Miss Fannie think of going to see her. She must be so sad and lonely at "Greenfield." Mrs. Bowyer would be anything but a pleasant companion. "Greenfield" is very much changed since Mrs. Bowyer became mistress. I have only been there once since Lulie was married and that was when I went to little Henry's funeral and saw his coffin in the very place that 20 months before Lulie and Dr. Meredith stood to be married.

Ma sent down to Buchanan for Emma, but the carriage returned empty, Emma being unable to come on account of a slight attack of sickness. Jimmy got a long sweet letter from Sister, but he thought it would be manly to appear to care nothing for it, and when Eliza offered it to him refused to take it, but Cary cried for it and seemed perfectly delighted when Eliza gave it to him. Eliza answered it for him tonight. He is such a sweet, little fellow.

Tuesday, Sept. 2nd, 1862

Ma started to Buchanan early this morning to bring Emma home. We all spent the morning reading. At dinner time we got the papers telling of our victories over the combined forces of McClellan and Pope. The battles were fought on the 28th and 29th of August on the plains of Manassas. General Ewell and several of our generals were badly wounded.[2] We feel so

2. Losses were heavy on both sides. Among those seriously wounded were Brig. Gen. William B. Taliaferro and Maj. Gen. Richard S. Ewell. Although Ewell lost a leg as a result of his wound, he, nevertheless, returned to active duty and continued to serve throughout the remainder of the war. Ibid., pp. 645, 711; Jon L. Wakelyn, *Biographical Dictionary of the Confederacy*, p. 181.

anxious to hear from our boys. Late in the afternoon we all walked to meet the carriage. It was a cool, delightful evening for walking, and we went quite far. About dark the carriage came bringing Emma, Miss Deborah Couch and Rev. Dr. George Woodbridge. We all spent a delightful evening. Miss Deborah drank two strong cups of tea which excited her very much and she excelled herself. She imitated Mrs. Fort's reading, told funny anecdotes, et cetera. Mr. Woodbridge was as sweet and charming as ever. I love him dearly. Eliza says she feels as if there was a blessing resting on the house when he is in it. I wish he was kin to us. Emma looks right badly since her attack. I am so glad to get her back. I commenced reading *Castle Richmond* by Anthony Trollope. I like it very much. Eliza is enjoying *The Mill on the Floss*,³ so much. Maggie and Tom are charming characters.

Wednesday, Sept. 3rd, 1862

I was not ready for prayers! Soon after breakfast Eliza and Miss Fannie went over to Greenfield. Emma, Miss Deborah and myself sat in the parlor for an hour. Then Ma came in. We chatted very pleasantly all the morning. Miss Deborah had heard of that report that the horrid creature had circulated about her *engagement*. That is almost more than I can forgive. The morning was passing very pleasantly, but Miss Deborah wished to make it more profitable, so she made me get *The Spectator* to read out and says we *must* read out some every day. Mr. Woodbridge brought the papers containing news of another battle on Monday.⁴ The accounts do not seem to be very reliable. We got letters from Mrs. Leyburn, Cousin Kate Breckinridge and Mrs. Lucy Yancey. Mr. Leyburn will be here on Friday to attend the Presbytery. Very soon after dinner Eliza and Miss Fannie returned. They found Lulie very sick. Mrs. Bowyer did not *press* them to stay all day so they went to Mrs. Grey's to dinner. The edibles were very bad, but Mrs. Grey was very cordial and gave them some beautiful flowers.

3. A novel by George Eliot (pen name of Mary Ann Evans, 1819–1880), published in 1860.
4. This is a reference to the battle of Chantilly on 1 September 1862, in which Jackson repulsed a federal advance under Reno, but failed to cut off Pope's retreat to Washington. *CMH*, 3, pp. 333–34.

After supper we started to church. As we were riding in the lane I looked out at the sky where the sun had just set, and saw what first looked like Venus, (the evening star), flying, but became every moment larger and more brilliant, and finally exploded and disappeared. It lasted long enough for me to show it to Eliza and Miss Fannie, and we all agreed that it was the most beautiful thing we ever saw in the heavens, and indulged in many conjectures as to what it could be. Eliza thought it might be a ball of fire sent from an avenging God to destroy Washington. Miss Fannie said it *might* be a rocket McClellan had sent up; and I thought it might be the spirit of some hero ascending on a car of flame—General Ewell, for instance, or probably a piece of the sun, which had lingered and lost the tract. We heard a very good sermon from Mr. Hart of Buchanan.

Thursday, Sept. 4th, 1862

This morning soon after we came up to get ready for church, Susan came in to tell us that Cousins Robert and Kate Breckinridge had come. Eliza and I stayed at home and the others went to church. We got acquainted with our cousins directly. Cousin Robert is very handsome, and unlike his father, has a gentle and sweet disposition. Cousin Kate is very pretty and has charming manners. Little Robbie, I must say is a spoiled little fellow, aged three. About 1 o'clock they all returned from church, bringing Cary home. He had received a sabre cut on his brow and nose in the battle of Saturday. Three hundred of our cavalry attacked eleven hundred Yankees, thinking they would not make a stand, but they did fight well and our troops had some trouble defeating them. It was a terrible hand-to-hand conflict, but we lost very few men. Cary says Brother James was in the thickest of the fight, and must have killed a great many of the enemy, but came through safely himself.[5] He had not heard of Fan's death when Cary left on Sunday.

5. The battle referred to was the Second Manassas, 30 August 1862. The report of Col. Thomas T. Munford, Second Virginia Cavalry, of operations 26 August-3 September 1862, gives the following account of the engagement in which Maj. Cary Breckinridge was wounded: " . . . My regiment in line of battle going at a gallop, we

Late in the evening Mr. Leyburn came. He and Cousin Kate
sang some hymns together. We spent a very pleasant evening.
Mr. Woodbridge is so sweet and kind.

Friday, Sept. 5th, 1862

This morning, Cousin Kate, Cousin Robert, Mr. Woodbridge,
Miss Fannie, Eliza and I went to Church. We heard a poor
sermon from a Mr. Windy. Mr. Woodbridge and Cousin Kate
went to sleep. All the young ladies rushed up very
affectionately to speak to me after church, and to inquire after
the Major [Brother Cary]!

We received further news of our victories at Manassas. It is
reported that General McClellan was killed. Miss Fannie
Burwell introduced me to the Rev. Mr. Blanton of Salem. I
begged him to come out to see Cousin Robert, but he is going
away tomorrow and cannot come. Cousin Kate, Miss Fannie,
Eliza and I went to church tonight. Mr. Blanton preached a very
good sermon. Sister Julia came this evening. Nannie is sweeter
and funnier than ever and so pretty.

Saturday, Sept. 6th, 1862

Sister Julia, Miss Deborah, Eliza and I went to hear Mr. Thomas
of Maryland preach. He looks so fat and animal that I could not
admire his sermon. Most people would think him very handsome. His profile is strikingly like Cousin Lindsay Walker's, but
he looks too much like a man of the world and pleasure. After
church we went shopping. At the post office we heard that
William Word and Alfred Gibbs were killed on Saturday. The

---

went through the first line of the enemy and engaged part of the second. Here a
terrible hand to hand fight ensued. The two commands were thoroughly inter-
mingled, and the enemy overpowering us by numbers (being at least four to one), we
were driven back; but as soon as the Seventh and Twelfth Virginia Cavalry re-
enforced me the whole of the enemy's command commenced a retreat. Had my
regiment been promptly re-enforced my command would not have suffered so
severely. My regiment went up in splendid order, and made as gallant a charge as ever
was seen. In this fight Lieut. Col. Watts, Maj. Breckinridge, Lieut. Kelso, Company
A., and Lieut. William Walton, Company C were severely wounded." *O.R.*, I, 12, pt. 2,
p. 748.

Fincastle Rifles have suffered terribly in this war.[6] Mrs. Anderson told us that Baldwin Allen's body had been brought home for interment this morning. It has hardly been a month since George died away from home, and with the same dreadful disease, typhoid fever. The last time I saw Baldwin was at John's funeral.

This evening we all sat out in the yard and ate ice cream. Sister Julia sang some for us. The parlor was so full after tea that it really looked like old times. There were so many of us, and we were having such a pleasant time that we could not make up our minds to go to church. We looked for Sister, Brother Lewis and Dr. Crenshaw, and Brother Gilmer until quite late, when Jim came from Bonsacks and said that they could not come as there was no stage until Monday.

Sunday, Sept. 7th, 1862

Soon after breakfast fourteen of us arranged ourselves in the two carriages and two buggies with a few riding horses and went to church. Mr. Woodbridge preached a beautiful sermon and read the whole service which we Episcopalians enjoyed very much. After church Mr. Godwin assembled us around him and read the news. And glorious news it is. Our army at Munson's Hill in sight of Washington! But the Yankees have been as near Richmond! We were so distressed to hear that Mr. Charles Spears had been killed. They told his poor wife about it just as she was coming out of church. Brother James sent a telegraphic dispatch. He was a fine young man and a good soldier.

After dinner we all went to church again and heard another splendid sermon from Dr. Woodbridge. Miss Fannie Burwell left us today. We shall miss her terribly. Tonight Mr. McGuire came. He certainly does not show off to advantage beside Mr. Woodbridge. After tea Mr. Woodbridge had services for the servants. He had quite a good congregation. Mr. McGuire, being our pastor, had to have prayers. Sister Julia and Cousin Kate sang some hymns.

6. The "Fincastle Rifles" were officially Company D of the 11th Virginia Infantry Regiment.

Monday, Sept. 8th, 1862

This morning we all sat in Miss Deborah's room for some time knitting, sewing, and talking. Cousin Robert left for Richmond early this morning, and soon after breakfast dear Mr. Woodbridge went away. At dinner time Pa brought the mail. Ma got a letter from Brother James. He had just heard of Fan's death. This affliction shows what a pure and noble character he is. He bears her death like a Christian. I am so sorry his letter did not come while Mr. Woodbridge was here, so that he could have written to him. Soon after dinner a Mr. Pettigrue called to see Cary. He paid Eliza such devoted attention that we teased her very much. Sister Julia and I went to walk, and Miss Deborah made Eliza and Mr. Pettigrue follow much to our amusement and Eliza's chagrin.

Brother Gilmer arrived from his travels in the Western counties about 9 o'clock. Cousin Kate is so sweet and lovely that she has completely won all of our hearts. We miss Miss Fannie so much.

Tuesday, Sept. 9th, 1862

This morning very soon after breakfast Emma Wilson and Mr. William Edmundson came out to see us. Emma would be so pretty if she would not be so disgustingly affected. Mr. Edmundson is not improved since that memorable night of Lulie's wedding when I had the honor of standing with him. Mr. Pettigrue bestowed some of his attention on me this morning, after which I excused Eliza's horror. In the afternoon Brother Lewis arrived, and about 9 o'clock Sister and the children came. Little Emma seems to have had a delightful time at the "Gomery White" [Montgomery White Sulphur Springs in Virginia]. Brother Lewis prescribed for Cary who has been suffering terribly from rheumatism. Miss Deborah continues sick. She is so smart and agreeable that we have made her sick chamber quite a sitting room.

Wednesday, Sept. 10th, 1862

We all amused ourselves this morning, reading and chatting. At dinner time we got the mail. The papers say that we have captured Cincinnati.[7] Jackson gained a victory at the "Relay House," 9 miles from Baltimore. I received a kind, affectionate letter from Miss Letty Burwell, and the first copy of *The Southern Illustrated News*, sent me by D. Gardiner from Richmond.

Late this evening Ma, Sister, Cousin Kate, Cary, Brother Gilmer, Sister Julia, Eliza, Emma, the little children, and myself walked over to the graveyard. Soon after we returned a Mr. Harris came to see Cary.[8] He is one of his V.M.I. [Virginia Military Institute] classmates, and is one of the handsomest men I ever saw, and seems to be a good sort of a fellow, very like Henry Allen. Sister Julia sang some for us after tea. Little Mary has whooping cough, and we have quite an exciting time keeping little Nannie out of her presence for fear she will take it.

7. This was a false report. Major General E. Kirby Smith commanding the Army of Kentucky in a dispatch dated 6 September 1862 stated that he was sending forces in the direction of Cincinnati and General Heth was at Cynthiana about 50 miles from Cincinnati with orders to threaten Covington. Newspapers reported Cincinnati under martial law with business suspended and the citizens fortifying the city. *O.R.*, I, 16, pt. 1, p. 933; Ibid., 16, pt. 2, p. 800.

8. Nicholas Cobbs Harris served as Third Capt. of Co. G. of the Second Virginia Cavalry and was retired at reorganization. He was later reappointed Fifth Capt. upon recommendation of Col. R. C. W. Radford. H. B. McClellan, *The Life and Campaigns of Major-General J.E.B. Stuart*, p. 436.

4

An Unexpected Visitor

Thursday, Sept. 11th, 1862

I spent this morning making envelopes and writing a letter to
Miss Letty Burwell. Miss Deborah continues in her room, and is
the centre of attraction. She amused us this morning talking of
marriage. She says she has tried the single life for 69 years and
thinks double life much happier. (But she has not tried that!)
The papers still bring us good news, but still I see no prospect
for peace.

This evening Mrs. Godwin and Ella came to see us. Ella sang!
After our visitors left Cousin Kate, Eliza, Mr. Harris and I
walked down to the garden to eat some grapes.

After tea we all talked, sang and tried to make the best of it until
bedtime. When we came upstairs we amused ourselves reading
some Yankee letters that Capt. Harris captured. They were very
amusing.

Friday, Sept. 12th, 1862

The morning was spent as usual, playing with the babies and
knitting. Brother Gilmer and George went to town. George
brought out the mail. Brother Gilmer says Rev. Whittle was at
"the hanging."[1] Jennie, I suppose, was there also. George, I am
thankful to say, had too much gentility to go to such a place.

1. In a trial held 11 and 12 August 1862 in Botetourt County, Virginia, before
Justice of the Peace John Q. A. Kelly, two slaves, Oscar Murry and James Burnett,

Brother Gilmer started over to Lewisburg this evening to see about his guerillas. He has been made Captain of cavalry in Floyd's army.[2] Robbie and Cary still keep up their battles, much to Sister's horror, who, of course, thinks her boy has not fair play.

We all started to walk this evening, but the rain drove us in. We made Sister Julia and Cousin Kate sing some and tried to persuade Capt. Harris to join them, but he would not. He and I got very well acquainted last night, far enough advanced to cast gentle and reproachful looks at each other, which does not mean in this case that we like one another very well. He does not speak good grammar enough to make him very fascinating, even with that beautiful face of his. He is an Episcopalian, though!

Saturday, Sept. 13th, 1862

Sister Julia and Miss Deborah left this morning. The house is very desolate without them. I miss dear, little Nannie so much. She is so beautiful and attractive. Cousin Kate is a real treasure in the house. She is always cheerful and agreeable. Late in the evening we all walked to the garden and discovered a tree full of soft, ripe peaches. Our enthusiasm at the sight of them amused Capt. Harris very much, who is accustomed to the delightful Bedford fruit.

Sunday, Sept. 14th, 1862

Mamma, Cousin Kate, Eliza, and Emma went to the Presbyterian church expecting that Mr. Ewing's funeral sermon would be preached there, but every church in town was closed, so that they had to return very early. I employed myself during their

---

were found guilty of the ax murder of one Samuel C. Tribbett. They were sentenced to die by hanging on 12 September 1862, between the hours of 10 and 4, the executions to be public. Burnett died in jail before the day of the execution; and it was the hanging of Murry to which this entry refers. Botetourt County Court Records.

2. Peachy Gilmer Breckinridge served as a Captain in the 28th Virginia Infantry until reorganization, at which time he joined the Company of his younger brother as a private. He served with distinction in Company C of the Second Virginia Cavalry and was promoted to Color Bearer. H.B. McClellan, *Life and Campaigns of J.E.B. Stuart*, p. 429.

absence writing to dear Brother James. I wish very much that I
could become a Christian and join the church, when he does,
but I am afraid to trust myself. I might not be able to prove
myself a consistent member of the church. So few people do,
and I am not as good naturally as other people. Eliza could not
help being good and gentle. Brother Lewis and Jimmy came over
today from Glencary. Jimmy is such a fine boy. He has not so
much approbativeness as Emma and Cary, and, therefore, is not
so easily spoiled and made vain and affected. It cannot be
denied that Sister spoils Cary very much. She makes such a
baby of him. He was one of the sweetest children I every saw
until lately.

Brother Lewis wrote a certificate that Cary (the Major) will not
be able to return to duty for 20 days, so I hope Ma will be able
to keep him. We took our usual walk to the grape vines with
Capt. Harris to reach the high branches. Eliza told Capt. Harris'
fortune tonight.

Monday, Sept. 15th, 1862
Capt. Harris left early this morning; so did Brother Lewis. We
shall miss the Captain very much when we go grape gathering.

Ma, Sister, Cousin Kate and Emma went to Fincastle. Emma
has commenced music lessons again. Mrs. Gould's school is
considerably decreased since Fanny Pitzer's courting Charlie so
assiduously.

Ma received letters from Uncle Will, Aunt Eliza, and Mr.
Woodbridge. Uncle Will is quite sick in Gordonsville; says he
will be here as soon as he can travel to help to nurse Cary. He is
the best Uncle that ever nieces and nephews were blessed with,
and such a devoted brother to Ma. Mr. Woodbridge writes to
tell us that Edwards will be here on Wednesday, and says he
will come, too, to preach for us on Thursday, Thanksgiving
Day. I do hope he will come.

I commenced the socks that Miss Deborah says I must knit for
George Woodbridge. We all went to the garden as usual. The

little children sat up late. We had several terrible battles between Robbie and Cary. Eliza and I sat in Cousin Kate's room talking until late. Eliza and Cousin Kate had a Robbie-and-Cary skirmish in which Kentucky beat Virginia all to pieces. I wrote a long letter to Miss Fannie Burwell today.

Tuesday, Sept. 16th, 1862

I knit industriously all the morning and nursed little Mary some. She is a sweet, good baby and I prophesy will be a beauty. Messers Bowyer and Radford spent the day here. The papers bring news that our army is at Hanover in Pennsylvania.[3] I am so glad! Eliza went to town this evening and brought Mary Johnstone and Coalter Logan home with her. I like Mary very well. We got a letter from Sallie Grattan. She says hers and General Garland's engagement is broken off. I expect it is only suspended. I do not think he would be a good match for Sallie. I have no confidence in him and few persons have. I answered Sallie's letter this evening and begged her to come to see us. She is so smart and agreeable that it would be delightful to have her here. I love Sallie dearly. 240 sick soldiers have arrived in Buchanan!

Wednesday, Sept. 17th, 1862

Eliza and I knit industriously on Mr. Woodbridge's socks. I slept last night in Cousin Kate's room, and a rat ran about on the bed so that I was in a constant state of terror. And even when I slept for a few minutes I dreamed that a rat was escorting me about the yard discussing moonlight, music, love and flowers, so that I felt very stupid all day. Late in the evening, Mr. Woodbridge and Edwards arrived. Edwards is a beautiful boy. He is looking very pale and delicate. The Woodbridges are a charming family. George and Edwards seem

3. The news was inaccurate. Action in Hanover, Pennsylvania, did not occur until June of 1863 during the Gettysburg Campaign. There was, apparently, considerable confusion in news reporting at this time. From the *New York Times* of 15 September 1862 comes the following: "Harrisburgh, Sun., Sept. 14th—Heavy cannonading was heard this morning at Hanover, Greencastle, and Chambersburgh, proceeding apparently from an action between McClellan's Army and the rebels south of Hanover." It is possible that what the Pennsylvanians heard on 14 September was the battle of South Mountain, Maryland, which raged all day on a mountaintop.

to get on very well together. Robbie staid in the passage with his Mamma most of the day. He is a fine boy and I think will make a splendid man. He has quite fallen in love with Jim. Poor Sister, I do pity her. She will not let us love or take any interest in her children, but makes them disagreeable to everyone.

Thursday, Sept. 18th, 1862

This is the day appointed by President Davis for Thanksgiving. Mr. Woodbridge preached in the Episcopal church to quite a large congregation. Bishop Johns arranged the services for the day. We read the 5th selection of psalms, the "Gloria in excelsis," the concluding anthem in the "forms of prayer to be used at sea," and sang the 82nd and 85th hymns.

Soon after we came home Walker came. Aunt Belle had some business to attend to and could not come. Cary dined with Dr. Meredith whom we saw at church. He looks wretchedly. Lulie is getting better, and little Virginia is improving since Arianna took her to her motherly bosom. Poor Mrs. Spears was at church. Walker brought her a likeness and some other things which Brother James took from Mr. Spears' pocket after he was killed, and a lock of his hair which Brother James cut off for her. Ma is going over to take them to her.

The papers bring news today of a victory at Harper's Ferry. General Garland is reported killed.[4] I feel so sorry for Sallie. She loved him devotedly. Tonight we all assembled in the parlor and Mr. Woodbridge talked to us so charmingly. He explained to us the 8th Chapter of Romans. He thinks the earth will be the habitations of the redeemed. St. John says, "And I saw a new heaven and a new earth; for the first heaven and the first earth were passed away and there was no more sea." From the 18th to the 25th verses of the 8th Chapter of Romans, the same idea is advanced. It is a very sweet thought that we shall continue on

---

4. Samuel Garland (1830-1862), prior to the War, was a lawyer practicing in Lynchburg, Virginia. He was not by inclination a military man, but entered the service as a matter of duty. He served as Brigadier General of the Fifth, Twelfth, Thirteenth, Twentieth and Twenty-third North Carolina regiments. Garland received a mortal wound during the Maryland campaign and died on the field. *CMH*, 3, pp. 595-97.

earth and that there will be no more sin, nor corruption, "and we shall have no need of the sun, neither of the moon to shine in it, for the glory of God shall lighten it, and the Lamb is the light, thereof." Mr. Woodbridge also spoke of the humanity of Christ. He says that we are too much inclined to forget it in thinking of His divinity, but if we remember that He is the Son of Man, it draws us nearer to Him, and in sorrow or temptation we can embrace Him in prayer so much more readily.

Dear Mr. Woodbridge! It is such a blessing and privilege to have him here and to hear him talk. Cary and George went to hear Mr. Grasty preach. It would have been better for them to have staid at home and heard Mr. Woodbridge talk.

Friday, Sept. 19th, 1862

I was sick all day and could not sit downstairs and see Mr. Woodbridge. He left soon after dinner. Late in the evening I went downstairs and found the family had resorted to the garden, so Edwards and I determined to follow. We feasted on grapes and returned to the house. I gave Walker and Eddie lessons in knitting, and little Emma taught her Uncle Cary. Cary is a great deal better and is getting into good spirits. He is a splendid fellow. I am proud of Cary and love him dearly, but I think I feel a more tender affection for Brother James. I don't feel as if I could ever make Cary love me much or let him know how very much I love him.

Saturday, Sept. 20th, 1862

Eliza and I both breakfasted in bed today. Eliza was quite sick. Jim came from Buchanan and brought some delightful peaches and damsons. Sister Julia always sends us something nice by return carriage. I read a good deal today and did not walk this evening. Walker brought me some grapes from the garden. George and Eddie hunted nearly all day. Eddie still looks badly, but is improving. He is such a lovely boy. I never saw a face so expressive of holiness and innocence as his. Mr. Woodbridge deserves to be blessed in his children.

The Lynchburg paper contained a long editorial about General

Garland today. His remains were brought to that city on Thursday. I do feel such deep sympathy for dear Sallie.

Just before supper, Mr., Mrs., and Betty McGuire came. Mrs. McG. had written to Eliza to tell her that she was coming on Saturday to stay some time, but we did not get the letter. Betty is a bright, smart child and very pretty. Mrs. and Mr. McGuire are the healthiest looking invalids I ever saw, but Mrs. McG. is very delicate.

Sunday, Sept. 21st, 1862

All of the family went to church today except myself. I spent the hours of their absence nursing little Mary and writing. Mr. Woodbridge sent a letter he had written to Brother James by Mr. McGuire, for Ma to forward to him. It is such a sweet, beautiful, and comforting letter that I feel strongly tempted to copy it. I hope Brother James will enter the ministry as Mr. Woodbridge suggests. I read a sermon of Mr. Woodbridge's.

They all gave amusing accounts of Mr. McGuire's sermon and congratulated me upon staying at home. Mr. McGuire dined at Mr. Godwin's and preached in the afternoon. None of us went. I had to entertain Mrs. McGuire all the evening. After Mr. McGuire came, Walker and I joined the rest of the young folks in the garden. The grapes are almost entirely demolished. After tea we all got into cliques about the room. Eddie, Walker, George and myself formed one, and were so charming that we soon drew Cousin Kate and Emma into our circle. The three boys have agreed to go to Kentucky in search of wives and propose to try first to win Cousin Kate's three sisters Lila, Helen and Ida. Cousin Kate has a way of charming everyone.

Monday, Sept 22nd, 1862

Mr. McGuire left this morning. Brother Gilmer and he discussed theological subjects last night and he made himself quite agreeable. *We* think Brother G. talked and argued more pleasantly, and Cousin Kate says she thinks he knows more about the Bible, etc., etc.

Today Sister Julia came. Cary went to town this morning and called on the Millers. He is just getting well and bright, and we enjoy so much having him at home; but he is going away tomorrow.

This evening we again assembled in the parlor and divided into little companies. Walker made me take my usual seat on a little ottoman by him and George. Eddie and Cousin Kate were on our side of the room. Sister Julia sang for us. About 10 o'clock we all told Cary and Walker goodbye, and came upstairs with sad hearts. Cary was so sweet and funny tonight. He amused himself drawing a likeness to put under the place where I had rubbed a very ugly picture of him out. I have been sleeping in Cousin Kate's room, and we have *"some* fun" talking to a late hour every night just like girls. I got a very sweet letter from Miss Fannie Burwell.

Tuesday, Sept. 23rd, 1862

I got up about daybreak today to see Cary and Walker start; and we have missed them sorely today. I came upstairs soon after breakfast and read some. I got a long and interesting letter from Kate Oden. They have suffered very much from the Yankees. The horrid creatures have been in Martinsburg during nearly the whole of the war. The papers today say that our army has returned to Virginia after terribly bloody battles near Boonsboro and Sharpsburg.[5]

This evening we all walked to the spring house and milked our faces. We sat in the passage all that evening and had a very pleasant time knitting and talking, but we could not get over Cary's and Walker's absence.

Wednesday, Sept. 24th, 1862

This morning Eddie left us. George took him to Buchanan in the

5. In the Maryland Campaign against McClellan, Lee's vigorous defense of the South Mountain passes near Boonsboro on 14 September 1862, bought the Confederate forces much needed time and allowed Jackson to complete the capture of Harper's Ferry. The battlefield of Sharpsburg or Antietam following an all-day battle on 17 September was a scene of carnage. Confederate losses were some 8,000 while Union losses numbered some 12,500. Ibid., pp. 335-59.

buggy. We all learned to love him very much, and shall miss him exceedingly. He improved very much, I think, and looked brighter and in better spirits in the last day or two. Little Emma and I are rival queens. We quarreled about which should have Walker for a sweetheart, and today she was quite broken-hearted at my saying that I was in love with Eddie. So, I had to profess only a sisterly affection for him to comfort her. We could not walk this evening as it was very damp and cold. George came back from Buchanan quite early. Mr. McGuire came up this evening. Cousin Kate and I took supper in her room. I had little Nannie and did not like to leave her.

Thursday, Sept. 25th, 1862

Soon after breakfast Cousin Kate, Eliza, Emma, Betty, little Emma, and Jimmy walked to town. Mrs. McGuire and I sat in the sitting room during their absence and talked very interestingly. Eliza and I stayed in Cousin Kate's room all the evening and enjoyed her charming conversation. I have not discovered a fault or a weakness in her yet. We all sat in the sitting room tonight. Eliza got Cousin Kate into such a laugh at supper that she could not drink her buttermilk, by telling her of Mrs. Amen's note to Ma requesting the following flowers: "pink corrinthians, flowery almond, snow cherries, and any other *scrubbery* she had to spare." Mr. McGuire made himself quite agreeable.

Friday, Sept. 26th, 1862

We all went chinquapin hunting today. We wandered about the forest near the sulphur spring, and went on to Foston. Cousin Kate got very tired and I stood the walk better than any of the party, though I took Cary a good bit of the way on my hips. Eliza and Cousin Kate laid down, but I sat up knitting all the evening, and felt very proud of my strength. Late in the evening I was looking out of the window and saw someone whom I thought looked like Captain Houston, but Eliza said he was a great deal taller and finer looking than the Captain, so I went downstairs to find out, and lo, it was he! We all sat in the parlor until after supper, when all except Eliza, the Captain and myself adjourned to the sitting room. About 9 o'clock all the family retired except the Captain and myself. We sat in the parlor reading the Bible and behaving ourselves for an hour longer. He is going back to the army in a few days, and I feel so sad about it. He thinks he will certainly be killed.

Saturday, Sept. 27th, 1862

I was ready for prayers this morning! Soon after breakfast Captain Houston left. I never felt as sorry to part with him before. We thought when we parted that we would meet again on Tuesday at the Natural Bridge; but we shall be disappointed as Cousin Kate says that she would rather not go until Cousin Robert comes from Richmond. Mrs. McGuire told me something that made me so mad with the Fincastle gossips that I wish Grove Hill could be taken up on the wings of an archangel and set down anywhere, *anywhere* but in Botetourt. Mr. McGuire went to town yesterday evening and came out soon after Captain Houston, and those nasty Fincastlevillians asked him if he was going to perform the marriage ceremony for———! I felt very badly and low-spirited today, and laid down most of the time. Late in the evening we all took a walk.

Sunday, Sept. 28th, 1862

I wrote a little note to Captain Houston and sent it by George. Ma read the service for us today and Mrs. McGuire read a sermon by Dr. Woodbridge on the inspiration of the scriptures. I felt so sad that I came upstairs and laid down and read some. Mr. Utz and Charlie came to dinner. After dinner we all went over to the graveyard and put some flowers on John's grave. I wish I was resting quietly beside him. I dreamed the other night of going up there and of seeing his grave with the white cross, and I saw him by it, and he put his arms around me and told me to lie down there by him. After we returned from walking, George and I went into the flower garden which had the additional attraction now of a peach tree.

Monday, Sept. 29th, 1862

I was not ready for breakfast this morning. I came upstairs and read two sermons by Dr. William Bacon Stevens,[6] one on "Faith

6. William Bacon Stevens (1815-1887), Episcopal bishop, historian and author, was born in Bath, Maine. Bishop Stevens was a member of nearly two dozen literary

Touching Christ's Garment." The other was called, "Christians Leaning on Jesus' Breast." Both of them are beautiful. Then I sat in Cousin Kate's room. Soon after dinner Joe brought the mail. I got a note from Capt. Houston and "Drainsville" which he "was constrained" to leave me. Cousin Kate, Mrs. McGuire, Eliza and I went to town. Eliza went to Mr. Carper to have her measure taken for a pair of shoes, and we teased her about the holes in her stocking, "necessary probably for ventilation." I sat in the parlor with Emma tonight while she practiced. I hope she will practice well this Fall and made a good performer on the piano.

Tuesday, Sept. 30th, 1862

I commenced the day by reading another of Dr. Steven's sermons called, "Causes of Unanswered Prayers." Mrs. McGuire was sick in bed today. Cousin Kate and I sat in her room playing with Robbie, and Eliza staid with Mrs. McGuire. Emma went to take a music lesson and brought the mail back. I did not go down to dinner as I felt right badly. I wrote a letter to Capt. Houston. Late in the evening we all took a walk.

and historical societies. In addition to his historical works, Dr. Stevens authored a great number of pamphlets and books on religious subjects. Allen Johnson, ed., *Dictionary of American Biography*, 17, pp. 628-29 (hereafter cited as *DAB*).

5

Melancholy Musings

Wednesday, Oct. 1st, 1862

I read a sermon by Bishop Butler[1] upon "Self Deceit." The text is from 2nd Samuel, 12th chapter and 7th verse, "And Nathan said to David, 'Thou art the man.' " It is a fine sermon as all of Butler's are. I commenced Robbie's socks today. Cary gave Robbie quite a severe wound today, pushing him against a wheel of Uncle Anderson's patent sugar press. Eliza is very busy working for little Nannie. She is a blessing to Nannie and her Mamma, as well as to us all. Pa does not seem to be well. He has no appetite at all. It is so touching to see his attention to a game rooster, which was a pet with our blessed Johnny. He feeds it after every meal, and it knows him and follows him all about, jumps into his lap and tries to talk to him. Cousin Kate expected Cousin Robert today, but he did not come. George is going to school to Mr. Logan, and says he is quite a strict teacher. I walked alone this evening, Cousin Kate and Eliza being lazy.

Thursday, Oct. 2nd, 1862

I am pleasantly aroused every morning by hearing the "Borders of the Delaware." Emma practices before breakfast in the morning. I was down sometime before breakfast this morning and

---

1. Joseph Butler (1629-1752), English theologian, served as clerk of the closet to Queen Caroline and later as bishop of Durham. His "Sermons on Human Nature" were published as *Fifteen Sermons Preached at the Rolls Chapel* (1726). Sir Leslie Stephen and Sir Sidney Lee, eds., *Dictionary of National Biography*, 3 & 4, pp. 519-24; *New Catholic Encyclopedia*, 2, p. 916.

employed myself knitting on Robbie's socks. After breakfast I came upstairs and read a sermon on "Human Nature" by Bishop Butler. Cousin Robert came today.

I have been thinking so much about poor, dear, Fan all this evening. Her death makes me so sad. Sister, Ma, Eliza, Emma and I walked down to the creek this evening. Ma gave me quite a severe rebuke for laughing at Emma's saying that she liked to ride in a "fagen" with two fine horses. I wish I did not like so much to tease. I am afraid no one will love me.

Friday, Oct. 3rd, 1862

Cousin Kate put the children into a state of great joy by giving them each a beautiful present and as much candy as they could eat. I found the sock I knit for Robbie was too small so I walked over to Amanda's and got her to knit one the right size for a model for Cousin Kate. Eliza got a letter from Rosa Burwell enclosing a letter from Brother James. Ma got a letter from Aunt Lizzie, telling us of poor Aunt Marianna's death. It is a happy release for her, for her married life has been a long term of suffering. She has been married about seven years and had five children. I never heard of anyone who suffered as much. Her death was very unexpected. They all thought she was doing well after the birth of a dead child, and Uncle Wilmer went to the bed and felt her hand and brow and finding they were very cold, he called the Doctor; they found she had died without anyone's knowing it. I cannot help thinking that Uncle Wilmer is a Bluebeard. I was saying the other day that some relative or connection of ours had died every month since June. John died in June, Aunt Watts and Cousin Edward in July, Fan in August and now Aunt Marianna in September, on Saturday, 27th.

I read over all of Capt. Houston's letters today. I think I love him more than I ever did. I do hope he will be a great man just to spite those persons who do not admire him now and who do not think it sensible in me to love him. I think if he is spared, other people will think I have cause to be proud of him. *I* think so now. Maybe some of these days I shall be fat, old Mrs. Jones, and he a settled down plain, old lawyer, married to *somebody*, and then I and my old man will amuse ourselves reading over this nonsense and wondering how I ever could have fancied such an uninteresting old fellow, or anybody, indeed, except Mr. Jones. But I shall excuse myself to Mr. Jones by telling him that at that silly period of my existence, I had not the pleasure of his acquaintance.

Though I am engaged to Captain Houston, I have no idea that we shall ever be married. I never have been able to imagine myself Mrs. H. How ridiculous it sounds. God bless him! I do pray constantly that he may pass safely through the dangers which surround him and come home to us very soon. I read Butler's second sermon on "Human Nature."

Saturday, Oct. 4th, 1862

Cousins Kate and Robert left this evening. We spent all the morning in enjoying their society and lamenting the necessity of giving them up. Cousin Robert told us a great deal about our Kentucky kin, and gave me one item of family history that I had never heard. That was that Pa had a brother, Robert, who married a first cousin, a Miss Meredith. This Uncle Robert of ours was very dissipated and Grandpa disinherited him. He was known in Kentucky as "handsome Bob Breckinridge" to distinguish him from "squeeling Bob Breckinridge" and "Devil Bob Breckinridge" (Dr. Robert J. Breckinridge). We have two first cousins there. One married a Mr. Birch and the other is a talented young man named James. They were here a long time ago. I did not know that Pa ever had any grown brothers except Uncle James and Uncle John. Cousin John Bartow Breckinridge interests me more than any of my kin. Cousin Robert says he is the most talented man of the name. I should like to go to Kentucky some of these days and see my relatives.

I got a long letter from Captain Houston today. This evening all of the family walked over to the graveyard. After supper I sat in the parlor with Emma while she practiced. George came in there and staid with us. He says he feels very sad tonight. I wonder what makes him feel so. He is a happy-tempered fellow, but he has no brother to stay with now, and it is a very desolate feeling to have no constant companion. John would have been such a blessing to him. I hope George remembers and thinks of him very often.

We miss Cousin Kate tonight. We girls used to have so much fun every night after we came up to our rooms. Cousin Kate is the most charming person to have staying with us that I ever knew.

Sunday, Oct. 5th, 1862

Eliza and I did not go to church today. I sat in the library all the time that the others were at church and read a sermon by Dr. Stevens on "The Soul Waiting for Jesus," and the services. Then I wrote a very poor letter to Capt. Houston. I know he will make fun of it. Mrs. McGuire says she thinks it is very wrong to write letters on Sunday, but I cannot see any harm in writing to people that you love. I think it would be sinful to write formal business letters. We all walked to the graveyard this evening. The sun always casts its last, lingering rays on Johnny's grave. It is such a quiet, beautiful spot. How I long to rest there. It is not the fear of the troubles and sorrows of life that makes me wish to die now. I am willing to bear my cross, but I feel such a yearning to be with Jesus. I wonder if it is wrong for me to think as I do. I am so sinful, so weak to resist temptation. I am always doing wrong, and yet my heart thrills with love for Christ. When I am alone I think of Him all the time, and resolve to lead a new life, but I always fail. There is so much to discourage anyone who tries to do right. May God help me!

Mr. McGuire came this evening. We had quite a pleasant time after tea. Mr. McGuire made himself very agreeable, talking of the habits of birds and insects. We have diphtheria on the place, now. It keeps Sister busy watching the children's throats. Little Mary opens her mouth very wide to show her throat. She's a sweet, little thing. The children are always good as long as they are under Aunt Maria's care. She ought to have their moral training to attend to. Eliza has such a bad stye. I wish I had it for her. It is so painful to me to see her or Ma or Emma suffer any pain.

Monday, Oct. 6th, 1862

This has been a very quiet day, the first we have passed for a long while without company. I read part of one of Butler's sermons on "Human Nature." They are so hard to understand that I have to study them very carefully. Ma sat up in our room fitting our dresses and talking with us, so the morning passed very

57

pleasantly. I did not sleep any last night or the night before, so I laid down this evening and took a nap. We all walked up to the gate. George came in from school quite late, and he and Jimmy amused themselves with a block house that Cousin Kate gave Jimmy. Emma and I came upstairs soon after supper and played with Mary until Sister came up. Mr. McGuire, lady and child left today.

Tuesday, Oct. 7th, 1862

I read Butler's last sermon upon "Human Nature" this morning. Pa and all of us got very much interested in the sugar press. It does very well. I have not seen Pa so much interested in anything for a long while. While we were all standing under the old apple tree watching Ephriam patiently going around and around pulling out the syrup, Nat Logan came up.[2] I was in my dressing wrapper, and, no doubt, shocked the dear, soldier boy very much. Nat has improved in appearance since I saw him. He has been away a year. I like Nat right well. He used to be so ugly and awkward that it was a source of amusement to us all. I remember the night of Sister Julia's "infar" here.[3] Mr. Houston asked Nat if he had been introduced to the bride, and upon his replying in the negative, took him up and making some remarks to make Nat appear ridiculous, introduced him. If I had been in Nat's place I should have "fit" him.

Sister Julia enclosed Ma a letter from Brother Gilmer who is still in Lewisburg. Colonel Swann has promised to get him a commission as major in Floyd's army. Ma and Sister went to see Aunt Matilda this evening. They saw Lulie in town. I am glad she is able to be out again. After supper tonight, George and I went out under the apple trees and ate sugar cane. George distressed me very much by some hard strictures on somebody that I love? I can't imagine what makes him so bitter in his judgment of late. It

2. Private Nathaniel B. Logan returned to Co. 1 of the 4th Virginia and received a severe leg wound on 1 April 1865 at Petersburg. He died on 6 April, following amputation of his right leg. U. S. National Archives (comp.), "Compiled Service Records of Confederate Soldiers Who Served in Organizations from the State of Virginia," Microfilm Roll 408 (hereafter cited as *CSR-Va.*).

3. "Infare" (often pronounced "infa") refers to a reception given by the groom's parents in honor of the bride and groom. Harold Wentworth, *American Dialect Dictionary*, p. 317.

distresses me more than I can express. I have to bear it on all sides, but until I know that there are good reasons why I should not love him [Captain Houston], my whole heart shall be his. And hearing him spoken of harshly will only make me more determined to be his friend. But the moment that I have reason to believe that he is not worthy of my love, that moment I shall banish all remembrance of him. My heart aches tonight, and I shall not sleep much.

Wednesday, Oct. 8th, 1862

After eating three biscuits for breakfast, Eliza and I went out to see the sugar manufactory. Ephriam seems to take a good deal of interest in his part of the business. I noticed that a chain was rubbing the skin off his shoulder, and Matilda and I fixed a piece of cloth on the chain to prevent it. I have a very warm affection for horses and I believe they know it, for they never seem afraid of me.

Ma, Sister, Eliza, and Little Cary went over to East Greenfield this morning. After they went Emma amused herself making some hoar hound candy out of our Chinese syrup. And I came upstairs and read one of Butler's sermons on the "Government of the Tongue." I feel like being quiet for the rest of my life. Many have been the sins of my tongue! I wish I could have that sermon ever before my mind. I will try to be more watchful over that unruly member. I also read a very interesting novel called, *The Laird of Norlaw*.[4] I like Scottish stories generally. Andrew came from Buchanan today and brought a letter from Sister Julia to Eliza. Sister Julia gives good accounts of the hospitals. The papers bring no news today from our Virginia army. We have had a victory at Corinth, General Price commanding our forces.[5]

They all got back from Greenfield just as we were having supper. Eliza says Lulie's baby is very delicate. Arianna does not take very tender care of it.

4. A novel written by the popular and prolific English author, Margaret Oliphant (1828-1897).
5. Undoubtedly a reference to General Sterling Price's successful attack on the entire line of federal outer works at Corinth which took the Confederate forces to within 600 yards of Corinth on 3 October 1862. The victory was short-lived. On 4 October 1862, the Confederates were met by an overwhelming force and had to retreat. *CMH*, 7, pp. 83-107.

Thursday, Oct. 9th, 1862

I read half of Butler's first sermon on "Compassion." I am so much interested in his ethical discourses. Light reading is almost disagreeable to me. I commenced a book of Miss Pardoe's called *The Confessions of a Pretty Woman.*[6] I do not like it at all, thus far. It is too much like French novels. I knit some on little Mary's stocking. She's a sweet little baby. But for one thing I should make a great pet of her. I am not such an enthusiastic baby admirer as I used to be. I have not the physical strength for it. There is one little baby, though, that I will love with all my heart. I think I shall even be industrious for that baby if Eliza gives me a chance. I took a walk this evening. After dark I got Eliza to play on the piano for me, and while she played, I sat on the sofa and thought sadly of the past. As usual, the future has no charms for me now. It is full of perplexity and uncertainty. The past I thought of tonight was not one that often comes to my mind. I very, very often think of my happy childhood when Johnny was my favorite playmate, and Eliza and I used to play dolls together sometimes, and she did all the sewing and was so unselfish and good. And frequently almost always when I hear Eliza play, I think of the last two years, since new feelings and interests have been awakened in my heart. Having so cheerless a future to look forward to makes me dwell very often on that happy past. The past, though, which occupied my thoughts tonight, was the "Grove Hill Seminary" times. I thought of Jennie Whittle and of my blind devotion to her, the first love of my girlhood. I do not think I shall ever again love anyone as unselfishly and entirely as I did her. With what rapture I used to listen to her music! And poor little, tearful Mollie Galt! Her form floated before me. We had much amusement at her expense. And good, merry, kind-hearted Kate. She was a sunbeam in the school; while Miss Oden was the fiery, little star, ever threatening to be a flying star. I leave tender and mournful recollections of her to the youthful minds of Emma and George. But she did try to do her best, poor little thing. Part of that happy year, dear John was at home, and he added so much to our enjoyment. All of the girls loved him. He was going to school then at Mr. Galt's. Oh, those were happy days!

6. This work was written by English author, Julia Pardoe (1806–1862).

I was not as bad then as I am now; that is the only part of my school life which I can look back to with pleasure. I studied hard then and tried to do my duty, but in the Wharton reign, I was a "leetle deevil," under the rule of a big one. I am not yet quieted down enough to feel true penitence for my rebellion and contempt for that woman and her dominion. But I do feel sorry that I was not better and obedient while under good Miss Benner's authority. Ah, there is no denying it, I was a bad child! I am afraid people who knew me then will not get over the impression I made on them and acknowledge that now I am a quiet good-natured sort of a girl. Sister thinks I am powerful bad and unruly yet, but her opinions are not always well founded. It is getting late. Eliza has shut up *The Laird of Norlaw*, and is saying her prayers. So, visions of past joy and fears of future unhappiness, take your flight, and let me soothe and calm my mind to read my Bible and fix my thoughts on holier and more peaceful things, on a future beyond this life, which though I am sinful and unworthy, yet is not dark or mournful to me, for Jesus, the Lamb slain, brightens it and makes it, when this life is full of trouble and dread, a refuge for my thoughts.

I am not unhappy tonight. I feel less anxious than usual about worldly things. One thing troubles me always, and that is the fear that I am doing wrong in not telling Pa all my affairs. I am afraid it is deception, and yet, I cannot make up my mind to do it. I am a coward! I try to reconcile myself to it by arguing that if I am silent now, there may something occur to make Pa favor my plan and if I told him now, it would distress and anger him and I would have to give up all my, what? Love? And then, all girls do it. Sallie Grattan did not even tell her mother! But that's small comfort. I'll think of it and try to make up my mind.

Friday, Oct. 10th, 1862

I finished the first sermon on "Compassion"; then I knit some. Eliza and Emma went to town. I read some of *The Confessions of a Pretty Woman*. It is not worthy of Miss Pardoe. Pa brought the mail today. I hope he will not do so tomorrow. Sister was the only recipient of a letter, and that letter Jimmy thought anything but agreeable as Brother Lewis wrote that he had sold Selim and

Caesar. They were pretty little horses and great pets with the children. The sugar business is still prospering. The syrup is really delightful.

The papers say that we have again driven the enemy across the Potomac. Our victorious season is almost over if it again proves that the Southerners cannot fight so well in cold weather, and the Yankees better. I am right despondent about the times. It is so hard to believe that war is a punishment to a nation, administered by a merciful and just God. If it was a fiery ordeal through which we would come out purified and humbled, I could see the mercy of it; but it seems to me that people are more reckless and sinful than ever. It ruins our young men and has an immoral effect upon everyone. But, of course, it is just and wise, as God orders it so.

Saturday, Oct. 11th, 1862

I read Butler's second sermon on "Compassion." I thought before I read those sermons that I understood human nature, but I find that I only understood human nature perverted. I was a hard judge of mankind. I got my notions more from books than from observation. I knit very industriously all the morning, and in the evening I read some more of that pretty woman's confessions. Eliza, little Emma and I went to walk this evening. We saw Preston coming up the lane, so we all ran and got into the meadow and had a very disagreeable walk over its rough surface. Eliza played some for us after supper. Eliza can scare one so badly sometimes with her great big eyes!

Sunday, October 12th, 1862

It rained today so that we could not go to hear Mr. Grasty preach. I read the services and a sermon on the text, "And all the days of Methuselah were nine hundred sixty and nine years; and he died (Genesis, 5:27). It is one of the best sermons I have read by Dr. Stevens. It was so cold today that we had to have fire. The cold weather makes me so sad. I dread this winter. I read over Fan's letters to me today and it brought her so vividly to my mind. Ma and the girls and children walked over to the graveyard this evening. I walked alone late in the evening. I dislike so much to be in the house between twilight and supper. It is the most doleful portion of the day to me unless I am walking or sitting in the porch alone.

6

Kate's Sad News

Monday, Oct. 13th, 1862

I read Butler's sermon, "On the Character of Balaam." It was a cold day, and we all sat in our rooms around a bright fire and had a right cozy time. Peter made some applebutter and we enjoyed the fun of looking at and tasting it as much as if we had been native-born Dutch. I read out a few chapters of the "Confessions" to Eliza and Emma, and we were very much amused at Eveleen's trials and triumphs. News of Gen. Stuart's raid into Pennsylvania.[1]

Tuesday, Oct. 14th, 1862

As usual I commenced the duties and pleasures of the day by reading one of Butler's sermons. I read half of his sermon on "Resentment" today. It rained all day so that we were confined to the house. I went out to meet Joe with the mail hoping to get a letter, but was disappointed. Emma has commenced writing some every day. Eliza is busy making winter dresses for Nannie. I think it is time to commence making another little baby's clothes. We have not heard from the boys for a long while. I read a good many chapters of that pretty woman's confessions out tonight. It is a great deal more interesting to read out. Eveleen's adventures are equal to Amanda Malvinia Fitzallen's.

Wednesday, Oct. 15th, 1862

Eliza was sick today so we sat upstairs all the time. I knit

1. A reference to General J. E. B. Stuart's daring raid into Pennsylvania, 9 October-12 October 1862. Penetrating as far north as Chambersburg, Stuart with 1800 men

industriously and finished Mary's little stockings. I finished
Butler's admirable discourse on "Resentment." Little Emma gets
one of us or all of us to hear her spelling lesson every day and we
have a good many laughs at her mistakes. I enjoyed this evening.
We all sat up here knitting, sewing and talking so comfortably
about old times— recalling to each other the exciting and
interesting events of our childhood. And then we talked of Jennie
Whittle's first appearance at Grove Hill, when she acted so well
"The Boarding School Girl." We had not read that little book
then, but I afterwards found that it was a favorite of Jennie's. I
love Jennie now sometimes when I think of how attractive she
used to be to me. I do not know what I found to admire in her. She
was very homely and repulsive in her manners, and not very
smart, and certainly her character was not so very admirable. I
can excuse myself for having loved Sallie; I love her yet. Brother
Lewis came this evening.

Thursday, Oct. 16th, 1862

Sister, Brother Lewis, and little Cary went over to Glencary
today. I came upstairs soon after they left and was soon put down
on the sick list. Mamma and Eliza sat up here all day. Emma went
to take a music lesson and waited for the mail. It was so late coming that she had to dine at Lulie's and had a very pleasant time.
I wish she had to visit alone more frequently. I knit a beautiful,
little red sock for Mary. It is the first clouded sock I ever knit and,
therefore, I think it is the prettiest I ever saw. I read Butler's
sermon on "Forgiveness of Injuries" and was very much
impressed by it. I almost wished someone would offend me that I
might have the pleasure of forgiving. I do feel a little resentment
to somebody now, but I try to keep that up to a certain point—I
am too inclined to be forgiving in this case. Susan came upstairs
last night to tell Ma that Agnes was dead but on inquiry it proved
to be that she was very low with diphtheria at Mr. Hillary
Ripley's. Ma sent a prescription and medicines as they could not
find a doctor. I had no idea that Susan was such a sensationalist.
Mr. Ripley lost two daughters within seven hours of each other. I
hope we escape that terrible disease.

---

captured a thousand horses, and circling around the Federal army, recrossed the
Potomac with the loss of only three men. H. B. McClellan, *Life and Campaigns of J. E.
B. Stuart*, pp. 136-66.

Friday, Oct. 17th, 1862

This was a bright, beautiful autumn day. Eliza, Ma, Emma and I
sat all day cozily and lovingly in one room. Eliza was busy making
a blue merino for Nannie. Ma was sewing on dresses for us, and
Emma was working on her scrapbook and knitting a pair of gloves
for me while I was doing nothing. I had a headache and sore
throat and thought seriously of diphtheria. I did not knit any
today, but made up for it by knitting late tonight. I have been
knitting so much that I hardly know how to write. At the end of
every line I imagine I have done a round, and at all of these
imperfectly formed letters "thinks says I to myself" I have
dropped a stitch. When I used to play chess a good deal I could
not help making people in church chessmen—Miss Mary Grey
would be a bishop checking Mr. Kyle who was a knight (errant),
and Lulie a queen check-mating Dr. Meredith and seriously
checking Mr. Ambler (a castle). Oh! dear, I am tired and sleepy
tonight.

Big Emma is sleeping in Sister's room taking care of Mary, who
cried piteously last night. George is sleeping in "the little room."
I wish he would not use tobacco so much; it will ruin his beautiful
eyes. Ma, Eliza, Emma and I went over to the graveyard this
evening and put fresh flowers on John's grave. It was a sweet
evening for walking. They had a meeting of "The Soldiers' Aid
Society" this evening. It is time the society was doing something
for the poor soldiers, who, I fear, will have an active and
disagreeable campaign this winter. Eliza advises me to stop this
nonsense, so, beloved page, adieu for 24 hours. I wonder if
nothing will happen tomorrow to help me to fill up a page with
more interest. I will do something desperate to make this journal
more interesting. I'll rest my fingers! I'll knit less and think more,
but, then, the poor soldiers! I must commence their socks. Alas! I
must resign myself to stupidity; my life flows on with such
unmarked tranquility that I must necessarily be monotonous.

Saturday, Oct. 18th, 1862

I sat all the morning in the sitting room and read a sermon on
"The Love of Our Neighbor," and knit a red sock for Mary. Big
Emma made some delightful brittle gingers and some molasses
candy. Late in the evening Brother Lewis and Sister came. Little

Mary seemed delighted to see her Mamma. We have been having so much fun with the little thing. Little Emma stays with us constantly and is, I think, improving. I wish we could keep her this winter. Little Mary is staying with us tonight, as Sister has a bad headache and does not wish to be disturbed.

Sunday, Oct. 19th, 1862

We all went to church today. We stopped at Lulie's to unpack, the carriage being very full. We were surprised to see Mrs. Kate Bowyer there and made an arrangement to go to Avenel with her next Tuesday. Today is the first time I have seen Lulie since the night Fan and I went to sit up with Little Henry. A good many changes have taken place since then. Fan and Henry have both died and little Virginia now lies in Henry's cradle. She is a pretty, bright baby, but the very "weeist," dainty little morsel I ever saw. Mr. McGuire preached quite a good sermon and gave notice that Bishop Johns would be in Fincastle on next Friday. I have determined to be confirmed then.

Monday, Oct. 20th, 1862

After breakfast today, Eliza, little Emma and I went to walk. It was a delightful day and, in spite of the plowed ground, Spanish needles, dead pole cat, etc., etc., we had a charming walk. About 1 o'clock, Mr. Bowyer, Mrs. Kate and Cousin Sue White came to spend the day. We had a very pleasant time. Cousin Sue is so sweet. Mr. Bowyer *aloud* and *before Pa* told me that Mr. Radford with a very long face and very lugubrious expression told him that I was to be married very soon. I took it very well and told him to relieve his anxiety by telling him that I had no intention of committing such a folly, as I really have not. Cousin Sue reproached him for teasing me so publicly, and he excused himself by saying that he knew there was no truth in the report of my being engaged or he would not have mentioned it. May he not have cause to change his opinion for a long while!

Griffith came home today bringing a letter from Brother James who was with Stuart when he went into Pennsylvania. Griffith says that they say in the army that he can beat Jim cooking. Eliza and I went over to the graveyard this evening. I sat in the parlor with Emma tonight while she practiced. George came home from school this evening and gave the startling intelligence that the Yankees were in Fincastle, but we soon found out that they were there as prisoners, lodged in the Court House, 26 in number. George sits in our room with us at night. We amused ourselves initiating little Emma tonight with a plate smoked with the candle, and also allowed her the privilege of sitting between the king and queen. She is very much interested in hearing of the games we used to play when we were little. Ma got a letter from Mrs. Leyburn. She says Bettie Campbell is married to Rev. somebody Hendrick. Eliza wrote to Mr. McGuire for me today. I was thinking of how I used to worry Eliza just before she joined the church, and she is so sweet and kind to me. George is suffering so much from a boil under his arm; it makes him right sick. We are so much in hopes that Brother James can meet us in Liberty. He says he wants to come home for a short time.

Sunday, Oct. 26th, 1862

I have had so much to do and to think of this week that I could not write any. I read the Episcopal Manual by Rev. William H. Wilmer. On Thursday, Ma, Sister, Eliza and I went to Buchanan to hear Bishop Johns, and to bring him home with us. We got down there just in time for services. Jennie and Sally Whittle were confirmed. Sally looked so sweet. Sue and Sally Jones dined at the Bank. Soon after dinner, Ma, Sister, the Bishop and Miss Julia Johns in the large carriage, Eliza and I in the little carriage, Mr. McGuire and Mr. and Mrs. Bacon in the rockaway, formed a procession and proceeded to Grove Hill. Miss Julia Johns is so bright and charming, and so good and useful withall.

On Friday, soon after breakfast, Mr. McGuire and I had some conversation. He gave me some excellent advice. We all went to church and heard a most beautiful and impressive sermon from the Bishop on the text, "Choose Ye This Day Whom Ye Will Serve." Robert Logan, Emma Wilson, Jimmie Miller, Jennie Godwin, and I were confirmed. The Bishop had a very large audience, and I was glad for so many to have the privilege of hearing such a sermon. I thought so often of Brother James, and wished that he and I could have knelt together to be confirmed. After church Lulie told us that Cousins Kate and Robert Breckinridge had returned to Fincastle, so Eliza and I ran up to

Woltz's to see her. She heard while in Knoxville that her father had died three months ago. Cousin Robert fears that her family was left in bad circumstances. It was a great disappointment not to get to Kentucky. Cousin Kate looks so sad.

We spent a delightful day. Mr. Bacon spoke so kindly to me about my confirmation. He and Mrs. B. both seemed to take quite a fancy to us (Eliza and me), and begged us to spend this winter with them in Richmond. Miss Julia and I had a long conversation in her room. She is so good, and talked to me so sweetly about John. Tonight the parlor was so full, and everyone so bright and smart that it reminded me of old times. Early Saturday morning they all left. I think they all enjoyed their visit, and all promised D.V. [*Deo volente,* God willing] to come to see us next summer.

Ma and Sister went to town to see Mrs. Kate Bowyer and brought Cousin Kate and Robbie out with them. Cousin Robert walked out in the evening. They are here now. Cousin Kate is not like her merry, happy, old self. I feel so sorry for her. Tomorrow we shall be busy packing to go to Liberty on Tuesday, so I shall not write anymore until I return. I put the events of this interesting week in a very small space.

7

Avenel

I shall try to write some of the events of our happy visit to Avenel.
We left here on Tuesday, the 28th of October, and went to
Bonsack's in the stage. One of our fellow-travellers was Maj. Nat
Witson [probably Major Nathaniel C. Wilson of the 28th Virginia
Infantry] who made himself very agreeable. At Bonsack's we met
Cousin Kate Bowyer, and continued our journey to Liberty with
her. We arrived at Avenel just in time for dinner. Mrs. Burwell
and Rosa met us at the door. Mrs. B. was just the lovely, gentle
lady that I expected her to be, but Rosa was much prettier and
more interesting than I had been led to believe from what I had
heard. She is very singular looking, and without having a pretty
feature, has a striking and pleasing face. I liked her very much.
Cousin Letty, though, was my favorite. She is just as lovely and
good as anyone can be. I never saw anyone who was so unselfish
and lived so much for others as she does. Now that Fan is gone,
Cousin Letty is the flower of the family. Upon entering the parlor,
we were introduced to Captain Frank Clarke of New Orleans, a
soldier who was slowly recovering from a wound received at the
battle of Sharpsburg.[1] He is a bright, smart, *nice* little fellow!
Then entered upon the scene Mr. Willie Michel of Washington, a
conceited, smart, handsome, interesting, diminutive gentleman,
whose most striking peculiarities were that he was a nephew of

---

1. Captain Frank Clark of the 6th Louisiana suffered wounds on two more
occasions. He became permanently disabled in April 1863 from wounds received at
Fredericksburg. Andrew Booth, *Records of Louisiana Confederate Soldiers and Louisiana
Confederate Commands*, II, p. 348.

Gen. Joe E. Johnston, and an accepted lover of Rosa's. Later in the evening the stage was rendered more thrillingly interesting by the appearance of Dr. Todd[2] and *Lieut. Richardson* (!) of Louisiana.[3] The former looks like a little good natured Scotch terrier. I like Dr. Todd—he talks of alligators! I believe he is a beau of Rosa's. Lieut. Richardson appeared that evening to be a bashful man, so they all said, but I was of a different opinion. I thought of *The Spectator* whenever I looked at him. He is one of the most perfectly handsome men I ever saw. I would describe him, but words fail. I did not get at all acquainted with him that night, but when I did I found him to be one of the least *bashful* and most charming persons I ever met.

Well, time wore on and each day found Avenel possessed of some new charm. At first I missed dear Fan so much that I could not be happy. Eliza, Cousin Kate, Cousin Letty and I walked out to her grave one evening. It is a very desolate spot. Cousin Letty seems to miss her more and think of her more than any of them. I studied Cousin Letty, and, diving beneath those frivolous, light-hearted little manners, found a fine, noble, little heart. I shall always love Cousin Letty. Little Lillie is one member of the household whom I have failed to mention. She was so sweet and pretty that she proved a source of great interest to Eliza and myself.

After we had been at Avenel a week, Capt. Hamilton Pike of Arkansas arrived.[4] He was a great acquisition. He is so bright and sweet that Eliza and I felt as if we had known him all of our lives. While he was there we made up a party to the Peaks.[5] Eliza,

2. This was probably a reference to Charles Henry Todd, an Assistant Surgeon who had served on the staff of the Moore Hospital at Manassas. Manassas was evacuated in May 1862 and the hospital was reestablished at Gordonsville. Wyndham B. Blanton, *Medicine in Virginia in the Nineteenth Century*, p. 308.

3. Frederick Richardson was at this time on sick leave. He was later promoted to Captain of Co. F of the Fifth Louisiana Infantry and was killed in action at Gettysburg on 4 July 1863. Booth, *Records*, III, Bk. 2, p. 309.

4. Captain Luther Hamilton Pike of Arkansas was the son of the controversial Brigadier General Albert Pike, Provisional Army, C.S.A., and captain of an artillery company in his father's command. For more complete information see Ezra J. Warner, *Generals in Gray*, pp. 240-41; *O.R.*, I, 13, pp. 869, 923, 977, 978, 980, 981; *O.R.*, I, 48, Pt. 2, pp. 1266, 1280; Margaret Ross, *Arkansas Gazette*, pp. 375-76, 397.

5. The Peaks of Otter are located in Bedford County, Virginia.

Rosa, Mr. Michel and I went in a wagon. Cousin Letty, Lieut.
Richardson, and Capt. Pike went on horseback. The day was
beautiful and the road very rocky and terrible, so we had a
pleasant trip with a little alloy of stones—anything *but precious*
stones we thought them. At one terrible jolt someone of the party
became poetic and parodied Longfellow's piece, "Some days must
be dark and gloomy" and we all agreed that "into each life some
stones must fall, some roads be rough and *rocky.*"Rosa, becoming
very tired, laid down in my lap and I sang "Rock a bye Baby" to
her.

At the Peak hotel we all stopped. I had been riding Cousin Letty's
pony, and gracefully dismounted, but getting out of the wagon
was rather an awkward thing. Rosa turned a complete some (sort
of) a set, but congratulated herself that everything was white and
clean! Ascending the Peaks was found to be somewhat fatiguing.
Rosa was carried by Mr. Michel, Cousin Letty rode on a mule, and
Capt. Pike, Lieut. Richardson, Eliza and I went up like men and
mountaineers. The view was magnificent and repaid us for our
toil. That was a very happy day!

I wish to commemorate one other happy evening at Avenel. The
Misses Smith, refugees from Alexandria, Drs. Moses, Letcher and
Blackford, and Lieut. R. spent a sociable evening. We had a great
deal of fun laughing at Capt. Clarke's telling Eliza "the cherubim
and seraphim" anecdote so often. At last, or at the end of two
weeks, we thought it was time to tear ourselves from Avenel. We
proposed to Cousins Letty and Rosa, Mr. Michel, and Lieut.
Richardson to come home with us, and to go from there to the
Natural Bridge,[6] to which they all agreed.

Another night at Avenel must be put on record. Rosa and I
determined that being awakened at the early hour of six was very
disagreeable, and to save ourselves that painful operation we
made up our minds to put on our cloaks and bring our bonnets
downstairs, and sit up all night—which we did most heroicly do.
We drew two large rocking chairs up to the fire in the parlor and

6. This natural phenomenon is located in Rockbridge County, Virginia, about
twenty-five miles from the site of Grove Hill.

seating ourselves therein most cozily and comfortably talked romances, discussed the "phantoms" and the propriety of marrying "phantoms" and being a Rosy "Phantom." At length, finally becoming tired of talking of phantoms at that late and fearful hour, we betook ourselves to reading out the first days of Pisistratus Caxton, and after laughing merrily over his infantile experiences, we resorted to apples. At last, even apples failed to interest and amuse us. Becoming desperate (at 3 o'clock) we thought we would arouse Cousin Letty. I neglected to mention that Eliza, becoming frightened at a ghost tapping at the head of Cousin Kate's bed, came down into the parlor at the 2nd hour. At 4 o'clock, Rosa and I had succeeded in awakening all of our fellow-travellers, and as "rosy morn purpled o'er the sky" we were all in the cars flying at the rate of 13 miles an hour to Bonsack's. At that place we encountered our old friend, Uncle Phil. We then got into the hack, and with Mr. Michel driving, we soon arrived at Amsterdam, where Cousin Letty got out and bought shoes, etc. We then proceeded to Grove Hill where we found everything very sweet and homelike.

The next day (Wednesday, Nov. 12th, 1862), directly after breakfast we started to the Bridge, Cousin Letty, Eliza, Emma and I going in the carriage, Mr. M. on Gazelle, and Lieut. Richardson driving Rosa in the buggy. About 3 miles this side of Buchanan, Cousin Letty and I got tired of the carriage and got into the buggy, and I drove to within 6 miles of the Bridge through cattle, rocks, broken bridges and other obstacles. Lieut. R. rode near and kept a tender and watchful eye over Cousin Letty. We took a guitar and flute to the Bridge and after coffee (pint cups of that article), we sat in the parlor and had music, poetry, and a very hot fire. We all went down to the Bridge the evening we got there. Lieut. R. was the only one of the party who went down the next morning. We left the Bridge after a hearty breakfast of "subdued sausage," and arrived at the "Bank" at 12 o'clock, and took a delightful dinner and some beautiful songs with Sister Julia. We then came home, arriving quite late. The gentlemen, being very much fatigued, excused themselves and took their tea (milk) in their rooms, but the ladies being of stouter constitutions came down and sat in the parlor until bedtime, when they came upstairs and serenaded the young truants, singing with the guitar the sublime songs, "Sleep

73

Fair Maidens" and "Good Night"—with an occasional interlude
of the flute played by Mrs. Breckinridge.

The party staid until Saturday. Lulie came on Thursday and staid
until Friday evening. She and Eliza went to town in the carriage,
Cousin Letty and Mr. Richardson were on horseback, and I drove
Rosa in the buggy, coming home alone. The traces came loose and
Rosa and I had to fix it all by ourselves. Cousins Robert and Kate
B. came home in the carriage with Eliza. Early on Saturday
morning they (the Burwells, the Lieut. and Mr. M.) left us—left
us desolate and broken-hearted. I felt so sad at parting with the
Lieut. He is so much like John was that it made us all take great
interest in him, and we can never expect to see him again. I
became so desperate at parting with those dear friends that I
solemnly said that I would never meet anybody anymore. Oh,
dear! 'Twas very sad! The clock strikes 12! I must pause in these
sweet reminiscences and close my weary eyes. Dear friends of
Avenel, I bid you a long, a drear farewell! May we all meet again.
Will we all meet again? Time, remorseless time will tell!

Tuesday, Nov. 18th, 1862
I must write a little more about Avenel and the acquaintances I
made there. Eliza, Rosa, Mr. Michel and I went out to Judge
Wingfield's and saw Miss Sis and her four maiden sisters. We also
went to Mr. Davies' to see Miss Muggy. One bright day we went
out to see "Ops," Donald and Lady. They have such a sweet,
pretty place. I enjoyed our little visit to them. While we were at
Avenel, Bettie Campbell, now Mrs. Hendrick, and her husband
spent a day there. Bettie is very much improved since she was
here. I think I shall pass over the other incidents of my visit now
and return to Grove Hill.

Today I wrote a letter to Cousin Letty and one to Capt. Houston. I
received two from him while I was at Avenel and did not have the
energy to answer them.

8

Quiet Days

I have been so busy and so lazy this week that I have entirely
neglected my friend, "H.R." I shall return tonight with renewed
zeal. All last week Cousin Kate interested me so much that I could
not write. She and Cousin Robert are staying with us now. They
are so bright and sweet that they are a great comfort to us. I got a
letter from Cousin Letty and replied to it. We also got letters from
Brothers Gilmer and Cary.

On Friday I drove Emma to town in the buggy to take her music
lesson. I staid at Lulie's and nursed little Virginia. I got some
cantharides and hartshorn, and mixing these articles with sweet
oil and alcohol, made an *infallible* remedy for falling off of the
hair, baldness, turning grey and other afflictions of the hair.
Cousin Kate gave me the idea of how to make it, and I proposed
naming it after her, "Bonnie Doen." I put some on Ma's head and
hope that she will soon have an abundant suit of hair.

On Sunday we all went to hear Mr. Grasty preach, and heard quite
a practical sermon on the subject of giving to the poor.[1] On
Monday we all went hard to work making shirts for the soldiers,
and I made the first whole garment that I have made in many
years—since I used to play "babies." Eliza went down to
Buchanan early in the morning, and in the evening returned

1. The Reverend Mr. Thomas Grasty was pastor of the Presbyterian Church in
Fincastle.

bringing Sister Julia and little Nannie. On Tuesday we all sewed on shirts and had a pleasant day. Nannie is so sweet and interesting.

Eliza got a very shocking letter from Cousin Kate Bowyer on the subject of Rosa and Mr. Michel, accusing us of encouraging Rosa in her love for "that young man." I got a note from Cousin Rosa saying that she, Cousin Letty, Capt. Clarke, and Dr. Todd would be here the first of next week. Red Fox returned from the army looking very badly, but spirited.

Today nothing has happened. We have sewed, knitted, and played with Robbie and Nannie. George went down to Uncle Harmer's at Gordonsville to bring Brother James' horse home. Uncle H. has sold Logan and bought Soldier's Joy, a place in Nelson County.[2]

Thursday, Nov. 27th, 1862

This morning we all sat in the chamber being industrious. I am getting over my unsocial habit of sitting in my room reading all day. I finished Nannie's little socks before dinner. Cousin Kate, Robbie, and I went to walk on "The Hill of Gloom" this evening, and found some beautiful white frost, shaped like lilies and feathers. I never saw any like it before. We brought some home, and Ma, who was quite a wood nymph in her youth, said she had never seen any before. After dinner we received a reinforcement of shirts, and all went to work upon them. I could have finished one tonight, but sewed a sleeve in wrong and had not the energy to rip it out. Eliza got a letter today from Cousin Martha Adams offering to pay us a visit. Nannie has been so sweet and funny today. Sister Julia told us one thing she said which ought to be put on record. She is accustomed to hearing the servants say that she is exactly like "Marse Jeemes." The other day she was holding a kitten in her lap, looking attentively at it, said very gravely, "O! Kitty, you are just zackly like Marse Jeemes." The little thing has never suffered from any of the ills that flesh is heir to except "pain under her apron" and being "chopped" (chafed). She was looking out and saw a dog lying very still and said, "Poor little

2. "Soldier's Joy" was the former home of Samuel Jordan Cabell (1756-1818), Revolutionary patriot and statesman. *DAB*, 3, pp. 388-89.

dog! It is dead." Jane told her that it was not dead, whereupon, she declared very pathetically that it was "chopped" then.

I read *The Lays of the Scottish Cavaliers,* today.[3] It is such a sweet little book.

Friday, Nov. 28th, 1862

It is late at night, and I am very sleepy. Eliza is sitting beside me rocking Nannie to sleep and singing "Three Little Kittens." Nannie is so much interested in the unfortunate little kittens who have lost their mittens and couldn't have any pie that she does not seem disposed to sleep. I think "Old John Brown" would probably be more soothing. I have just left Cousin Kate's room. She and I have been discussing matrimony very earnestly and she made me promise never to marry "D." I wrote a letter to Rosa this morning expressing my joy at the prospect of seeing them so soon. Eliza does not seem disposed to answer Cousin Kate's [Bowyer] letter.

Eliza, Cousin Kate, Robbie and I walked to the shop today, and watched Joshua mending a plowshare. Last night some men broke into the mill and stole flour and some of the batting cloth. They also tried to take Gazelle, but she threw the man and refused to be a party to the theft. Pa's mill has been the Egypt of the county, and I am surprised that anyone should treat him so. They are deserters from the army and, therefore, bad men.

Tuesday, Dec. 2, 1862

I have been so deeply interested in Tennyson's poems for the last few days that I forgot "H.R." I admire his poetry. "The Princess" is splendid and "Locksley Hall" is a little gem. On Saturday morning when we arose the ground was covered with snow, so we were confined to the house most of the day. Nannie was our little sunbeam. She has won my heart more completely than any child ever did. She sleeps in our room and stays awake until late at night amusing us.

---

3. A collection of ballad-romances published in 1849 by William Edmondstone Aytoun (1813-1865).

On Sunday we went to hear Mr. McGuire preach and he gave us quite a good sermon. Robbie went to church for the first time. Lulie gave him an immense apple which kept him quiet until the sermon was nearly ended. After church we all went and sat with Lulie for an hour hoping the mail would come in, but it was later than usual. On Monday we all played with Nannie and read. Brother Gilmer went to Buchanan Monday morning, and in the evening Sister Julia got a note from Dr. Kean saying Mr. Anthony was ill. She went down too, so we feel quite desolate. Robbie and I went down to the stable and fed Little Dorrit. Eliza, Cousin Kate, and I walked to town today. Cousin Kate went to see Mrs. Hodge and Eliza and I went to see Lulie. After sitting with her an hour we thought it was time for Uncle Phil to return from Buchanan and we wanted to ride home, so Eliza and I started *down* street to meet the carriage. We walked below Mr. Grasty's but still saw nothing of Uncle Phil. We stopped at "Aunt Milly's" and inquired if she had seen the carriage pass. She had not! We then walked *up* street and seeing Emma Nelson standing on the porch, we went in to see her a few moments. Still no carriage! We then proceeded to wind our weary way *up* street. We went to Woltz's for Cousin Kate, found she had gone *down* street looking for us, went *down* street to look for Cousin K. We stumbled upon her at a corner. We heard glad tidings of the carriage. The carriage soon appeared winding its rumbling way *down* street. We got into the carriage, got safely home, got a good dinner, and so on.

Wednesday, Dec. 3rd, 1862

Read all the morning. After dinner, Cousin Kate, Eliza, Emma, Robbie, and I went to the mill. We examined all the works and had ourselves weighed. We were respectively: 134, 142, 187, 37, 152. We enjoyed the walk very much.

Thursday, Dec. 11th, 1862

Another long interruption! On last Saturday late in the evening Cousin Kate got a dispatch which made her determined to go to Kentucky immediately, so that night she packed up and on Sunday morning left us. We felt so sad at parting with them. Cousin Kate is certainly the finest woman of her age that I ever saw.

On Monday the 8th, Cousins Letty and Rosa, Capt. Frank Clarke, and Dr. Todd came. On Tuesday they all went to town and invited Messrs. Walter Staples, Thomas Michie, and Randolph Tucker out to spend the night, but the important case of "Va. versus Rucker" prevented their coming.[4] I wrote Sallie Grattan a long letter, and wrote a note to Brother James.

On Wednesday the 10th, we all spent a memorable day. Cousin Letty, Dr. Todd, and Capt. Clarke went to Fincastle to attend Rucker's trial, and returning brought Lulie! She kept us laughing all day, but when Mr. Tucker came I never did know such a funny time. He is perfectly charming and one of the most amusing persons I ever saw, and quite as bad and vile as Lulie. Mr. Tucker, Capt. Clarke, and Lulie kept the company convulsed with laughter all the evening. Somehow, Mr. Tucker got to talking about Lulie's baby, and Capt. C. begged her to carry it to Liberty and said if she would do so that he would nurse it all the way down for her, so they called him "the nuss," and got to talking dreadfully. Lulie laughed about how small the baby was and Capt. C. said it weighed nine pounds, but Lulie insisted upon it—that it only weighed six. Mr. Tucker said very gravely, "Why, Mrs. Meredith, it ought to have commenced with that!," which silenced her for a minute. Everytime Lulie spoke to the Capt. she called him "nuss," and he whispered to Eliza that he was a "dry nurse." Mr. Tucker seemed very much surprised at Lulie's having so young a baby at home, and kept on asking her how she managed to leave it so long or how the baby got on without her. Lulie told him she could leave her baby whenever she chose at which Mr. T. said, "Oh! the nuss can take it in the bed with him if you bring it out with you." Lulie said he was not moist enough to which "the nuss" retorted that he guessed he would be moist enough by morning if Virginia slept with him. This morning Capt. Clarke was singing and had his hand in his bosom. Lulie looked at him for a moment and said she wondered what he was feeling for. Dr. Todd said, "He is getting

4. A lengthy and involved case brought before the Circuit Court of Botetourt County as the result of a change of venue from the Circuit Court of Alleghany County. The case concerned the trial of a man indicted on ten counts: murder, treason, arson, five counts of larceny, and two counts of enticing slaves to run away. Botetourt County Court Records.

something for the baby, I expect." Dr. Todd said worse things than anybody else. He helped Lulie to her supper and told her to take a sausage, that she had to eat for two. Mr. Tucker told me a good deal about the Grattans. Gen. Garland left Sallie a legacy of $10,000.

Thursday (today) Capt. Frank Clarke, Lulie, and Emma went to Fincastle in the carriage, and Dr. Todd and Rosa went in the buggy. Dr. Todd has made me his confidant, and we like each other very much. I have a terrible headache today, and hardly think I can go to Roanoke. Capt. Clarke got such a smart, well-written letter from Lieut. Richardson today. I have neglected to mention that Mrs. Carrington and Mrs. Campbell have been to see us. They spent last Thursday with us. On that day I got a letter from Capt. H. which I answered immediately. The engagement is broken off and I don't love him any now. "Oh! woman, fair woman, light as a feather, false as fair weather. Who will believe her?" Today Eliza and Rosa dressed up like old ladies. Eliza acted her part so well that they all said they should never have recognized her. She looked exactly like Mrs. Carrington. Ever since they assumed that costume they have been acting old Aunt Dinah and Aunt Elizabeth; and they amuse us children very much talking of their acquaintances, Jacob, Moses, Methuselah, etc. This evening Cousin Letty and Dr. Todd took a ride on horseback.

Thursday, Dec. 18th, 1862
On Friday, Dec. 12th, Rosa, Dr. Todd and I got into a hack, and Eliza, Capt. Clarke and Cousin Letty into the carriage and went up to Oaklands. We had a very pleasant trip. Dr. Todd and I got very confidential. I like him so much better than I expected to. About 8 miles from Oaklands Capt. Clarke stopped to light his pipe and we all heard a violin in the house he went to. We all followed and found upon entering the "back parlor" of a small cabin, a very pretty girl playing with all her might upon a fiddle. We staid there about half an hour and had a great deal of fun. About dark we arrived at Oaklands. There were so many ladies there, all dressed in deep mourning, that we felt as if we were at a convent and formed a sisterhood. There were Cousins Alice, Emma, Anne,

Letty, Mrs. Gwathmey, Cousin Sara White, Lizzie Holcombe, Miss Fanny and Lucy Johnstone, making, with the two Burwells and two Breckinridges, 14 ladies dressed in black. Cousin Alice had a very devoted beau, Judge Robertson of Charlottesville. Rosa and I were so restless that we walked up and down the pavement most of the time.

On Saturday morning Rosa finally and decidedly discarded Dr. Todd, and he left immediately. I missed him very much. Rosa has broken off her engagement with Mr. Michel. Capt. Clarke and I got better acquainted at Oaklands. He called us his little family, and we were very devoted children and staid with the old patriarch constantly.

On Sunday everyone went to church except Rosa and myself. While everyone was gone, Col. Carr came in and scared Rosa and me nearly to death. Dr. Blackford came on Sunday.[5] I like him very much. On Monday Dr. Blackford vaccinated everybody and then we sent for the carriages; and Rosa, Capt. C. and I got into one carriage, Dr. B., Eliza and Cousin Letty in another, and we all went over to Buena Vista. The Tayloes were charming and we spent a delightful day and night. Cousin Mattie Adams was there and could not come home with us. I shall always remember my visit to the Tayloes with pleasure. They promised to come to see us in the Spring.

On Tuesday morning Capt. Clarke, Cousin Letty and I got into our carriage, Eliza and Rosa in the Tayloe equipage, and Dr. Blackford on a "recalcitrating" horse, and went to the depot. We got there just in time. Eliza and I bid a sad farewell to them all, went back to Oaklands to tell them all goodbye, and then we came back home. We arrived just about sunset and found everything

5. Dr. Benjamin Blackford entered the war as Assistant Surgeon with the 11th Virginia Infantry. He was promoted to Surgeon, 26 May 1862. At this time Blackford was in charge of the hospital at Liberty (Bedford City), Virginia, where he remained until Hunter's Raid of June 1864 forced him to evacuate the hospital. Blackford was under orders from Surgeon General Moore to vaccinate people in the vicinity because of the outbreak of smallpox. Wyndham B. Blanton, *Medicine in Virginia in the Nineteenth Century*, pp. 305-10, 395.

just as we left it. Brother Gilmer was here. I found a letter from Sister and a note from Sue Jones asking us to spend Xmas with her.

On Wednesday Eliza and I rested from our labors and took breakfast in our room. The battles of Fredericksburg keep us all right uneasy. I was so sorry to see that Gen. Tom Cobb was killed, but he gained a brilliant victory.[6] Early this morning Eliza and Ma went down to Buchanan. While they were gone I walked and wrote. At dinner time Brother Gilmer came up from the Bank and went on from here to the Warm Springs. Ma got a letter from George saying the reason he did not come home was because he had a "boil on his seat of honor." We miss him so much. I got a letter from Rosa Burwell enclosing one from Mr. Michel. Capt. Clarke promised to write to Eliza and I hope he will remember to do so. Ma returned late this evening leaving Eliza in Buchanan, which makes me very mournful. Emma and I sat up a long time tonight making Roman Catholic wafers between two flat irons. They are really very nice. I want to begin going to bed early now, so I must stop scribbling for tonight and reserve further communications for———

Friday, Dec. 19th, 1862

It is late at night. Emma is already folded in the soft arms of sleep, man's sweet "lastory." In spite of my good resolutions I find it impossible to retire early. I have been reading *The Spectator* today and enjoy it so much. Tonight I picked up "Salad for the Solitary" and thinking it appropriate to my feelings and position, took quite a large "slice" of it. I feel very low-spirited tonight. Let

6. The Battle of Fredericksburg, 12-15 December 1862, was one of the bloodiest of the war. In the *New York Times* of 17 December 1862, a special correspondent reports on the fighting of Dec. 13th: "... The result thus far leaves us with a loss of from ten to fifteen thousand men, and absolutely nothing gained. Along the whole line the rebels hold their own. Again and again we have hurled forward our masses on their position. At each time the hammer was broken on the anvil!" The strategy of General Ambrose Burnside, Commander of the Army of the Potomac, was regarded as "a manifestation of daring untempered by the slightest prudence."

Although the Confederate losses were less than half of the Federal losses, numbered among their dead were Brigadier Generals Thomas R. R. Cobb of Georgia and Maxcy Gregg of South Carolina. *CMH*, 3, pp. 360-74; A. L. Long, *Memoirs of Robert E. Lee*, pp. 224-45; *O.R.*, I, pp. 21, 545-56; Wakelyn, *Biographical Dictionary*, p. 142.

me think now of the causes. I have laid down my pen and looked
at the fire and reflected that I am mournful, 1st because Eliza is
away, 2nd, because of the war and the danger and discomforts the
boys have to endure. Oh! for peace and a large family circle again,
though the dearest of our band may never more be with us. I have
yearned so to see Johnny once more. He was dearer to me than
anyone on earth and I shall most probably be separated from him
for years. I cannot hope for an early death. I wrote to Eliza today.
I think Eliza and I are more devoted to each other than we ever
were before and so it is harder to be separated from her, but poor
Sister Julia needs her more than I do. I wish I was as useful and
necessary to someone as Eliza is to Sister Julia. I also wrote a long
letter to Rosa Burwell. The papers today give further particulars
of the victory at Fredericksburg. I do not think we had any
acquaintances or friends wounded. I have been thinking about
my last letter to Capt. H., and am really sorry I wrote to him so
unkindly. His letter did not justify so stern a proceeding. I am
going to write him a kind letter and apologize, if he does not cut
me all to pieces in his next letter. The wind has commenced to
blow so mournfully, so dismally, and I feel so alone. I can't people
the room with sweet fancies and imaginations now. I shall have to
have recourse to sleeping dreams. When I was in love, some four
or five months ago, I always had something interesting to think
of, but now that I have cast aside all such follies and settled down
to discreet, matter-of-fact old-maidism, I have nothing to think of
but darning socks and working for poor soldiers. I'll be a sweet old
maid. I won't have any cats or lap dogs or parrots, but will have
ice-cream, nieces and nephews and such a bright, happy home.
I'll be one of those joyous spirits that ever "make sunshine in a
shady place!" How quiet everything is. I feel a superstitious chill
creeping over me. How foolish! I must write down that sensible
little piece I saw in *The Spectator* about superstition. Here it is!

"I know but one way of fortifying my soul against those gloomy
presages and terror of mind, and that is by securing to myself the
friendship and protection of that Being who disposes of events
and governs futurity. He sees at one view the whole thread of my
existence, not only that part of it which I have already passed
through, but that which runs forward into all the depths of

eternity. When I lay me down to sleep, I recommend myself to His care; when I awake, I give myself up to His direction. Amidst all the evils that threaten me I will look up to Him for help and question not that He will either avert them or turn them to my advantage. Though I know neither the time nor the manner of the death I am to die I am not at all solicitous about it; because I am sure He knows them both and that He will not fail to comfort and support me under them.''

Now, I am much more comfortable and will say my prayers and go to sleep.

9

Year's End

Saturday, Dec. 20th, 1862

Read *The Spectator*. Wrote a good deal in my quotation book. Washed my hair! Took a walk. A man came by with a wagon to take some things to Sister. Mr. Nat Burwell came to spend the night. Baked some apples on the hearth and am now going to eat them!

Monday, Dec. 22nd, 1862

Yesterday, Sunday 21st, we all went to the Presbyterian Church and heard a poor sermon from Mr. Grasty, who told the audience that, "*We* are not well today," and, therefore, could not preach this evening. I like Mr. Grasty very much and went right far to speak to him very affectionately. We parted with Mr. Nat Burwell at church. He is so talkative and amusing, but I am constantly afraid he will suddenly become deranged and pounce upon me. Emma and I went to see Little Dorrit and gave her some corn.

How very matter of fact and uninteresting my journal is. I only write about people and have no ideas. Some of these days my "little daughter" will be reading this charming work, sitting in her little arm chair beside me. She will come to Mr. Nat Burwell's name and will say, "Mamma, who was Mr. N. B.?" And I will tell her he was an uncle of Miss Coalter Logan's, a very good man who was deranged and used to go about buying turkeys and eggs. Then looking at another portion she will see something else she wants explained. I will hear the dulcet tones of her youthful voice and

look into her beautiful, inquiring, blue eyes as she says,
"Mamma, was Mrs. Walter Pike (Rosa B.) ever engaged to Mr.
William Michel?" "Yes, dear." "Well, Mamma, why didn't she
marry him?" (Little innocent has not seen enough of the world to
have found that engagements are lightly made and lightly broken)
"Because, dear, she found she did not love him." Looking down
into that sweet, childish face I shall find the large eyes wide open
with astonishment as she exclaims, "Oh! Mamma, here is
something so curious. Were you ever engaged to that Mr. H. who
was here the other day?" "Yes, child, put up that book and get
your knitting!" "But, Mamma, did you really love him so much?
Had you ever seen Papa then?" "No, dear, there's your Papa
now. Run and get his slippers and don't ask foolish questions!"
(Takes the book and hides it where little blue eyes won't find it)
"Mamma" does not enjoy such inquiries. Mine is a very smart,
precocious, little daughter. She inherits her father's talents and
her mother's *sweetness* of disposition! I ought to be ashamed to
write such nonsense—I who have so solemnly promised myself to
be a good, charming old maid and devote my affections to nieces
and nephews, and to be a sweet, loving old "Auntie." Long since I
bade farewell to the dreams of my youth. Capt. Clarke said I must
not be an old maid, that I would be too good a wife and mother to
sacrifice myself on the altar of Diana, but I do not agree with him.
I don't want any grumblesome husband to be sewing and cooking
for all the time, nor any disagreeable, colicky little babies, always
getting their little noses and mouths soiled and keeping me awake
all night. I beg to be excused. Help me, chaste Diana, to keep
resolutely this wise determination!! And may all the young
maidens who are disposed to laugh at old ladies of my class be
brought to believe that there can be such a thing as a happy,
contented "old maid" when they look upon the happy face of old
"Miss Lucy Breckinridge!"

I wrote a note to Eddie Woodbridge this morning and tonight we
packed a box to send him and Bob Saunders. I received a very
funny letter from Eliza which I answered. This morning I
occupied myself writing a piece of literary mosaic and read *The
Spectator*. Ma is sleeping upstairs with Emma and me. E. has a
very bad cold.

86

Tuesday, Dec. 23rd, 1862

Ma sent the wagon to Buchanan today and tonight we got notes from Eliza and Sister Julia. Emma has been sick in bed all day. I sat upstairs with her and read *The Spectator*. The 26th number is so beautiful on his visit to Westminister Abbey. About 12 o'clock I went to walk on "Cedar Hill." "The air was as soft and balmy as a woman's sighs" (Mr. D. Davies), and everything looked so still and beautiful. The haziness of the atmosphere made the mountains look so far off and softened the outline of the hills and everything. I was very happy over there. I am always happy when I am out of doors and alone. "I am never less alone than when alone!" (L.R.) It is quite late at night so I must stop writing—"sic gloria transit Tuesday."

Wednesday, Dec. 24th, 1862

This is Christmas Eve and how have we spent it! Pa, Ma and I sitting in the dining room talking as gravely as if there was no such thing as Xmas. No little socks to hang up at Grove Hill now! Just think how desolate it must be! Not a brother! And only one sister, and she *sick*! I have been restless and I think wretched today. I tried my cure for mournfulness—walked over to "Cedar Hill" which rose so much in my return today that I christened it "Bushnell's Mountain." My spirits were a little raised by receiving a letter from Rosa Burwell and Eliza got very funny letters written to "Old Aunt Elizabeth" by "Frank," "Benny Blackfoot," "Charlie Todd," "Little Letty," and "Old Aunt Dinah." "Benny's" letter was so perfect an imitation of a little boy's style of writing that it was very hard to decipher. All of "the little ones" wrote very sweet, funny letters to "Aunt E." I posted Nelson to town immediately to have the letters forwarded to Eliza. I won't write any more now until Xmas.

Thursday, Dec. 25th, 1862

George came home today. He looks very badly and does not seem to have enjoyed his visit to "Soldier's Joy" very much. The servants have all been busy in the kitchen making cakes, etc., for Jim's wedding. Emma and I both have such bad colds that we could not help them much. Ma, Emma and I walked over to the graveyard this evening. Tonight we all sat in the dining room and talked with George. After supper Matilda and Virginia came in to let us see how nice they looked dressed for the wedding. Both looked lovely, attired in white muslin with black trimmings.

Monday, Dec. 29th, 1862

The last few days have been very peculiar, they reminded me of a piece of Hood's poetry called *"November."* We had *no* servants, *no* dinner, *no* supper, *no* comfort, *November*! When the holidays are over I think I'll write an Ethiopian parody on it, having *de* servants, *de* carriage, *de* fires, *de* dinner, *de* cook, *de* light, *December*.

We miss Eliza so much. On Friday Emma and I really worked hard helping Matilda to make cakes for her party. I learned all about baking. In the evening I made a beautiful head-dress for Serena and carried it over to Aunt Sukey's. They all begged Emma and me so hard to come to the wedding that we went. The bride looked very pretty dressed in pink tarleton with the artificial pink and white roses I fixed in ivy leaves for her. The Episcopal service was read by "Uncle Ned" at Dolly's house. After the marriage Dolly and Susan begged us to go to Polly's house to see the dancing. They had banjoes and fiddles and danced quite prettily.

Major Lewis came here Friday night and there was not a servant about the house, so Ma "got" supper and she and I fixed the room for him. Saturday Messers Utz and Logan dined here with Major Lewis. I was more than ever struck with the awful solemnity which attends gentlemen's eating and drinking.

Saturday night Matilda's party came off. She begged very hard that Emma and I would go, but no whites went except George and Charlie Utz. They say that everything was in elegant style.

On Sunday, we all went to church. The congregation was immense and communion had been appointed. We all waited for Mr. McGuire until 12 when the people dispersed. Cousin Lizzie Preston had brought her baby in to be christened. It is a sweet little thing and some think like Eliza. After church, Mrs. Hudson came up and invited George, Emma and me to spend Monday with her. George was not well enough to go, and I do not associate with such young, giddy creatures as the Pitzers, Wilsons, Millers, etc., and declined going, so Emma had to go alone. She returned late this evening and said she spent a very pleasant day. Mary H. sent me an elegant apple which quite touched my sensibility. All the servants gone to a party at Santilaine kept me busy writing passes.[1] Joe came for one and while he was waiting said, "Miss, Marse Tom (Col. Swann) say he wish you would send him some preserves and good things if I go back." He and "Marse Tom" seem to be very good friends.

Tuesday, Dec. 30th, 1862

Nelson started today to Nelson Co. to bring Brother James' horse home. Ma got a letter from Brother James, I got letters from Eliza and Capt. H. Eliza enclosed her vaccine—I vaccinated Emma tonight. When Capt. H.'s letter was handed me I opened it with fear and trembling, expecting to have anathemas showered upon my wicked head, but I was astonished to receive a gentle, apologizing letter, very long and interesting. He will *not* quarrel with me. What shall I do! Oh! for Eliza to advise me. He is a smart, fine, magnanimous young man, but I do not want to be Mrs. H., and I will tell him so honestly and gently.

Wednesday, Dec. 31st, 1862

It is late tonight—almost 1863. This time last year I was at Mrs. Miller's talking to Capt. H. This time I have just finished a letter finally and decidedly breaking off our engagement. This world is all a fleeting show! 1862 has been an eventful year for me. How I wish I could just take a little peep into 1863. God grant it may not be so sad a year! Poor Brother James, 1862 will never be forgotten by him. In March he was married, in June lost his dearest brother, and in August his lovely wife. So much has happened since he was at home in March. I got a letter from Eddie Woodbridge today. Ella and Jennie Godwin, Damaris and Chigg Wilson spent today here. George is quite sick. Tonight I wrote to Eliza.

1. According to the Criminal Code of 1848 enacted by the Virginia State Legislature, slaves or free Negroes going from home without a pass were punishable by stripes, not exceeding thirty-nine. June Purcell Guild, *Black Laws of Virginia*, p. 168.

1863

1

Lonely Days

Friday, January 2nd, 1863

January 1st I read a life of Addison, also of Steele, Hughes and other writers in *The Spectator*.[1] I take more interest in the writings when I know the character and history of the writer. Today I read *The Spectator* industriously. I also read some of Cowley's[2] poetry which *The Spectator* criticises under the head of Wit. I do not admire Cowley. I cannot appreciate him. Tonight I read a play in *The English Theater*, "Oroonoko," by Thomas Sotherne.[3] I have done little else than read for the last week or two. Today I did fix my bombazine and vaccinate myself and re-vaccinate Emma. I got a letter from Eliza yesterday and one from Rosa B. today. Ma got a letter from Sister saying that Emma and Jimmy have scarlet fever. I have taken my maid, Virginia, about the house. She does very well and seems to be a cheerful, sweet girl. Smallpox is said to be only five miles from here.

They sent up a large balloon in Fincastle last night. We went out into the yard to see it and it was very brilliant and beautiful. The papers are very encouraging. We are beginning to hope for peace.

1. Joseph Addison (1672-1719), Richard Steele (1672-1729), and John Hughes (1677-1720) were the three major contributors to *The Spectator*, considered the best of all periodical essays of the eighteenth century.
2. Abraham Cowley (1618-1667) wrote essays in the style of Montaigne. At the end of the Restoration period, Cowley appeared "briefly and thinly" as a comic writer. After 1660 his poetry was very influential.
3. This eighteenth century play by Thomas Southerne was a dramatization of the novel, *Oroonoko* or *The Royal Slave*, written in 1688 by Mrs. Aphra Behn (1640-1689).

We have had another victory at Vicksburg and one at Murfreesboro.[4]

Saturday, January 3rd, 1863
I read *The Spectator* and two plays, "Cato," by Addison and "Zara" by A. Hill. Emma and I went to the stable to see Little Dorrit. I feel right uneasy about Sister's children having scarlet fever. I hope dear little Mary will be spared—it is so dangerous for babies. I should like to see her now.

Tuesday, January 6th, 1863
On Sunday none of us went to church except George who went to hear a new Methodist preacher. I was sick in bed all day. Vaccinations had a singular effect upon Eliza, Matilda, Virginia and myself. Ma sat upstairs with me writing all day. I read 1st and 2nd Eccleas. The three wise men's proverbs amused me very much. I think the one who said wine was strongest might take the prize now.

At dinnertime George brought the mail. Ma and Eliza got letters from Miss Lelia Saunders who says Miss Agnes Coles spent Xmas at the Rectory. I hereby prophesy that she will be Mrs. George T. Wilmer. She is very sweet and would make a good stepmother to the little ones. I got a beautiful letter from Sallie Grattan. She says Lucy is to be married the 10th of this month to Major Will Alexander. He will be a very good match for Lucy. I liked him so much. I do wish Sallie could come to see us. I love her so dearly.

Later in the evening Amanda came down from the "Gomery" White bringing a letter from Sister. Little Emma still continues very sick with scarlet fever and longs so to see "Grandma" that Ma determined to go up immediately. She and Emma left this morning. I feel very uneasy about the little thing.

4. The Vicksburg reference concerns the Confederate victory under the command of Brigadier General Stephen D. Lee over the Union forces under the command of General W. T. Sherman at the battle of Chickasaw Bayou, Mississippi, on 29 December 1862. *CMH*, 7, pp. 101-7. General Braxton Bragg commanded the Confederate forces in the battle of Stone's River, Kentucky, or Murfreesboro, on 31 December 1862-3 January 1863, and General William S. Rosecrans commanded the Federal forces. Ibid., 5, pp. 112-19.

I have been quite lonely today. Pa, George and I are the only ones at home now. A letter from Eliza cheered me somewhat. I sent her my answer to Capt. H.'s letter for her to criticize and she comforted me very much by her warm approval. I think she is having quite a pleasant time driving out with the Joneses, McGuires, Haneys, etc., but I miss her so much that I think I shall make her come home. I must stop writing my journal now and write to Emma and Eliza. But for my companions, the Japonica, Luna and violets, and my beloved friends, Addison, Steele, etc., I think I should die of ennui. The former interesting companions are living in the window, and *The Spectator* is constantly before my eyes. Lieut. Richardson is very much like Addison.

Thursday, January 8th, 1863

Yesterday nothing occurred worthy of note. Nelson returned bringing Brother James' horse. I got a letter from Eliza. Sister Julia can't come until the 20th of this month and I cannot take Eliza from her, so I resign myself to Pa, George and loneliness. *Boys* are no comfort. George is away at school all day and Pa riding out.

Esdras interests me. He asks God the only questions I have been trying all my life to solve, for instance—"I answered then and said, this is my first and last saying, that it had been better not to have given the earth unto Adam; or else, when it was given him, to have restrained him from sinning. Oh! thou Adam, what hast thou done? For though it was thou that sinned, thou art not fallen alone, but we all that come of thee."[5] Esdras was a great genius, a *very* talented man, but I don't think he was a prophet. Addison's "Vision of Mirza" is very like the writing of Esdras. I think Esdras must have been written after Christ came into the world.

We got two letters from Cary today.

Friday, January 9th, 1863

Today I have been as busy as "A.B." packing things to send to Cary by Jim. I did not have time to read much. I wrote a long letter

---

5. From the *Apocrypha*, 2 Esdras, regarding the mystery of human destiny.

to Cary. We were disappointed when the mail came not to get a letter from Ma, but I hope the children are better. I got a letter from Rosa Burwell, as usual, nothing in it. I answered it tonight. I expect she will pass the same judgment upon mine—it deserves it as it has nothing in it except nonsense about Dr. Todd and her beaux generally. The art of writing and conversing pleasantly, I have found, is to write and talk only of your correspondent's own affairs, and mention only the things which will please their vanity. I intend practising that art, not with any desire to be popular, but just with the kind intention of pleasing people with themselves. Some persons flatter from no other motive than kindness of heart and the wish to give pleasure. I do not think, though, that I shall ever be adept in the art of flattery, as I am naturally so honest and candid in expressing my opinions and sentiments.

George is sitting up here wishing there was no such thing as Friday night, and that Saturday, January 10th would make haste and come.

[Saturday, January 10th, 1863]
Here it is—the 10th!

The ground is covered with snow, so George cannot take his grand hunt. Heard from Ma today. The children are better for which I am very thankful.

Strother came today and brought me a letter from Eliza giving me some advice relative to the "little toe-nail" of the army as Dr. Lazarus would probably call Capt. H. Pa got hold of the letter and read it and then sent for me to get it, a very bad thing in Papa.

My Japonica looks badly. I feel very uneasy about it. The luna is flourishing. I read a great deal today and enjoyed it exceedingly. Tonight I wrote a long letter to Ma. George sat in my room with me a good while tonight.

Monday, January 12th, 1863

Pa and I did not go to church yesterday. George went, but Mr. McGuire did not come so he went to hear Mr. Grasty. I read the

Apocrypha; "The Wisdom of Jesus, son of Sirah," is beautiful. I read some pious numbers of *The Spectator*. One chapter interested me particularly, it is the 237th on the ways of Providence. There is a Jewish tradition concerning Moses which I must write down. That great prophet, it is said, was called up by a voice from heaven to the top of a mountain, where in a conference with the Supreme Being he was permitted to propose to Him some questions concerning His administration of the Universe. In the midst of this divine colloquy he was commanded to look down on the plains below. At the foot of the mountain there issued out a clear spring of water, at which a soldier alighted from his horse to drink. He was no sooner gone than a little boy came to the same place and finding a purse of gold which the soldier had dropped, took it up and went away with it. Immediately, after this, came an infirm old man, weary with age and travelling. Having quenched his thirst he sat down to rest himself beside the spring. The soldier, missing the purse, returned to search for it. He demands it of the old man who affirms he has not seen it, and the soldier, not believing his protestations, kills him. Moses fell on his face with horror and amazement when the divine voice thus presents his expostulations: "Be not surprised, Moses, nor ask why the judge of the whole earth has allowed this thing to pass. The child is the occasion why the blood of the old man is spilt; but know that the old man whom thou sawest is the murderer of that child's father." That's not my idea of justice.

Sunday, January 18th, 1863

It has been more than a week since I wrote in this dear, stupid old book. There is something in the very appearance of it that takes away all of my ideas. I must sum up in as short a space as possible the events of this week.

On Monday, I had salt petre put on the bacon, and read a great deal. On Tuesday, I got a letter from Eliza and one from Lizzie Woodbridge enclosed in a long letter from Mr. W. to Eliza. I also received a letter from Ma. I am beginning to think I can't do without her any longer. Papa misses her so much, too. On Wednesday, I read industriously and attended to my dear flowers, and practiced medicine on Aunt Betsy. She is still very poorly, but better. Wrote to Eliza, Miss Jane Harvey and Sue Jones. On Thursday, I sent Strother and Joe over to Bath[6] with what few things I could fix for Brother Gilmer.

George is a great comfort to me. I tried to write Sallie Grattan, but find it hard to do, probably from the exalted admiration and love I feel for her. I love her just as a human girl would be supposed to love a goddess. Besides my arduous duties as housekeeper, I have to practice medicine. Ella has been quite sick and I had to treat her for *violent affection of the summits* of her lungs. Lydia's baby has diphtheria, the croupal form, I think. I applied instant and severe remedies and think it will probably recover. I can make or take a diagnosis now as quickly as any M.D.

A letter from Uncle George announces the birth of a little daughter who opened her eyes upon this world on the 3rd of January. He has named her Mary Peachy.

Monday, January 19th, 1863
I dreamed of peaches last night and upon waking this morning lay in bed thinking of Dolly's mournful interpretation: "to dream of fruit out of season is trouble without reason," and in my own mind trying to establish the fallacy of it. The truth of it was most painfully impressed upon my mind by looking around and finding my precious Luna frozen, the sweet little bud that I had watched over with maternal tenderness and anxiety nipped just as it was ready to repay my care. Life is full of sad disappointments, full also of rich blessings—my Japonica was not much injured! I have moved from the room over the chamber to the room over the parlor, and feel that I am entirely removed from the world and a warmer climate to the north pole, where I and all my floral companions will soon be blocks of ice. Instead of calling this room, as I proposed to George, "No. 363 corner of Pictorial Street and Main," I shall henceforth term it the end of the Pole, as it will probably prove the end of me.

I got a long letter from Rosa Burwell on Saturday and one from

6. Bath Alum Springs, Bath County, Virginia.

Ma. Today I received a letter from Ma saying she, "Big Emma,"
"Little Emma," and Cary would be at home on Monday. Jimmy is
not well enough to come. I also received one of the saddest and
most touching letters I ever read from Capt. H. It almost breaks
my heart to have to cause him so much distress, but he will get
over it very soon and laugh at his ever having fancied he loved
me, and tell his future spouse that he cannot express his gratitude
to the Ruler of hearts and events for having so ordered his lot—
that she, lovely and beautiful, is his wife instead of that
uninteresting Lucy Breckinridge. Such, I hope, will be the case. I
wrote to Eliza today. I cannot see her until Friday. Pa opens all
my letters since Eliza's alluding to Capt. H., and I have not a
doubt was very much interested in the Capt.'s letter today. The
Capt. has left the "Fincastle Rifles" and is Asst. Adjt. Gen. of the
Stonewall Brigade.

I have been enjoying the wit and wisdom of *The Spectator* today,
and am sorry to be getting through it so fast. My room, in spite of
its being so terribly cold, looks very sweet and cozy. I have fixed
everything so nicely and tastefully. It is very late now and I must
put up my pen. I feel so tempted to tear this book up, but I intend
to keep it until the 11th of next August, as a reflection of my
faults and follies, inconstancies and inconsistencies. Whenever I
wish to try my blushing faculties I can read the first month of my
journal. Yes, I'll keep it as an antidote to vanity.

2

Ma and Eliza Come Home

Wednesday, January 22nd, 1863

On Tuesday, I sent the carriage to Oaklands for Ma and the children. I spent a very idle day. I tried to read and write, but could not command my thoughts, so I just sat looking in the fire and thinking of the past and future with all my might. I received a letter from Eliza. She says she has *Whittle* news to tell me. I hope it is something good about that unfortunate family. I cannot help taking a deep interest in them. Though I cannot but think they have behaved very badly, I confess, we acted too hastily.

On Wednesday, (today) about four o'clock, Mamma, Big and Little Emma, Jimmy and Cary came. The children look weak and pale but are improving rapidly. Cousin Alice told Ma that she is to be married in March to Judge Robertson! Cousin Letty and Rosa Burwell and myself have cause for shame—we laughed at the Judge so unmercifully before all of the Watts family. I cannot see the fascination about him which caught Cousin Alice—he is dry, old, a widower, and the father of 4 children.[1] Cousin Alice says she could not get a position as matron in a hospital, so she thought she would take an orphan asylum. I wrote a long letter to Rosa Burwell today. I wish I had waited until I could announce

1. A reference to William Joseph Robertson (1817–1898), noted lawyer and jurist, elected to the Supreme Court of Appeals of Virginia in 1859. *DAB*, 17, pp. 29-30. Little did Lucy realize that her beloved niece, Nannie, would some day marry Judge Robertson's son, William Gordon Robertson.

100

that engagement. I am so rejoiced to see Mamma again! Emma has been quite sick and looks very pretty.

Thursday, January 23rd, 1863

Enjoyed the children today. Wrote to Sister, Eliza and Capt. H. I sent my letter to the Asst. Adjt. Gen., to Buchanan by Uncle Phil. Everything looks busy and comfortable since Ma came. Sister gave Ma a little book which interested me very much, a life of Dabney Carr Harrison. One thing that made it peculiarly interesting to me was that I was breakfasting with his father at Miss Deborah Couch's when he received a dispatch informing him of the death of a young and beautiful daughter whom he was just going to see and half an hour later received another dispatch telling him that his noble and talented son, Dabney, was killed at Fort Donelson.[2] I am always interested in observing the emotions and passions, and thought without any reflection on the subject that Mr. Harrison's grief would be doubled upon hearing of the death of his son, but I believe from my limited observation that it was more natural that his first sorrow should be decreased by having another to direct his mind from the one. He could not apply his mind and feelings sufficiently to either one to feel the same intensity of grief.

Eliza will be here tomorrow. She has been away so long that I do not know what I shall do to repress my joy when she comes. I don't like to be so glad when anybody comes.

Friday, January 30th, 1863

Eliza has been at home a week today and I am just setting down the events of her arrival. Little Nannie has not been well since she

2. Captain Dabney Carr Harrison had been an instructor in Hebrew at Union Theological Seminary, Chaplain at the University of Virginia, and a supply minister in Hanover County, Virginia, before the war. He entered the Confederate service as a member of the 56th Virginia Volunteers on 23 September 1861, and was killed leading a charge at Fort Donelson on 16 February 1862. His father was Reverend Peyton Harrison, D. D., a Presbyterian clergyman of Baltimore, Maryland. Rev. Harrison lost three sons during the war in the service of the Confederacy. Richard McIlwaine, *Memories of Three Score Years and Ten*, pp. 102-4; William Wilkins Glenn, *Between North and South*, p. 360.

came. She is as sweet and funny as it is possible for a baby to be. Eliza and I have been busy all this week making beautiful worsted hoods. We made Little Emma a blue one and Eliza's is purple and mine snow white. The ground was covered with deep snow for two weeks and we have been feasting on snow cream. Ma has been quite sick all this week and is not well yet. We were afraid she would have an attack of fever. I got a long letter from Cary which I answered tonight. I also got a letter from Sue Jones in answer to my assertions, avowals, affirmations, etc., that I was not engaged. Brother Lewis came here last night and left this morning to go to the Sweet Springs. He was delighted to see how improved the children were. I have been teaching Little Emma to write and she commenced a letter to Sister yesterday without help from anyone. Dolly got a letter from Joe written by Col. Swann. Major Dick Maury[3] came out here from Fincastle yesterday.

I got a good joke on Emma this evening. She and I pulled the breast bone of a guinea hen to see which would marry first and she got the shortest one. She put it over the chamber door, saying she would marry the first gentleman who came in the room, and she was very certain no one would go in. About an hour afterwards George came in bringing *Robert Logan!* Emma is not at all pleased with her intended. I have not had time to read any this week which distresses me very much. A letter from R. B. She is engaged to Walter Pike.

Thursday, February 12th, 1863
I have been sick with diphtheria for some time and have not written or read any. Ma nursed me while I was sick and I did not see anyone else. Brother Lewis came by to see the children on his way to the Springs.

On Wednesday, February 11th, Sister Julia had a little boy. I have not seen him yet but hear he is a fine little fellow. I will go in to see him this evening. Nannie is very much pleased with "little bubber," as she calls him. Ma and Eliza went to see Mrs. Sue Maury on Tuesday. They were very much pleased with her and

3. Richard L. Maury was later promoted to Lieutenant Colonel of the 24th Virginia Infantry Regiment. *CMH*, 3, p. 565.

Eliza intended going to bring her out here today, but she is not well enough. I got a letter from Capt. H.—the last!

Saturday, February 14th, 1863

The little boy is so sweet and interesting. I never saw a three day old baby. Sister Julia got a letter from Mrs. Pendleton yesterday saying that Uncle Jordan and all of them thought she ought to call the baby John after the dear lost one. His name alone would make him a great darling with us all. I hope he may be like his uncle. There never was a purer or nobler character. Little Nannie was quite sick yesterday, but is well today. Eliza looks so badly and weak that I feel right uneasy about her. Yesterday, I received a letter from Mr. Willie Michel accusing me of breaking off his and Rosa's engagement. I suppose the Burwells, who have no more regard for truth than Ananias, told him that I used my influence with Rosa to make her flirt with him. They have not the moral courage to take it upon themselves. I never said one word to Rosa against Mr. Michel, and if I had Mrs. Kate Bowyer's letter accusing me of using my influence (after an acquaintance of two weeks!) with R. to make her marry him, I should send it to Mr. M. and let him see what a nest of snakes Avenel is. I wrote to Rosa a plain and candid opinion of their treacherous conduct and told her I could not stand an ambushed foe, that if she disliked and abused me when she was away from me she could not pretend to be my friend. I wrote to Mr. M. also, but I could not excuse myself without implicating the Burwells, which I did not want to do. I do not feel like being on friendly terms with such mean, dishonest people, but for Fan's sake must keep up an appearance of kindly feeling.

Thursday, February 19th, 1863

I wrote the above when I was in a most intense and ardent state of mad. I don't think Mrs. K. Bowyer herself could excel it. Yesterday, I received a perfect avalanche of letters from the Burwells, all furious with Mr. Michel and declaring that they never gave him any reason to infer that I was the cause of the sad estrangement. Rosa says she will get her true and manly Walter to cowhide Willie genteelly. She sent me a copy of her letter to Mr. M., a most stupid affair. They all wrote so devotedly to me that I answered Rosa's letter today. I shall write to Cousin Letty as soon as my cold gets better. I owe her two letters. Mrs. Bowyer's letter is very funny and excited.

A Mr. Denton[4] of Brother James' company came by here today and brought likenesses of Brothers James and Cary, drawn in India ink by Mr. Marcus Ammen of Fincastle. They are pretty pictures but horrid likenesses. I hope Brothers Gilmer and James will be here in a few days. Little Nannie stays in our room and is so sweet and funny. She sings six or eight songs and knows her alphabet. Little Johnny gets sweeter every day. He is beginning to take notice now. We got invitations to Mr. John W. Jones' and Miss Marion Alexander's wedding, to take place on the 24th of this month. Eliza and I have a great mind to go to see the old couple married. Ma heard from Sister tonight. The Davies are still giving Brother Lewis a great deal of trouble and proving that they are more serpentine in their characters than their names would infer. Eliza is taking music lessons and is improving very much.

4. James W. Denton, a young carpenter of Fincastle, was 3rd corporal in Company C of the 2nd Virginia Cavalry. Denton was later severely wounded at Beverly's Ford on 9 June 1863. H. B. McClellan, *Life and Campaigns of J. E. B. Stuart*, p. 428; *CSR-Va.*, Roll 17.

3

The Battle of Kelly's Ford

Tuesday, February 24th, 1863

On Friday the 20th, Brother James came and we were perfectly delighted to see him. He looks very sad most of the time, but is so kind and sweet that he very often tries to be merry and amusing. The children keep him busy drawing all the time.

On Sunday there was such a deep snow that none of us went to church. It was well we did not as no church had opened. Brother James and I got letters from Rosa Burwell. She implores Eliza and myself to go over to Avenel with Brother James, and we have decided to do so if the weather permits. Ma received very sweet, nice letters from Annie and Mary Wilmer. I should like so much to see them. They say Uncle George's little Mary is like Ma.

On Monday, Eliza got a letter from Miss Deborah. She says Mr. Anthony is worse. I fear he will not recover. Ma had a letter from Aunt Belle giving an account of little Maria Walker's death. I, as usual, got a letter from Rosa, still begging us to come. I wrote to Joe (or Col. Swann, as the case may be) to inquire about Brother Gilmer. We feel right uneasy about his not coming or writing. Little Johnny is becoming a lovely baby. He is so good and strikingly like Bishop Johns. Eliza and I made 90 envelopes last night after supper. Brother James cut out a good many.

Friday, March 20th, 1863

So much has transpired since I wrote that I scarcely know what to

105

put down. The Friday after I last wrote Maj. Maury and his wife came to see us. While they were here the Major heard of the death of his brother, Johnny, who was drowned in the Mississippi.

On Thursday, the 5th of March, Brother James, Eliza, Major and Mrs. M. and myself went to Fincastle to stay all night at Price's and start from there early in the morning to Bonsack's. Brother J., E. and I spent the evening with Lulie. Early on Friday morning we started to Bonsack's and went over the worst roads I ever experienced. At Liberty we parted with the Maurys who went on to Lynchburg. Brother James was very sad at seeing them all, but they were very kind and affectionate, and he became more cheerful before he left. On Monday, Brother J. and Mr. Burwell left. We miss Brother J. very much. He was so sweet and kind to us all that we love him, if possible, more than ever. Rosa is very proud of a splendid set of jewelry Brother James gave her. Rosa confided all her love affairs to me. She is at this moment engaged to Walter Pike and seems to be very fond of him. We got to playing whist a great deal and that cheered us up very much during the dreary, dismal weather we had.

One night Eliza puzzled Mr. Harvey Allen completely. She dressed up like an old lady and came into the parlor and was introduced as Mrs. Carrington. He was so respectful and talked so gravely to her about her brother, John Preston of S. C., that Rosa and I almost killed ourselves laughing, and his astonished and perplexed look made it all the funnier. Eliza acted her part so well that I do not think he would have found out, but Mrs. Burwell took pity on him and told him who it was. The last night we were at Avenel Dr. Blackford gave a candy stew. Dr. Letcher, Moses and Harris, and Harvey Allen were there. Dr. Blackford presided over the stew. We spent a very pleasant evening and sat up until 2 o'clock. Everyone at Avenel was so kind to us, and we enjoyed our visit so much that it was very sad to leave.

On Tuesday, the 11th, at daybreak Eliza and I went down to the depot. Mr. Burwell intended coming to Bonsack's with us, but he saw his cousin, Mr. William Burwell of Franklin, and put us under his care. He was very kind to us and we got safely home that day by dinner. We found everything at home in a prospering state. During our absence both the Ballards had been sent off of the place.

Little Johnny is much improved and is a big baby now. Nannie is as sweet as possible. I found two letters from Mr. Michel awaiting me. He enclosed Rosa's letters to him for me to read, thereby explaining his own conduct, and convicting R. of a deliberate falsehood. R. has acted badly in that affair, but she is weak and could not help it, so I shall not get angry, but will let the matter rest.

The day after I got home Emma, Little E. and I walked to Foston. It is such a convenient, nice place. E., George and I are crazy to go up there to live. Since I came home I have received and answered letters from Brother James, Sallie Grattan and Rosa. Sallie gave me an account of Miss Talley's second transgression.

We heard yesterday that Cary was captured in the fight at Culpeper, and the papers today confirm the report. We feel miserable and anxious about it and hope to hear soon a more circumstantial account of it.

Monday, March 23rd, 1863

Saturday there was a very deep snow. I received a letter from Rosa Burwell, Mamma one from Aunt Belle. She is miserable about Walker; he is 18 years old now and is very anxious to join Brother James' company. Cousin Lindsay had offered him a position as Asst. Quartermaster, but Walker is intent upon going in the cavalry. On Sunday we received letters from Mr. Ran Tucker, Mr. William Burwell and Lieut Biggs,[1] all writing to us about Cary's capture. They all gave different accounts of it—but all agree in extolling his gallantry. Today we got letters from Uncle John, Cousin Robert Breckinridge and Brother James. They all say that Cary was captured and not wounded, and we

---

1. This is probably a reference to James W. Biggs, Third Orderly Sergeant in Company C of the 2nd Virginia Cavalry; promoted to First Sergeant. Biggs was at home recovering from wounds received at Sugar Loaf Mountain, Maryland, 8 September 1862. H. B. McClellan, *Life and Campaigns of J.E.B. Stuart*, p. 428; *CSR-Va.*, Roll 15.

were feeling very hopeful about him when Uncle Bowyer sent Pa
a letter he had just received from Mr. William Robinson saying
that Cary was certainly killed, that an officer told Mr. Allen
Caperton that he saw him fall. We cannot but feel very uneasy
about him, but still hope that Mr. R.'s account is without
foundation. I received letters from Cousin Letty and Rosa
Burwell. Cousin Letty said she had written to Mr. Robert Falls
whose wife and family are in Baltimore to write to them and get
them to find Cary out—if the prisoners are carried there, and pay
him some attention.

Brother James' letter is so interesting that I shall copy it down
here. It was written on the 19th:

"I could not find an opportunity to write after the fight and sent
word to Col. Munford to write you a note about Cary's capture
and suppose he did. I shall miss him sadly both in the field and
camp, but after that terrible day I really feel thankful that he is
safe and sound in Washington or somewhere else and not exposed
to such dangers as I saw him pass through. I was in command of
the picket at this point and under orders dismounted all my men
and placed them in rifle pits to hold the ford to the last extremity;
with 15 men in little holes in the ground I kept back 5,000 cavalry
an hour and a half. Four times they charged through our
stockades and some of them with drawn sabres mounted the
parapets. At last we had fired all of our ammunition, carbines and
pistols, but kept our post until almost every hope of escape was
past and 12 of my little band were captured by the overwhelming
force. I then, with two or three others, broke for our horses—300
yards off—exposed to a perfect hail of shot from both sides of the
river, reached a stray horse nearly exhausted, mounted while the
cavalry was almost up to me, and got off safe. 40 men of another
Regt. were sent to reinforce me and got there just at the opening
of the fight, but they had to pass over a wide meadow to reach the
pits and no human persuasion could make them go. In vain I ran
from the pits to them and back again, coaxed and threatened.
They would not follow me. Some of them I got out into the
meadow. The balls would plough up the earth around them. They
would then fall flat and I suppose never get up until the Yankees

picked them up. We heard from prisoners that we killed or wounded between 20 and 40. I fired 12 shots with my pistol and saw one Yankee fall at the first fire. At one time I saw my men falling back from one of the pits. I rushed over the bank and they rallied and fought with a desperation I never saw excelled. I saw Cary later in the day when he came up in command of our Regt., saw him lead it in the most desperate charge I ever saw. Some of the Regt. saw him completely surrounded firing right and left, his horse wounded and broken down, saw him lift his hat in the act of surrendering, and saw a Yankee lead him off by the arm. Today a citizen from the opposite side of the river said he saw the Major riding very composedly along with one Yankee close by him and ten more following some distance behind, the rest of our prisoners were compelled to walk. Our Regt. made another desperate charge against great odds after Cary was taken and it was probably for the best that he was not there. The Yankees soon fell back and gave us the field and I have the same ford to guard. Our loss in killed was slight, a good many wounded—'The battle of Kelly's Ford.' "[2]

Tuesday, March 24th, 1863

We have heard nothing more about Cary. I feel more hopeful now as I am sure that if Mr. Robinson's account was true, we should have heard it from some other source. I wrote several letters today, one to Rosa, Mr. Michel, etc.

Wednesday, March 25th, 1863

No news from Cary today. I wrote to Mr. Burwell and enclosed copies of Brother James' and Mr. Robinson's letters. I know he

2. The Breckinridge brothers distinguished themselves at the fight at Kelly's Ford, 17 March 1863, as the following account reveals: "Captain James Breckinridge, of the 2nd Virginia Cavalry, commanded the picket at Kelly's Ford. There was no more efficient officer of his rank in either army, and had he been properly supported on this occasion, he would probably have succeeded in preventing General Averell from crossing at that point. . . . The brunt of the fight fell upon Breckinridge's little band of about a dozen men. Gen. Lee says that he detained the enemy at the ford for an hour and a half. . . . In one of the charges, Major Cary Breckinridge, of the 2nd Virginia Cavalry, leaped his horse across a wide ditch which separated him from the enemy. His horse was killed, and Major Breckinridge was compelled to surrender to Lieut. James M. Fales, of the 1st Rhode Island Cavalry." H. B. McClellan, *Life and Campaigns of J. E. B. Stuart*, pp. 207–12.

will make inquiries and write to us soon about Cary. Mamma is so
anxious that it makes me wretched. Little Johnny improves
rapidly and we all think he is like his Uncle Cary. Today the sun is
shining brightly for the first time since last Friday

Friday, March 27th, 1863

This is the day appointed by President Davis for fasting and
prayer. We went to hear Mr. Grasty preach; he gave us a very
good disconnected sort-of a discourse. I like Mr. G. very much. I
wish we could have been at our own church—the psalter for the
29th day is so appropriate for the occasion. I felt miserable at
church today and was perfectly certain we would hear bad news of
Cary, but, oh, how joyful!! There was an extract from a Northern
paper saying that among the prisoners was a "Major B., relative to
John C. Breckinridge the traitor"[3]—I have been really happy
since I heard that. This evening Emma, the little Woodvilles and I
walked over to the graveyard; we found some violets there. These
days of wretched anxiety have recalled so vividly the time when
our darling Johnny was killed. We are so distressed now about
Brother Gilmer—his regiment has sent a petition to Legislature (I
believe) to have him turned out. It is a most mortifying thing and
seems so outrageously unjust. Some man wants to get his position
as Major, and resorted to that dishonorable way of doing it—he is
a Mr. Kesler, I think.[4] Mamma received an answer to my letter to

3. This is a reference to John Cabell Breckinridge (1821–1875), vice-president
under President James Buchanan; Democratic candidate for president in 1860; United
States senator from Kentucky from 4 March 1861 to 2 October 1861, at which time the
legislature requested him to resign from the Senate. He served in the Confederate army
as a brigadier-general and later as a major-general until his appointment by Jefferson
Davis as secretary of war, on 4 February 1865. Cary Breckinridge was a cousin of John
C. Breckinridge, their respective grandfathers, James Breckinridge (1763–1833) and
John Breckinridge (1760–1806), having been brothers. *DAB*, 3, pp. 5–10.
4. Peachy Gilmer Breckinridge, a Unionist, had been a candidate for the Virginia
State Convention which convened 14 February 1861 and passed the secession
ordinance on 17 April 1861, five days after the firing on Fort Sumter. In a lengthy
circular addressed "To the People of Botetourt and Craig Counties," he stated his
passionate belief in the Union: ". . . Has every spark of patriotism died out in the
soul of the people? If exiled in a foreign land, would the heart turn back to Virginia or
South Carolina, or New York, or to any one State as the cherished home of its pride.
No, we would remember only that we were Americans. We would pine for the land
whose goddess sits triumphant on her throne, her foot upon the neck of tyrants, her
ensign welcoming beneath its shelter the oppressed of distant nations. Away with your

Mr. Burwell today; he wrote very comfortingly about Cary. I shall always be grateful to Mr. B., he has been so kind to us. Little Johnny is getting lovelier every day. I never did love any baby as much. Nannie had a good cry this morning when Sister Julia told her that she (Sister J.) could eat no breakfast—that Jefferson Davis would not let her have anything to eat today. *The Whig* [Richmond] yesterday contained an account of the battle of Kelly's Ford, in which Brother James and Cary were highly complimented for their gallantry—

Saturday, March 28th, 1863

We expected Brother Lewis and Dr. Archer today but they did not come. Sister Julia went down into the parlor tonight and sang some for us. It reminded me so sadly of the past. Ma got letters from Maj. and Mrs. Maury. The Major says he thinks Cary will be paroled and can come home soon. Eliza and I took a terribly muddy walk this evening. Dear little Johnny!—

Tuesday, March 31st, 1863

On Sunday we went to hear Mr. Grasty preach, and he has improved his style of preaching. We saw a Capt. Crank at church who is very much like Cary. After dinner, Brother Lewis and Dr. Archer arrived. Dr. A. is from Maryland.[5] He is like Uncle Wilmer and Dr. Meredith. We all liked him very much and though his likeness to Uncle W. made me stand a little in awe of him at first, we finally became quite well-acquainted. He taught me how to make ivy wreaths and crowned me with the victor's crown.

On Monday, Brother L. went to town and left us to entertain Dr.

Palmetto flags. Let the banner under which Washington fought wave over every blow I strike in battle, and if I die the death of a soldier, let me be wrapped in the 'Star Spangled Banner.' "

His reputation as a Unionist and a "submissionist" undoubtedly was a factor in the above-mentioned affair. He continued to serve with distinction in the army of the Confederacy until he was killed in action at Kennon's Landing on 24 May 1864. Breckinridge-Preston Papers, Roanoke Historical Society. The gentleman seeking his position was Captain Joseph R. Kessler of the Virginia State Line.

5. Dr. George Washington Archer of Belair, Maryland, served for a brief time in the war as an army surgeon.

111

Archer. Physical geography helped us out considerably. I got two letters from Rosa. She sent the notes to "Rock me to Sleep." Today, Brother L. and Dr. A. left. Brother Gilmer and a Mr. Lyme came. Ma got letters from Brother James and Uncle William. Brother James is very indignant about that report about Cary. He says that the cause of it was that *he* (Brother J.) was reported killed in camp and that Cary went into the charge in which he was captured under that impression. Cary is in Washington confined in the old Capitol. I wrote to Rosa today and feeling very badly spent most of the day lying down reading the old play, *Douglas*.[6]

Saturday, April 4th, 1863

Nothing has happened worth recording today or this week. Little Emma and I have taken delightful walks in the woods every day. Yesterday, with Joe's and Strother's help, we moved two tall, young, white pines into the yard. They are beautiful and highly ornamental, but I am afraid they will not live. Little Johnny becomes more beautiful and interesting every day. I have been very lazy about reading. I commenced Plutarch's *Lives* again today. I never could get entirely through it. Today, I got a letter from Rosa. Cousin Letty enclosed a note saying she had written to Cary and sent the letter to Baltimore to be forwarded from there to Washington. All of our friends hold out the hope to us of Cary's soon being exchanged. Dr. Letcher sent me a copy of Mr. Burwell's opera, *The Maid of Vancluse*. It is very amusing to us who know all of the characters. Mamma made a good many purchases in Fincastle the other day. Among other valuables, she got a Jew's-harp for me, but I find I do not appreciate it as I would have done some *20* years ago.

Tuesday, April 14th, 1863

On Thursday, the 9th, Cousin William Watts and Allen came. They left on Saturday, the 11th, and on the same day Cary came. He looks better and handsomer than I have ever seen him.

Thursday, April 23rd, 1863

We have been so busy enjoying Cary and the beautiful spring

6. *Douglas*, first produced in 1756, was a romantic tragedy by Scottish minister, John Horne (1722-1808).

weather that I have not thought of reading or writing. I never knew Cary to be as sweet and cheerful. He told us a great deal about his sojourn in Washington. The only disagreeable parts of his captivity was being forced to wade the Rappahannock. He was so fatigued and ill from that and the march that though he had a chance to escape he could not move to do it. The fight at Kelly's Ford is one of the most remarkable of the war. Col. Duffié,[7] who commanded the Yankee brigade of 3,000 men struck one of our prisoners and with a French oath asked him how dared 15 or 20 of those d——d rebels keep back his brigade for three hours. The first night Cary got to Washington he was put into a small cell with 20 men. The water was two or three inches deep on the floor and there was only a bench which a few of them could sit on. At the Capitol, though, he had a very comfortable time. The ladies sent him clothing, flowers, and every sort of delicacy. Mrs. Bullock, John C. Breckinridge's sister,[8] offered to do anything she could for him. Cousin Kate Buckner was in Washington while Cary was there and applied to the Secty. of War for permission to visit him, but was positively refused. Cary was exchanged after 12 days imprisonment. Ma got a letter from Cousin Kate Buckner a week ago. She says she will be here about the first of June. On Saturday, the 18th, Sister came. On Sunday, the 19th, I communed for the first time. On Tuesday, the 21st, Sister Julia and Brother Gilmer left. We miss our darling Little Johnny and Nannie so much. On Wednesday, Mrs. Carter, Mary Hudson and the Millers came to see us. Early this morning Cary left and we miss him terribly.

7. Alfred Napoleon Alexander Duffié, an officer in the French army, married the daughter of a prominent New York family in 1859. When the Civil War began, he resigned his commission and joined the Union forces. He served as colonel of the 1st Rhode Island Cavalry at the engagement at Kelly's Ford, and was promoted to brigadier on 23 June 1863 for distinguished service. His rash temperament later earned the enmity of General Philip Sheridan, who requested his dismissal for allowing himself to be captured in October 1864. Ezra J. Warner, *Lives of the Union Commanders*, pp. 131–32.

8. John C. Breckinridge's sister was married to Reverend Dr. J. J. Bullock of Alexandria, Virginia, who, some years after the war, became chaplain of the U. S. Senate during the Democratic majority. Richard McIlwaine, *Memories of Three Score Years and Ten*, pp. 278–79; William C. Davis, *Breckinridge, Statesman, Soldier, Symbol*, p. 585.

This evening the girls returned to Fincastle. We talked to Fanny a great deal about her intended marriage on the 12th of May. Eliza gave her a lovely green silk for a bridal present. Sister has not been well lately. She brought a great deal of poetry by Dr. Archer. I should not have guessed he was a poet. We all went up to Catawba on Tuesday. It is such a pretty house, but the overseers have injured it very much. I have two such pretty new dresses, one a grey with black trimmings, and a lovely calico which we only gave $3.50 per yard for.

4

Dark Days

My journal is such a stupid thing that I do not like to look at it. I
never write in it except late at night when I am so tired and sleepy
that I cannot think. I do not recollect anything that has happened
except that on Saturday I worked all day in my scrapbook, and
received a very *flattering* letter from Miss Letty Burwell. On
Sunday, Eliza and I went to the Presbyterian church and heard a
very good sermon from Mr. Bocock.[1] We dined at Lulie's and
went again to hear Mr. B. On Monday, Lulie, Eliza and I went
shopping. Lulie got a beautiful dress. Then we walked all over the
Methodist churchyard, saw Jennie Godwin's grave. She died on
Friday, the 24th, and was buried Saturday. Her illness was a long
one. We also walked all about the Presbyterian cemetery. In the
evening Ma came for us, and Lulie, Mr. and Mrs. Copeland and
four children came home with us. Mrs. C. and family stayed until
Tuesday. On Wednesday, Lulie, Eliza and I went to Mrs. Gray's
and got some beautiful flowers. We then went to Amsterdam and
made some purchases. From there we went to Greenfield, arriving
at two o'clock. Lulie immediately informed Mrs. Bowyer that we
had had no dinner, but she listened unmoved. When Lulie found
we would get no dinner she begged for an early supper, but a long
ride and long fast made us so sick that when supper came we had

1. The Rev. Dr. John Holmes Bocock, chaplain of the 7th Virginia Infantry
Regiment in the first year of the war, returned to the Shenandoah Valley in 1862. He
later became pastor of the Presbyterian church in Harrisonburg, Virginia. Richard
McIlwaine, *Memoirs of Three Score Years and Ten*, p. 235; *CSR-Va.*, Roll 453.

no appetites. Little Wilmer and Mary Brockenborough are both pretty children. We staid all night at Greenfield and had to sleep without our usual night gear. The next day directly after dinner we returned to Amsterdam but, though Mrs. Hutcherson's goods had arrived, we found nothing we wanted, so we came home. Lulie staid in Fincastle.

I forgot to mention Lieut. Shuett, a young German who has been in this country only three years and has distinguished himself in our army, came Sunday and left today. He had received orders to take his company immediately to the Rappahannock, where a battle is expected.[2] The Lieut. is a fine little fellow. I feel so uneasy about the boys. Eliza, Emma and I walked to the graveyard this evening. Everything there looks so sweet and bright. The flowers are blooming on Johnny's grave.

Saturday, May 2nd, 1863
I busied myself making some honey soap. Emma and George went to see Fanny Pitzer. We got two letters from Sister Julia. Mr. Anthony continues very sick. Brother Lewis and Dr. Archer came. Dr. Archer has beautiful feet and hands and is a fine looking gentleman.

Tuesday, May 5th, 1863
On Sunday we all went to church. Mr. McGuire preached a better sermon than usual. Lulie was very much struck with Dr. Archer's appearance. He is strikingly like Dr. M. [Meredith] in person and, as far as I can judge, in character also. In the evening we all walked down to the garden.

Early on Monday morning Brother Lewis went over to Glencary. After breakfast Eliza, Dr. A. and I went down to the front gate and practiced pistol shooting. I was considerably out of practice, but made one very good shot. In the evening we walked over on the cedar hill to show Dr. A. the view. Mr. McGuire came out on Sunday evening. Dr. A. amused himself and all of us by getting Mr. McGuire to tell us about the effigy that was thrown from the

2. A reference to the campaign of Chancellorsville, 27 April–6 May 1863. A. L. Long, *Memoirs of Robert E. Lee*, pp. 246–66.

Natural Bridge. Today, soon after breakfast, we all took a long
walk out in the woods near the graveyard and got a few flowers. In
the evening Eliza and Emma went to take music lessons and Dr.
Archer and I went to practice shooting. My instructor
complimented my shooting very highly. From that amusement
we proceeded to get some most beautiful wild flowers from the
forest opposite the house, and were caught in a heavy shower. I
did not enjoy the walk as much as Dr. A. as I was conscious all the
time that my beautiful grey dress was being spoiled.

The papers today bring news of a great victory in Spottsylvania
county; the battle was fought on Saturday, the 2nd of May.[3] Gen.
Paxton was killed, Gens. Jackson, D. H. Hill and Heth wounded. I
feel so anxious to hear further particulars of the fight.

Friday, May 8th, 1863

On Wednesday, it rained incessantly, so we had to stay in the
house all day. I had a very bad headache and Eliza and Dr. Archer
were heartless enough to tease me all day. In the evening Dr. A.
and George got to showing each other puzzles and telling
anecdotes, so we spent a very pleasant evening. On Thursday
Sister, Cary, Mary and Dr. Archer left after an early dinner. We
miss them very much. I got a letter from Rosa Burwell. She is the
most stupid girl I ever saw, but not so deceitful as the smarter
members of the family. Eliza got a letter from Dr. Blackford and
from Sister Julia, who says Mr. Anthony is improving. I am so
anxious to see Johnny and Nannie.

The papers bring further accounts of the terrible battle of
Chancellorsville. Messrs. Godwin and Hinkle spent the evening
here. I wrote to Sallie.

Saturday, May 9th, 1863

A bright, beautiful day once more. I spent the morning writing
and reading. Wrote to Miss Letty Burwell, also to Jennie Miller to
tell her that Eliza wished to be excused from waiting on Fanny.
Jennie, in her answer to my note, alluded quite tenderly to Capt.
Crank. She will follow Fanny's example soon. This evening Eliza,

3. Chancellorsville.

117

Emma and I walked over on the hill opposite the front porch and gathered a great variety of flowers. That forest is a perfect flower garden at this season of the year. Dr. Archer would have been charmed with that walk. I wish we had gone there instead of going to the graveyard woods the day we took that long walk with him. I miss the Dr. very much. The papers, as yet, give no list of our killed and wounded in the late battles.

Thursday, May 14th, 1863

On Sunday all of the family except Pa and myself went to the Presbyterian church. I walked and read and tried not to be miserable. In the evening we all walked over to the graveyard. The lilies of the valley are blooming beautifully around Johnny's grave. I miss him more than I ever did and find it harder to be reconciled to the death of one who might have been so useful and an honor to his country. Monday passed quietly and gloomily. On Tuesday the papers announced the death of Gen. Jackson. No event of the war has cast such a gloom over the country.[4] I felt so sad about it that I objected more than ever to going to Fanny Miller's wedding, but we thought we ought to go. In the evening we went to Julie's and from there to Mr. Miller's. Fanny was the prettiest thing I ever looked at in her bridal attire. Capt. Crank[5] and Jennie stood together. The Capt. is quite an agreeable gentleman, and Jennie seems to be very much in love with him. I hope he will court her. We staid all night with Julie. Mr. Montgomery Miller told me that Capt. Houston was not in the late battles, but had rejoined his company and was at Suffolk. Today Mamma, Emma and Little Emma went to Buchanan.

Tuesday, May 19th, 1863

We have been arranging to go see Sister, but I am afraid our plans will be defeated. I got a letter from Rosa Burwell yesterday saying she, Miss Letty and the surgeons would be here the last of this or

4. The death of General Thomas J. "Stonewall" Jackson on 9 May 1863 was grievous to soldier and civilian alike. Jackson died as the result of wounds inflicted 2 May at Chancellorsville by his own men who mistook his reconnoitering party for Federal cavalry. Long, *Memoirs*, pp. 246–66; Heros Von Borcke, *Memoirs of the Confederate War for Independence*, 2, pp. 233–61.

5. This was probably William H. Crank, who commanded a company in the 5th Virginia Cavalry.

the first of next week. Fortunately (I hope), Eliza had just sent a letter before Rosa's came telling her of our intended trip, so I hope they will defer their visit. I wrote to Rosa today telling her *how glad* I was they were coming. Lulie has gone to see Dr. Meredith. She took by violence Cousin Kate Breckinridge's beautiful summer bonnet. I do not know what Cousin Kate will think of us for letting her do it, but Lulie is a self-willed woman. I heard that Capt. Crank is certainly engaged to Edmonia Woltz. Poor Jennie, from the way she talked I thought the Capt. had given her every reason to believe he was in love with her. Oh! girls!, girls!, they are enigmas. The beautiful flowers I loaned Jennie to wear in her hair at the wedding she took as a gift and put them in her summer bonnet.

Thursday, June 25th, 1863

On Friday, the 22nd of May, Eliza, Emma and I went up to Oaklands to stay all night, and go from there to the M. White [Montgomery White Sulphur Springs]. Cousin Letty Rives treated us with great kindness, but I think it is my last visit to Oaklands. Annie Gwathmey was there. I do not like her at all. On Saturday, the 23rd, we went to the Lick and took the cars. We had a very pleasant trip down and met Dr. Archer at Shawsville, and got to the Springs about eleven o'clock. I will write down a description of the *mess* for fear I shall forget. Mrs. Poelnitz (Herren Means) was one of the first persons I saw. She and her husband are both silly and uninteresting. Dr. and Mrs. Caperton I liked very much. Mrs. C. is one of the loveliest persons I ever saw, both in character and person. Her little children interested us very much. Harry is a beautiful boy. Dr. Archer was very attentive and kind to us and very bright, constantly making puns and *trying* to be smart. I liked him very much at first, but my admiration has decreased daily, though I must do him the justice to say that he is an honorable, noble gentleman and a *very good* friend of mine. Dr. Holloway[6] struck me as a very dignified and

6. Dr. Robert G. Holloway served as Assistant Surgeon in the 38th Georgia Infantry and in the military hospitals in Richmond. He was stationed at this point at the hospital at Montgomery White Sulphur Springs under Lucy's brother-in-law, Dr. J. Lewis Woodville, Surgeon. Wyndham B. Blanton, *Medicine in Virginia in the Nineteenth Century*, pp. 308, 405.

fine looking man. He has such fine and gentle manners that I felt acquainted with him directly, and liked him from the first. Cousin Jimmy Preston took it into his nonsensical head to take quite a fancy to me, and worried me to death. Cousin Willie Cochran is charming, so bright and handsome. Among the most pleasant acquaintances we made were the Sisters of Mercy. Sister DeSales, Sister Frances and Sister Agatha were my favorites. Mother Theresa reminded me somewhat of Aunt Watts. Bishop Lynch of S. C. I took a great fancy to. He is so learned and so entertaining. I forgot to mention Dr. Ellett, one of my favorites. He is so bright and boyish that no one could help liking him. We paid only one visit. Eliza, Drs. Archer and Holloway, Cousin Willie Cochran, Cousin Edward Preston and I went to Smithfield and spent a day and night very pleasantly. Nannie Preston and Laura Gardner are two as consummate flirts as ever I saw. I saw Mr. Waller Staples for the first time at Smithfield. We used to amuse ourselves in various ways at the Springs. Sometimes we would take long walks to the top of the mountain and down on the banks of the Roanoke River. Sometimes we would play tenpins and at night play euchre and whist. Drs. Archer and Holloway were our most attentive *gallants.* I wish I had had my journal with me so I could have written down some of the minor points, such as being caught in a heavy rain at the top of the mountain, and having Dr. Archer run after me with a caterpillar, and going to gather wild strawberries, and some of the incidents at the tenpin alley. We had so much fun. It was very hard for us to tear ourselves away, but on the 12th of June we came home, accompanied by Drs. A. and H. Cousin Kate Breckinridge was here to meet us. We got home to dinner on Friday.

On Saturday Fanny McCue, Jimmie Miller, Miss Mary Grey, Misses Ella and Sallie Caldwell (of Fredericksburg) spent the day here. On Sunday, the 14th, we all went to the Episcopal Church. Sunday evening Emma, Dr. A., Dr. H. and I went to walk. Early on Monday morning the Drs., Cousin Kate, Eliza, George and I started to the Natural Bridge. We stopped at the Bank and took lunch. Dear little Johnny was so sweet that I could hardly tear myself away. I rode as far as Buchanan in the buggy with Dr. H., and went the rest of the way in the hack. We arrived at the Bridge about four o'clock, and had time to view it from all points. I think it much more magnificent seen from the top. We all had terrible headaches when we got to the Bridge. Eliza was really sick. All of the party retired early except the M.D.'s and myself; we sat out in the second story porch looking at the stars, glow-worms, etc. I had so much fun. I made Dr. Holloway tell all about his love affairs, much to Dr. Archer's amusement. He would not have enjoyed it so much if he had suspected who Dr. H.'s second love was. Those two gentlemen flattered and petted me so much that I was right much spoiled. On our way home on Tuesday we stopped again and took lunch with Sister Julia. She played the harp for us. I played with Johnny all the time. I never saw such a white, fat, lovely boy in my life. I came home in the buggy with Dr. H. and found it excessively warm. We found Miss Letty and Rosa Burwell, Drs. Blackford and Letcher here when we came. Col. and Mrs. Pendleton came on Wednesday, so we had quite a houseful, and had a very gay and pleasant time. Poor Miss Letty looks right sad. She is engaged to Capt. Clarke. The Burwell and Pendleton parties left on Friday. We did not miss them very much. Dr. Holloway and I took a ride in the buggy in the evening. Dr. Archer looked so miserable Friday night that I sat out in the porch with him until late and had a very affecting little interview. Cousin Kate and Ma and Eliza accuse me of trifling with his affections, but I think I have acted very honorably. On Saturday Cousin K., Eliza and Dr. A. went to Foston and Catawba. Dr. H. and I staid in the parlor and entertained each other. On Sunday we all went to hear Mr. Grasty. I was surprised to see Lulie at church. Sunday evening Dr. Archer made me take a long walk with him and quarreled with me about Dr. Holloway's preference for me—poor fellow, he's jealous! After supper Dr. H. and I walked down to the front gate together. I almost promised to be Mrs. H., but am not engaged exactly and don't intend to be for sometime. He took my likeness which Capt. H. returned with my ring while I was gone. On Monday, the 22nd, the gentlemen left. Cousin K. and Eliza and I have been studying French ever since and have had a nice time.

Thursday, July 2nd, 1863
Cousin Robert Breckinridge came a few days ago. He gives very

121

interesting accounts of his campaign in Kentucky. He is a fine fellow and we all love him so much. The same day he came (on last Monday), Brother Lewis came. He looks so sad and quiet. I love Brother L. better than I ever did. He left early on Tuesday morning taking Jimmy with him. On Tuesday night all of us went to a concert given by Mrs. Gould's scholars. It was very poor, Emma being the best performer. We have been studying diligently this week. I have been reading DeQuincey's works. I like *Klosterheim* very much. *The Opium Eater* makes me long for a dose of laudanum.[7] On Wednesday I answered Cary's, Rosa B.'s and Sister's letters and wrote to Rosa Tayloe. I have received no letter from Dr. Holloway. Dr. Archer sent me a copy of *The Southern Illustrated News*, full of poetry and an allusion to vines, of course. I am sorry I ever talked unkindly of Dr. A. I do like him. Eliza and Emma intend going to Buchanan on Saturday. Sister Julia enclosed a letter from Mr. Burton Harrison for Ma to see. He alludes to my "lustrous eyes which have haunted him for nearly four years" in such a way as would most assuredly turn my brain and banish all recollection of surgeons if it were not for the report of his being desperately in love with Miss Connie Carey. Tomorrow we are all going to spend the day with Mrs. C. P. Gray. Grove Hill looks so sweet now—how thankful I am for such a lovely home, and such sweet, dear parents and brothers and sisters. I am sure I never can survive having to leave Grove Hill. I miss and think so often of my precious Johnny. In the Spring and Summer I always think more of the past and feel more mournful. This season recalls the time when Fan was with us just a year ago. I can almost imagine I see her sometimes in her little sky blue organdie with flowers in her hair. Poor little Fan, it was so sad for her to die. She had so much to make life desirable and joyful.

Saturday, July 4th, 1863

Yesterday Cousin Kate, Eliza, little Rob, and I spent at Mrs. Gray's and ate as many cherries, green apples, ice cream, etc., as we could, and borrowed *Lavinia* by Ruffini, Ossian's poems, and

---

7. *Confessions of an English Opium Eater*, by Thomas DeQuincey (1785-1859), was first published for *Blackwood's Magazine* in 1822; a later, enlarged edition was published in 1856. *Klosterheim*, a novel written by DeQuincey, was published in 1832.

The Listener by C. Fry.[8] Mrs. G. is a sweet, little woman and the only person about here who is at all literary. Today Ma, Eliza and Emma went to Buchanan. Ma will return tomorrow evening. I have been sick all day. The rain I was in at the Springs gave me a cold and I have felt the effects of it severely today. Cousin Kate felt badly, too, Cousin Robert having gone fishing with John Woltz, George and Capt. Frank. We have spent the day reading and sleeping. I read "Suspira de Profundis,"[9] which I like better than *The Opium Eater*. I never witnessed such a thunderstorm as we have had today. The peals made the house shake. I enjoy a thunderstorm intensely, especially at night when the flashes of lightning are more vivid and the darkness and quiet make it more sublime. A letter from Col. Pendleton came for Ma today enclosing Gens. Buckner's and Tilghman's travesty on McClellan's, "On to Richmond!"[10] It is very amusing, they wrote it while at Fort Warren. One of the white pines I had set in the yard in the Spring is growing beautifully. It is about 30 feet high, I expect, and very becoming to the yard.

Sunday, July 5th, 1863

Little Emma and I spent the day together reading the bible and learning hymns. She wrote a note to her Mamma, but the poor child shows very little literary taste and cares for nothing but Ella. She has depreciated very much of late. I missed Ma, Eliza and Emma very much. I read all of Capt. H.'s letters. I ought to destroy them, but cannot make up my mind to do so. I wonder if I shall ever love anyone as much as I did him. I am afraid to think of him much, the old love comes back; but I am so thankful that our

8. *Lavinia*, a three-volume work by John Ruffini (1807–1881), was published in 1860. *The Works of Ossian*, published in 1765 by the Scottish "translator," James Macpherson (1736–1796). Macpherson's so-called translations from the works of the third century bard, Ossian, were challenged by Dr. Samuel Johnson and others. *The Listener*, a work by Mrs. Caroline Wilson, better known as Caroline Fry (1787–1846), was published in 1832.
9. "Suspira de Profundus," an essay of dream visions, was written by Thomas DeQuincey (1785–1859).
10. General Simon B. Buckner, while in Fort Warren prison in July 1862, wrote a satirical poem about McClellan's 1862 Peninsular Campaign entitled "On to Richmond, or the New Hohenlinden." Arndt M. Stickles, *Simon Bolivar Buckner*, pp. 189–91.

engagement is broken off, for all of my family objected so strongly to the match, and I should not have been happy if I had married him. Ma came late this evening having had a pleasant visit. Poor Johnny Clarke was drowned in the river on Thursday; two of his brothers met with a similar fate. Mr. Anthony sent me the only ripe apricot, dear, old gentleman! Oh, dear! how dismally the frogs are singing. There is something in the idea that ever since I or anyone else can remember those or some other frogs have been singing that very same song, which always reminds me of eternity. I love to hear them, but it has the same effect on me that drowning is said to have—recalling all the incidents of the past, more particularly those of my childhood, to my mind, and it is impossible to think of the past without being melancholy—even when we remember happy things. We are generally alone and in some private place when we indulge in the pleasures of memory, and the very contrast between what we are recalling and our present position produces melancholy. It is very sweet to look upon "the blue mountains of our dim childhood" as Richter calls the past, and a very good little simile it is. The farther we get from the mountain the more softened is the outline, the less distinct the rocks and rugged places. The mountain is not *blue* enough yet for me to be thinking so sadly. What will my reflections be 10 years hence if I begin so early to moralize, then I'll have cause, I expect, for mournfulness, being quite a desolate old maid or still worse a married woman with ever so many crying babies and a cross, horrid husband as all husbands are. Oh, dear! Oh, dear!! How gloomy the prospect.

Tuesday, July 7th, 1863

It has been raining all day so I have spent my time quietly reading Ossian and *Lavinia*. Ossian is so beautiful I cannot read a great deal at a time, but will make the treat last me a week or more. I received letters from Rosa Burwell and Sister. Sister says Dr. Holloway is suffering from a very sore finger which accounts for his not having written before this. Sister DeSales says Dr. Archer is so much changed, that he looks so sad all the time. I know they want to lay the blame on me. He ought to be very bright now as Lee and his army are almost in Baltimore. We have good news from all quarters, Grant has been whipped at Vicksburg and Lee's army splendidly victorious at Gettysburg in Pennsylvania.[11]

Friday, July 10th, 1863

Vicksburg has fallen! No encouraging news from any quarter. I could not get interested in reading today. I got a letter from Kate Oden. She had just heard of Johnny's death. She begs Eliza and me to go to see her, but I am afraid Martinsburg will very soon be in the enemy's lines again. Dr. Archer sent me another *Illustrated News*. I want to return the compliment by sending him a *Fincastle Express*, but Ma and Cousin Kate think he would be offended. We sent the carriage to town this evening for Uncle Wilmer and family, but they did not come. They will probably be here tomorrow. I wrote letters to Sister, Sallie Grattan, and Eliza. Last night Little Dorrit gave birth to a lovely colt. This evening Cousin Kate, Robbie and I went to see it. Little D. came running to me directly, tried to kiss me then turned around and gave me to understand that she wanted me to see her baby, which was lying down asleep. I went up to it and it jumped up and met me, and let me pat and rub it a long while. It is the darkest possible bay and has the softest, blackest mane. Oh! the precious little thing, how I wish it could sleep with me. Little Dorrit looks so proud of it, but she seemed a little jealous of my petting it and would try to make me rub her nose some. Cousin Robert, George, Capt. Frank, etc., went on a deer hunt today, so I shall sleep with Cousin Kate tonight.

Saturday, July 11th, 1863

Mrs. Gray and Miss Anne Meredith dined here. We sent early this

11. The news regarding Vicksburg was false. Three days later Lucy learns of the surrender of Vicksburg on 4 July 1863 by General John C. Pemberton after a seige of more than six weeks. *O.R.*, I, 24, pt. 2, pp. 399–418; Henry C. Deming, *The Life of Ulysses S. Grant*, pp. 209–97.

The reference to the Confederate victory at Gettysburg is undoubtedly a reference to the successes of Generals Heth, Rodes, Pender, and Early in driving the Federal forces in disorder through Gettysburg and up into the hills beyond on 1 July 1863. The news of the terrible losses sustained by the Confederate forces in the bloody fighting of 3 July, and General Lee's decision to retreat had not yet reached Grove Hill. A. L. Long, *Memoirs*, pp. 267–302; *O.R.*, I, 27, pt. 2, pp. 317–25, 357–63, 439–73, 545–61.

morning for Eliza and Emma. Joshua returned this evening with a note from E. saying the carriage was broken and she was at Fanny McCue's. Ma sent Uncle Phil down for them immediately, so they will probably arrive late tonight. I feel so sad tonight, having heard that Capt. Houston is mortally wounded.[12] I still hope it may be a mistake. I cannot help still taking peculiar interest in him. This time last year his life was despaired of; he is a fine officer and will really be a loss to the service. No cheering news from the army. George got a letter from the Institute [Virginia Military Institute] saying he must be there on the 25th of this month. Lizzie Woodbridge cannot come to see us this summer. Sent again for the Wilmers, but they did not come.

Tuesday, July 14th, 1863

This is my precious Johnny's birthday. He would have been nineteen today. I try to imagine how he would have looked as a man, but it is very sweet to think that however old I may be I can always think of him as a bright, happy boy—will always have one little brother. On Sunday, Eliza and Emma came. We sent to Bonsack's for Miss Lelia, Annie and Mary, but they stopped at Greenfield and got here on Monday. Annie is beautiful and Mary is very sweet looking. Miss Lelia is so charming. On yesterday evening Mrs. Reynolds (who is so like Sallie Grattan), Mrs. Floyd, *Mrs. John Woltz(!)*, and Col. Reynolds[13] came out. They went into ecstacies over the beauty of the place. I got a very devoted letter from Dr. Holloway yesterday. I like and admire him so much, but cannot make up my mind to marry him. Sister Julia was charmed with him, and wants me to accept him. I expect it would be better, but oh, dear! The papers all concur in stating that Capt. Houston is mortally wounded, and in the enemy's lines. Major Nat Wilson was killed and Lieut. Grayble.[14] Ma got a letter

12. David G. Houston, First Captain of Company D Eleventh regiment, Kemper's Brigade, Fincastle Rifles, was killed in battle at Gettysburg on 3 July 1863. Robert Douhat Stoner, *A Seed-Bed of the Republic*, p. 466.
13. Colonel Samuel H. Reynolds commanded the 31st Virginia Infantry regiment. *CMH*, p. 566.
14. Major Nathaniel C. Wilson, a native of nearby Craig County, was serving with the 28th Infantry regiment. Ibid., p. 565. Lieutenant James A. Graybill of neighboring Amsterdam, Virginia, served in Company K of the 28th Infantry regiment. He was killed at the Battle of Gettysburg, 3 July 1863. *CSR-Va.*, Roll 740.

from Uncle William. He says the boys were safe up to the 8th. I
wish we could hear more directly from them. Cousin Kate spent
today in Fincastle, and I missed her terribly, bless her dear heart!
Gip died yesterday! Poor little fellow.

Thursday, July 16th, 1863

On Wednesday I knit while the others read and studied French.
In the evening I took Miss Lelia to ride in the buggy, and George
rode beside us on Red Fox. I drove up to Foston and turned into
the meadow, and came home by Catawba. This evening we took
the same ride, but instead of Fan I drove Robbin, and found him
much easier to manage. I wrote to Cousin Letty Burwell today.
Cousin Kate and I stay together most of the time, and I do love
her so dearly. George heard in town that Tom Godwin was
mortally wounded. Both Aunt Lizzie and Aunt Eliza lost brothers
in the battle of Gettysburg, Cols. Taz Patton and Henry
Carrington.[15] I cannot hear anything certain about Capt.
Houston, and feel so anxious about him. Annie and Mary are such
lovely girls. The time is almost arrived when George must leave
us. I do not know what we shall do without him. I am very glad
Walker got an appointment. I am so anxious to hear from the
boys.

Monday, July 20th, 1863
1 o'clock

I am so wretched tonight that I cannot sleep, and so will write
some in my journal. I have been thinking of my past connection
with Capt. Houston, and it makes me so sad to think that I ever
caused him any sorrow. I would give anything to hear the
circumstances of his death. If I could only hear something about
him I would not feel so miserable. Ma thinks I ought to send his
ring back to his family, but I do not know any of them and it
would be very hard for me to do. On Sunday we all went to the
Presbyterian church and Miss Pauline Price caused me two hours
of deep distress by telling us that Walker was mortally wounded,
but a letter from Uncle William relieved our anxiety by telling us

---

15. Colonel Waller Tazewell Patton served with the 7th Virginia Infantry regiment
and Colonel Henry A. Carrington served with the 38th Virginia Infantry regiment.
CMH, pp. 561, 567.

it was Cousin Christopher's son. I do hope dear Walker will be spared to us. When we returned from church we found Cousin Letty Rives and Allen here. Cousin Letty wants to take my precious Cousin Kate away tomorrow. Uncle William came today; he is very bright and funny. I wrote to Drs. Archer and Holloway and to Cary. This evening I took a delightful buggy ride with Miss Lelia. We were caught in a shower and had to drive as fast as Fan could go. Annie and George rode on horseback. Oh! dear, I used to be so happy. I feel now as if my life was darkened forever.

5

Diversion amidst Dejection

Friday, July 25th, 1863

This week we have spent quite pleasantly, knitting for George and having little riding parties. We borrowed Mr. Logan's sidesaddle so three of the girls ride on horseback and two in the buggy. George is very attentive to Annie and Mary—seems quite fascinated with Annie. Mary is rather my favorite. I got a letter from Sallie Grattan—she cannot come as soon as I hoped. I wrote to her yesterday. Yesterday evening Capt. Frank came out and sang very sweetly for us. Cousin Kate and I had been busy all day unravelling a skein of silk. I am thoroughly convinced she is the most patient woman I ever saw, and the most persevering, bless her heart! Uncle William is so sweet and funny. He and Cousin Robert get on splendidly, and he is as charmed with Cousin Kate as everyone is. Miss Lelia has quite captivated me. She is so highly cultivated and plays so sweetly that her music "is like the memory of joys that are past, pleasant and mournful to the soul." We got a letter from Cary today. He writes for clothes—the boys lost all of theirs in Maryland. Eliza, Miss Lelia, Annie and Mary spent today at Greenfield. Lulie has been quite ill, having had a little dead baby. They all stopped at Mrs. Gray's and got some beautiful flowers and delightful apples. Cousin Kate, little Emma and George rode to Foston this evening on horseback. It is so late that I cannot write. I must really turn over a new leaf of my journal—it is so stupid. I do nothing but sit in the room over the sitting room and knit, and think sadly of the past. I have not read any since Miss Lelia came. After George goes I shall have to read

129

to be comforted. Little Dorrit and Bonnie have been staying in the yard, and are so sweet and pretty. I am going to leave Little Dorrit and family to Johnny when I die. I wrote to Aunt Belle to send Walker by to see us when he goes to the V.M.I. [Virginia Military Institute]. How glad I shall be to see the dear boy.

Saturday, July 26th, 1863

Cousin Kate and I finished off George's socks. This evening Little Dorrit was brought up for the girls, and I rode her down to the creek. The colt is so gentle and perfectly lovely. Annie, Mary, George, and Emma rode to Foston. Emma looked terribly frightened when she mounted Red Fox. Cousin Kate and I went to meet Cousin Robert. When he came up he exclaimed to me that a young gentleman was in Fincastle waiting for a horse to be sent for him. My first thought was that it was one of the boys, but he said he was a gentleman just from the Natural Bridge. Oh, so many thoughts and hopes rushed through my mind in that instant, but, alas, it was only Dr. Archer. He looks very well and quite handsome (Miss Lelia thinks). He came from Avenel this morning, having escorted Miss Letty Burwell home from the Montgomery Springs. Cousin Robert got orders to go to Kentucky on Wednesday. I have promised Cousin Kate to go to Oaklands with her on Tuesday if Cousin R. is obliged to leave the day after they get there. I did not intend ever to go there again, but would do anything for my sweet cousin.

Saturday, August 8th, 1863

On Tuesday the 29th, Cousins Kate and Robert, little Rob, and I went up to Oaklands. We got there quite late, found no strangers except Lucy Minor and Miss Seaton. They were so kind and sweet that we had a delightful time. Cousin Robert and Capt. Frank (who came Wednesday evening) intended leaving on Thursday, but stayed until Saturday. The Capt. sang and made himself very agreeable. I made several very pleasant acquaintances. Two of Cousin Alice's daughters (Lucy and Sallie), Lizzie Holcombe and Nannie Fickett came up with Judge Robertson. I like the Judge much better than I expected and his daughters are very nice girls. Lucy and Mr. Frank Morehead of Kentucky had a nice little flirtation. On Thursday evening as Cousin Emma, Capt. Frank, and I were sitting in the porch enjoying ourselves, who should I

see walking up to the house but Dr. Archer! I was not at all
pleased to see him, and treated him so badly while he was there
that on Friday evening he very seriously took me to task about it,
and scared me considerably. He left on Saturday. On Monday
Cousin Letty, Cousin Kate, and I went to Salem. Cousin Emma
was so sweet that I loved her very much and her babies are lovely.
Allen is a fascinating boy. Lucy and Pat Preston spent a night at
Oaklands. Lucy is very bright and pretty. Cousin Kate charmed
everyone at Oaklands—she and I love Cousin Letty so much. On
Wednesday Miss Lelia, Eliza, Annie, and Mary came. On
Thursday we intended coming home, but staid one day longer.
Col. French,[1] such a kind, good, old fellow, left for the
Montgomery.

Friday evening Cousin Kate, Rob and I left, got home right late,
and found dear, little Sister Agatha and Sister Mary Peter here.
They left this morning for the Old Sweet. I am so glad I went to
Oaklands. I love all my cousins better and I think they like me
more than they did. I miss George dreadfully. Mrs. Ninninger
brought me some huckleberries today. She says she likes me
"monstrous." Dear Ma is so sweet. I am glad to get home. Little
Emma has two beautiful white rabbits Sister Frances sent her.
Cousin Kate and I went to ride, went to the mill and weighed, she
weighed 130½ and I 142 pounds. Little Dorrit went so nicely and
Bonnie is prettier and more spirited every day.

Wednesday, August 12th, 1863

On Sunday we all went to Sunday school. Mr. Godwin wants me
to join his class. Ma has an interesting little class. Her sweetest
scholar is little Lucy Stamps, a niece of President D.'s [Davis'].
We waited for some time for Mr. McGuire, but he came not—we
went to the Presbyterian church. On Monday Cousin Kate and I
read all morning. I commenced *Pendennis*.[2] In the evening Ma and
I went over to call on Mrs. Kate Bowyer. We went first to

---

1. This is possibly a reference to Colonel S. Bassett French of the staff of Governor
John Letcher of Virginia. In 1862 Bassett served as a volunteer aide-de-camp at the
headquarters of General Thomas J. "Stonewall" Jackson. Henry Kyd Douglas, *I Rode
With Stonewall*, pp. 152–53, 367–68.

2. *Pendennis*, a novel by William Makepeace Thackery (1811–1863), was published
serially in 1848–1850.

Greenfield and finding they were not there proceeded to Mr.
Copeland's where we found her and Lulie. Mrs. B. gave me a very
decided cut, but I was prepared for it and did not receive a great
shock. Lulie had intimated to Eliza that Mrs. B. had some story on
us. I don't care—let Mrs. B. nag as she will, I'll be gay and happy
still. On returning we found Mr. Burwell here. He is so pleasant
and I like him so much. On Tuesday Ma and Mr. Burwell spent
the day at Mrs. Gray's. Cousin Kate and I had a quiet day lying
down and reading. I enjoyed it, as I am always happy with her. We
got letters from Brothers James and Gilmer. I got a sweet letter
from Sallie. Cousin Kate, Emma, Rob, and I went to ride on
horseback yesterday evening—rode to Mr. Hinkle's. Late at night
Miss Lelia, Eliza, Annie, and Mary came. We have been expecting
Brother Lewis and Dr. Holloway, but they came not. Eliza got a
letter from Sister Julia. Mr. Bowyer and Dr. Meredith dined here
with Mr. Burwell. They seemed to have a very funny time, and
Mr. Burwell said a great many funny things. Mr. Burwell says
Capt. Richardson received a very severe lung wound, and is
expected at Avenel as soon as he can travel. Cousin Kate, Miss
Lelia, Eliza, and I rode to town this evening. This is my last night
with dear Cousin Kate. I wrote George a long letter while Cousin
Kate packed. Robbie is a sweet boy!

Thursday, August 13th, 1863

Soon after breakfast my darling cousin and Robbie left. I have
spent a wretched day missing Cousin Kate, sitting in her room
trying to read *Pendennis*, but looking up I always would see
something to remind me sadly of her—hanging in the screen was
"the garment *she* used to wear," and when I would fall into a doze
visions of "brows of beauty and bosoms of snow and trinkets and
tresses of hair" would appear before me. Oh! it is so sad to part
from those whom we love. The little rabbits are a source of great
pleasure for me. I attend to them more than Emma does and think
they are beginning to know me. Eliza, little Emma, Mary and I
went to the graveyard this evening. Eliza pinned some beautiful
crimson and green leaves together with thorns and made a
beautiful wreath for John's grave. I do not think our prospects for
peace were ever so dark. We have met with so many disasters of
late. I wish the women could fight, and I do think they might be

allowed to do so in the mountains and in the fortified cities. Their lives are not more precious than the men's, and they were made to suffer—so a leg shot off or a head either wouldn't hurt them much. I would gladly shoulder my pistol and shoot some Yankees if it were allowable. Mary Wilmer is a lovely girl.

I have not gotten any letters for so long. This evening at suppertime Ma wanted the lights gotten and some arrangements made about the house and inquired for Susan and Matilda, but Virginia said they could not be found as they had gotten religion. We all agreed that religion had a singular effect and hoped the rest of the servants would wait until after supper to get it. Eliza asked Nelson if they were having a revival. He said, "Yes, they always have 'em at this time of the year"—singular creatures they are! Mr. Breckinridge Cabell spent today here. He and Mr. Cocke wish to rent Catawba and Foston.

Friday, August 14th, 1863
Sewed some. Read some. Wrote to Rosa Burwell and Cousin Kate Breckinridge. Got such a sweet letter from Cousin Kate. Miss and love her awfully. A letter came from Rosa directed to Eliza commencing "Dear Lucy." After reading some of it I found it was intended for Lucy Burwell and returned it immediately. Wrote to Sallie Grattan—Petted the rabbits—Went to see Little Dorrit and found her sides very sore where the saddle girth had rubbed it. Sent salt to all of the horses. It rained, could not walk. Miss Lelia played for us tonight. Susan is really so much better and kinder since *she* has been converted. I hope she will be a firm Christian. Cut my hair.

Saturday, August 15th, 1863
This morning Emma Woodville and I had a great misfortune. We missed Bonnie and I sent Ella to look for her. She soon returned bringing the little corpse. We held a post-mortem examination, Nelson acting as coroner. His verdict was "died of a hard fall from Little Emma's arms," no external injury could be found but on dissection it was found to have some bruises on its side. Poor Little Emma's cries were heart-rending. She could not make up her mind to look at the body, but declared she would bury it with her own hands.

Mrs. Saunders, Page and Bob arrived this morning. Mrs. S. looks sadly broken. Page is so sweet and innocent. Bob is a handsome, bright fellow. I got a letter from Dr. Holloway, which I shall answer soon and settle the question. I cannot love that fellow! I can never learn to love any man. Oh, what would I not give for a *wife*! Some pure, lovely girl who would be mine and never learn to love any male, but the poor, weak things will do that. Women are so lovely, so angelic, what a pity they have to unite their fates with such coarse, brutal creatures as men, but some of them are *right* good. Miss Lelia and I walked to the creek together. Ma got a letter from Sister J. She speaks of coming up. How glad I shall be to see my little Johnny.

Sunday, August 16th, 1863

All of the family went to the Presbyterian church except Pa, Mrs. Saunders and me. We retired to our apartments and read. I took Frank (the rabbit) to my room, and he was a sweet, merry, little companion. He is a gay, little widower, eats as much cabbage and apple as if Bonnie was living and beside him. I have set my affections too much upon him, I fear, and am seriously afraid that my little idol will be taken from me. But for my devotion he would certainly have joined his little departed today. I found him shut tight in his little cage, then put in the warren and four or five planks put over it with the purpose, no doubt, of excluding air and light. Miss Anna Braxton came home with Ma from church. We spent a very bright, merry evening. Page is a little sunbeam, and much sweeter and more agreeable than Miss Lelia. All of the girls and Bob sang hymns after tea. I love the Litany hymn so much.

Monday, August 17th, 1863

Miss Lelia, Page and I escorted Miss Anna Braxton home this morning. I do not admire her. The girls and Bob are all down in the parlor dancing. The music and merry peals of laughter make me so sad. Page is so bright and sweet, even Pa and Susan are charmed with her. Eliza got a letter from Sallie today which I must answer now. I wonder if I shall ever be merry again. I look on in silent wonder when I see those *merry children*. My life is a quietly happy one, but we have had so little gayety, such as most young people have; no one would think that Page is older than I, her life has been such a joyous one. I shall be so glad to see Cousin Kate. She is a great comfort to me. Emma got a funny letter from dear George. I wish he was here to dance and laugh with the others. I miss him terribly; it is mighty sad not to have *one* boy.

Thursday, August 20th, 1863

I have been sitting in the parlor seeing the young folks dance. They are still at it, but I am tired of such frivolity, and so have taken off my dress to answer such a long, sweet letter from George. We have been spending this week very pleasantly, reading and walking in the morning, riding in the afternoon, and dancing every night, little and big Emma's dance. I really do enjoy Bob—he is so bright and such a splendid looking fellow.

I was so sorry to hear of Cousin Nannie Cochran's death. She died at the birth of her little boy. She and Cousin Hovie were so devoted to each other, I have heard. This morning soon after breakfast, Ma, Mrs. Saunders, and Miss Lelia got into the little carriage, Page and I in the buggy, Eliza and Little Emma on Gazelle, Emma B. and Annie on "the brown mare," Mary on the pony, Bob on a bay—all went about four miles from here, near a large spring and had a picnic. We spent a very pleasant day, eating, drinking (cider and wine), and reading. Late in the evening I drove Miss L. back. When we got home I found letters from Sister, Cousin Kate, and George. Cousin Kate's was a very flattering letter and very sweet. Sister's, as usual, is interesting and contained the startling intelligence that Dr. Archer and Cousin Willie Cochran will be here tomorrow evening. Cousins Kate and Robert are coming then, too.

Tuesday, August 25th, 1863

On Friday we all went to hear Mr. Crenshaw preach, and fasted diligently. On Saturday Miss Lelia, Page, Eliza, and I went down to Waskie's to shop, and were quite successful. We were caught in a very heavy shower returning, got home very wet and tired and found Cousin Willie and Dr. Archer here. We took dinner in our room, and I did not go down until sunset, so saw very little of the gentlemen. The young folks danced splendidly until after eleven. We then bade the gentlemen goodbye and retired. They left early next morning. Dr. A. looked very bright and happy, gave me a beautiful little piece of poetry called "Alone." On Sunday we all went to hear Mr. McGuire. Eliza, the Wilmers, Bob and I went in the hack—the horses ran off and we had to walk from Waxe's hill to church. On Monday I read diligently. The girls and Bob went to ride. They danced until very late. A sick soldier came and is here now. Today Mrs. Saunders and Bob left. Annie and Mary went as far as Greenfield with them. We miss them all terribly, particularly Bob. I am going to write down my prophecy that Bob will marry one of the Wilmers. I got a letter from Brother James!!!! Wonder of wonders!! I read, "Bitter Sweet," a little poem by [Josiah Gilbert] Holland—did not like it much. I commenced *Rutledge*, it is very interesting, something like *Natalie* and *Beulah* and *Jane Eyre*.[3] Eliza got an interesting letter from George.

Saturday, August 29th, 1863
Sat up until nearly Wednesday morning to finish *Rutledge*—it is deeply interesting. It is so singular that the heroine has no name. On Wednesday I commenced *The Quiet Heart*[4]—it is very sweet, but not so interesting as *Rutledge*.

On Wednesday Miss Lelia and Page went over to Greenfield to spend the day. Soon after they left a man came out to tell us that the Yankees were almost in Fincastle. I felt right uneasy about Little Dorrit; all day we looked for them—cannons were heard over the mountains. On Thursday directly after breakfast we all walked over on the hill opposite the front door—expected deserters to attack us, but met with nothing more formidable than a cow peeping out of the bushes.

Friday we walked in the morning. About dinner time Cousin Willie Cochran came, minus Dr. Archer, who had gone to the

3. *Rutledge*, a novel published in 1860, was written by American author Miriam Coles Harris (1834–1925). *Natalie* or *A Gem Among the Seaweeds*, a novel published in 1858, was written by Miss E. V. Hallett, whose pseudonym was Ferna Vale. *Beulah*, a novel published in 1859, was written by American author Augusta Jane Evans Wilson (1835–1909). *Jane Eyre*, the popular novel written by Charlotte Brontë (1816–1855) was published in 1847.
4. *The Quiet Heart*, a novel first published in *Blackwood Magazine* in 1856, was written by the prolific English author, Margaret Oliphant (1828–1897).

Greenbrier White to attend the soldiers wounded in the battle there.[5] This morning I spent playing with Cousin Willie—he is so sweet. He left soon after dinner. Before he went Pa's niece, Mrs. Betsy Burnett, husband and two children came. I do not like any of them. Mrs. Gray, Jennie and Miles Miller and Mary Hudson called this evening. Just before dark Cousin William Watts and a Mr. Langhorne came.

I got a letter from Cousin Kate. A note from Sister Julia announces Brother Gilmer's arrival in Buchanan. We are crazy to see him. All of the girls are desperately in love with Cousin William Watts—say he is like a novel hero. I like him so much. Lulie spent Friday here, she was quite cool to me, and is certainly the greatest gossip I ever saw—has *the* most venomous tongue. I must try to be more guarded in my intercourse with her. I will read again Butler's sermon on "The Sins of the Tongue," and avoid Lulie, and I think I shall be a happier and a better woman. Miss Lelia is a fine woman, and I love her very much.

Monday, August 31st, 1863

Yesterday morning Ma went to Buchanan to see Brother Gilmer; Annie, Mary, Little E., and I rode as far as Waxe's hill with her and walked home. I sat in the room over the sitting room in the morning and read Butler's sermon on "The Government of the Tongue." In the evening we all assembled in the parlor. Just before supper I went into the porch and heard a mighty rumbling of wheels, and in a few moments a large stagecoach with four white horses drove up to the door. The "austere form of Archer" leapt forth. He whispered in sepulchral tones that the Sisters were within. Eliza and I ran down the steps and earnestly besought them to stay all night. After considerable hesitation on account of their large party, Sister Agatha, Sister Mary Peter, Miss Anna Lynch, Miss Brennan, Miss Kelley, and Miss Hurley emerged from the darkness of the stage, and Eliza and I received them with great cordiality. We spent a charming evening, and everyone seemed to enjoy it. Dr. Archer brought us some trophies from the battlefield. He, with the Sisters, went to the battlefield, and got there just in time to see our soldiers marching

5. Greenbrier White Sulphur Springs. The battle of White Sulphur Springs, 26–27 August 1863. *O.R.*, I, 29, Pt. 1, pp. 32, 34–35, 53–55.

to the Springs triumphant. I liked Dr. A. *so* much better this time. Miss Lynch is a nice lady. They all left this morning soon after breakfast. Ten persons left today, the seven in the stage, Mr. Burnett, Miss Lelia and Page—the two latter went over to Greenfield to stay until tomorrow. After all had left, Annie, Mary, Sandy Birch, Jimmy Burnett, Little E., and I went blackberrying. On my return I called to see my darling Little Dorrit. She came rushing up to me, and followed me to the house, leaving Bonnie under Gazelle's care. I gave her some salt and apples, and conducted her back to the meadow. She and Bonnie both look wretchedly. I feel so anxious about them.

Just before dinner, Ma, Sister J., Brother Gilmer and the babies came. Brother G. looks very well. My blessed little Johnny is too sweet and lovely. His face is the most interesting I ever saw, the expression changing every moment. He is so loving in his ways, hugs me and pulls my hair so sweetly. I really think, impartially speaking, that there never was such a baby. He is a little bit like John sometimes, when he looks earnest and sad. God bless the little darling. Nannie is very sweet and pretty. She is sleeping with us tonight. I like Cousin Betsy better today. I wrote a long letter to George tonight. It is so sweet to have babies in the house!

Thursday, September 3rd, 1863
On Tuesday I read *The Quiet Heart*. It is a sweet, prettily written book. I like Scotch stories generally. I wrote to Sister. Annie, Mary, Emma, and I took a long walk, and I forgot my dignity so entirely that I waded in the creek. When we came home we all went to work paring peaches, and arranged a beautiful fruit and ice cream dessert. About 11 o'clock Mr. Tucker and Mr. Michie came. Mr. T. certainly is the *most* charming, amusing, and handsome man I ever saw. We all forgot the existence of Mrs. T. and fell in love with him. Mr. Michie is a fine old gentleman. Mr. Tucker admired and petted Nannie and Johnny very much. He thought Little Emma exactly like me except the color of her eyes. Late in the evening Miss Lelia and Page came. Miss L. had to spend the day at Mrs. Carter's to have her teeth fixed. We spent a pleasant evening. Sister Julia sang a great deal for us, then Miss Lelia played for the others to dance. We had four couples to

dance, Cousin Betsy and Page, Sister J. and Eliza, Annie and
Emma, Mary and Little E., who is learning to dance very well.

I got a very interesting letter from George. He had just returned
from a march of 50 miles in 48 hours with little to eat, and having
had a very hard time. The cadets were ordered to Millboro to meet
the Yankees, and George said the march would not have been so
hard but for the failure to find a Yankee. I commenced *Barnaby
Rudge*.[6] Mrs. and Miss Harris from Richmond called last evening.

Today we all walked in the morning. I missed Little Dorrit and
Bonnie a great deal. Little D. never seemed as devoted to me as
she does now. If she sees me at a distance, she calls me as she does
her colt and runs to me. I love her too dearly—I am afraid she'll
die. Mr. B. Cabell and daughter came. She is a right nice girl and a
fine musician without ever having had any teaching. Aunt
Matilda and Mrs. Carter called. Jimmy Burnett is devoted to Page
and me now. He is a very sweet boy, but I like Sandy best. Page
looks right sick and low-spirited—she is mighty sweet. The girls
danced tonight. It always makes me sad to see anything like
gayety; I feel as if dear Johnny was being forgotten, and the
contrast between the quiet and sweet solemnity of the graveyard
with the moonbeams resting on his grave, and us in his home so
full of life and spirits, is too painful. Beverley Whittle has joined
Brother James' company.

Saturday, Sept. 5th, 1863
Yesterday we spent very quietly, no visitors and no letters. Today
Miss Deborah came. She set me to knitting immediately, so
farewell to *Barnaby Rudge* and peaceful contentment. She is a
stirring old lady. Annie and Mary got letters from George and
Bob; both of the boys write so well. Bob says the Breckinridges
are the most charming people he ever saw. He likes Emma very
much. Little Emma is very much in love with Bob. She sent him
word that she was almost 9 and would soon be 12, and after that
girls got on so fast.

6. This novel by Charles Dickens was published in 1841.

Brother Gilmer and the girls made some cakes this evening and I made some elegant peach ice cream which was handed around about 10 o'clock after the girls had gotten tired of dancing. Sister Julia sang so beautifully tonight. It reminded me too sadly of our happy, happy past, of the sweet, beautiful castles in the air that I used to build. How intensely I used to enjoy sitting out in the porch at night dreaming bright dreams of a future without a cloud. How thankful we ought to be that a kind Providence hides from us the destiny in store for us; sorrows that I never dreamed of have come upon me in the last year. I know it is all for the best, but oh, it is so hard to be resigned sometimes. God has been more merciful to me than to most people; I still have a sweet home and kind friends and relatives and I am more grateful for the blessings I enjoy now than I was in those days of unalloyed happiness.

Sunday, Sept. 6th, 1863

All of the girls and Mr. McGuire are down in the parlor singing hymns, but it is late and I am wearied and so have retired from the parlor. Brother Gilmer drove some of us to church today in the hack with his four mules, two of them are named Annie and Mary because *they draw* so well. I saw and spoke to Capt. Frank and Willie Beale, and got acquainted with Sallie and Nannie Munford. They promised to come here tomorrow—they are both very pretty. I can't imagine what makes Cousin Kate stay away so long. It is nearly a month since she left. Capt. F. said he has written twice to Cousin Robert and gets no answer. I have not spent today very profitably. I had to entertain Cousin Betsy all evening. Miss Deborah seems to like Cousin B. very well. Brother Gilmer had intended leaving tomorrow, but we all begged so hard that he determined to stay until Wednesday.

Our church will not be open again for a month unless Uncle Wilmer preaches for us. We wrote to him to beg that he would hasten his coming so as to be here in time to christen little Johnny. He christened dear John and for that reason we would prefer his doing it for the baby. Sister Julia certainly is blest in her children. They are both so lovely. Miss Lelia thinks Johnny the prettier of the two. We have not heard from Sister for two weeks. I begin to feel uneasy about her and the Springs.

Thursday, Sept. 10th, 1863

On Monday the Munfords came; Eliza and Page went for them. Sallie is beautiful and very sweet. Nannie is perfectly lovely and most persons here think her prettier than Sallie. I never saw two people more alike than Sallie Munford and Sallie Whittle. Monday evening Willie Beale came and just before supper Cousins Linn, Jimmy, and Mittie Cochran came. Cousin Mittie is very pretty and very charming, and I learned to love her very much. On Tuesday the girls all came upstairs and left Eliza, Cousin Mittie and me to entertain Willie Beale. Soon after dinner Cousin Jimmy had his ambulance, and took all the girls to town except Sallie and Page who went to ride with Mr. Beale on horseback. I staid at home to help make ice cream. Cousins Kate, Robert, and little Rob came. The girls and Willie B. danced until late on Tuesday night. On Wednesday before breakfast Brother Gilmer went away. About twelve o'clock Willie B. left; the girls were all so charmed with him. He is mighty handsome and sweet. After dinner the Cochrans left. Sallie and Page went to ride, and Cousin Kate and Cousin Robert went to town on horseback. The young folks danced again last night, and Cousin Lelia made me laugh until I was right sick, dancing like different people. Eliza, too, mimicked some gentlemen. I have been sleeping in the third story with Emma, Annie, Mary, and Nannie Munford, and have had a very nice time. The light comes into the large window so brightly that I get up right early. Cousin Bettie Catlett, husband, and child came.

Sunday, Sept. 13th, 1863

I have read the services for the day and a sermon, and now I must recount the events of the last two or three days, though they are not at all interesting. Friday we all spent the morning talking and eating peaches. The Munfords were so sweet that I fell in love with both of them. In the evening they said they must go, so I fixed a bunch of roasted corn, etc., and about two o'clock they, with Annie, Mary, and Page got into the hack, drawn by four mules and driven by Wilson. As I was sitting at dinner mourning over the girls and wishing I had told them more explicitly how much I loved them, I heard a scream of delight and rushing to the door saw the five dear girls walking up the hill. All of them,

perfectly breathless with fast walking and excitement, began at
the same time telling the whys and the wherefores of their return.
As they were going down Waxe's hill (the scene of many similar
disasters) they met a man all dressed in blue on a white horse. The
mules, unaccustomed to such a sight, wheeled suddenly around
nearly upsetting the hack, and wrenching a wheel off; so the girls,
much to my delight, had to return. They were all very tired, and I
would not let Nannie, Annie, and Mary come down to tea, but
sent it up to them. I took every opportunity to let the girls know
how much I loved them, and when on Saturday morning the five
got into the carriage and went away, I felt easier about it. Sister
Julia, Miss Deborah, and the children left at the same time. I miss
my little Johnny terribly. He is without doubt the sweetest baby
that anybody ever saw, even Miss Lelia used to go into ecstacies
over him. Nannie is lovely, too, and it is right touching to see how
devoted she and Brother Gilmer are.

Cousin Bettie Catlett also went to Greenfield on Saturday. She
did not have a pleasant visit; poor little Maria suffered so terribly
from a toothache. The little thing hardly slept at all. She is a week
younger than Nannie, and looks at least two years older. Cousin
Bettie is very strikingly like Fran though she has black hair and is
a brunette. Saturday was a very quiet day; I staid in the deserted
room over the sitting room reading *Barnaby Rudge*, which is
charming. Cousin Kate sat out in the passage packing her trunks
with "malice prepense," as I afterwards found. While she and
Robert, and I were sitting in the dining room eating supper she
announced her intention of going to Price's to stay on Monday. I
fired up like anything at that, and declared solemnly and truly,
too, that I never would love her a spec if she did, and I really was
so mad and distressed that she promised not to do it. I do love her
so dearly though I do not think either she or Cousin Robert like
us very much. I got such a sweet, sad letter from dear Sallie. She
cannot come to see us. She and Lizzie think of opening a school
for young ladies. Lucy Alexander expects a baby about Xmas. I
had quite a long, interesting letter from Cary, bless his dear heart,
he is so sweet about answering my letters. Bob Saunders sent his
likeness to Annie and Mary. It is very good, but not so handsome
as he is. This evening and last evening we went to the garden and

ate as many peaches and grapes as we possibly could, our peaches are better than Mr. Utz's. It is reported, bye the bye, that Mr. U. and Miss Margaret Glasgow are to be married. I hope she will send us peaches!

Thursday, Sept. 17th, 1863

This week has passed very quietly and comfortably. *The rat* disturbed us so much in our own room that Miss Lelia, Eliza, Emma, and I adjourned every night to the opposite room where we had very merry nights, laughing at nothing, and Miss Lelia's witticisms until a late hour, and even waking up in the night to laugh some more. But "even in laughter the heart is sorrowful, and the end of that mirth is heaviness." I dreamed sad dreams about the boys and felt low-spirited all next day. I have enjoyed reading *Barnaby Rudge* intensely. Dolly Varden and Joe Willet are very interesting lovers. Sir John Chester is a well-drawn character. There is too much of the horrible in it— the descriptions of the riot, and minute detail of the execution of the hangman, Dennis, are painful. Mrs. Gray, Miss Annie Scott (her sister), and Miss Cross called to see us.

The times are very gloomy now; we are unsuccessful everywhere. Stuart's cavalry had a fight at Culpeper C. H. which made us uneasy about the boys, but our having heard nothing more of it assures me that they are safe.[7] Ma sent down to Buchanan yesterday to send things to Sister Julia and to get some sugar and shoes. We have been expecting Uncle Wilmer for two or three days. Sister Julia thinks of bringing Johnny up on Saturday to have Uncle W. christen him, and asked me to stand for him. It was so sweet and kind of her to confer such an honor upon me; I am in favor of waiting until his father can be his sponsor.

I got such a funny, sweet letter from George. He has been invited to a dinner and to a party by Lilly McDowell—he and Bob room together. Page and the Wilmers returned today; they say the

7. A reference to the Federal cavalry's attack on General Stuart's headquarters at Culpeper Court House on 13 September 1863. In the face of the enemy's large force, General Stuart retreated to Rapidan Station. H. B. McClellan, *Life and Campaigns of J.E.B. Stuart*, pp. 372-74.

Munfords were charmed with Grove Hill and its inmates. The
Cochrans went over to Greenfield and laughed at every person
and thing they saw here, so Lulie says. I am inclined to think she
did a good deal of it herself.

Saturday, Sept. 19th, 1863

Uncle Wilmer and little Georgie came today. Uncle W. is
somewhat like Dr. Archer, but I don't think he is as handsome.
Georgie has changed very little since he was a baby—he is an
earnest, interesting little fellow. Little Emma came home last
evening from school. We were delighted to see her—she certainly
is a funny child. The other day she went to Mary and said very
earnestly, "Cousin Mary, please tell me how to flirt. I wish to flirt
with Sandy." Mary told her she must appear to like him very
much and do all she could to be entertaining, so away she ran,
soon returning with a rosebud, sat down by Sandy and
commenced a conversation, and offered the bud with a sly look
worthy of Cousin Alice.

Ma got a letter yesterday from Mrs. Burwell which explains the
reason the Burwells have treated us so curiously. I knew Lulie
had been telling stories on us, but I had no idea she could
manufacture so mean a one. She told Mrs. K. B. that we were very
angry with them for not sending back the bridal presents we gave
poor, dear little Fan, whereas, we had never thought of them, and
if we had, would have been opposed to their being returned. I am
glad our eyes are opened at last, and we see what a bad and
dangerous woman she is. I had decided last night to go to
Richmond on Tuesday with Cousin Betsy to stay two days; it
would have been charming, but Pa would not consent. I would
give a great deal to see my precious Sallie, but it cannot be until
next summer. The one thing I hoped for and longed for is denied
me. There is *no* hope now of seeing her for a year. Miss Lelia,
Page, and I went to see Jennie Miller and Mrs. Carter today. Mrs.
C. wished Page and me to sit in some tableaux to be had for the
soldiers on Monday night at the C. H. Of course, we declined
showing ourselves to the public. This evening we took a merry
ride up to Foston in the fixed, newly painted hack. Cousin Kate

and I sat in Aunt Betsy's room talking to her.[8] Dear Cousin K.,
she takes as much pains to make the servants like her as she does
ladies and gentlemen. I wonder how long we all shall love her; I
am so afraid of being disappointed in her, too. I expect too much
of those whom I love—I must stop hoping or looking for
perfection. Cousin Kate and Cousin Robert have evidently heard
something about Lulie—they both so solemnly warned us against
any intercourse with her.

Thursday, Sept. 24th, 1863

On Sunday we all went to church. Eliza and I walked most of the
way there, then got into the hack. Ma, Miss Lelia, Page, and
Cousin Kate went in the large carriage. When they got to church
it was found that the carriage door could not be opened. Messrs.
Logan, Godwin, Bowyer, Uncle Wilmer, and Pa tried to open it
but in vain. Ma said she must hear the sermon, so she made Uncle
Phil drive up to the side door of the church and there succeeded
in squeezing out of the window. Cousin Kate had on immense
hoops, and had more difficulty than the others. We all at last got
into church and heard such a sweet, comforting sermon from
Uncle Wilmer. He alluded so appropriately to the times and
addressed some remarks particularly to those who had lost dear
ones in the terrible conflict. I do love and admire Uncle Wilmer
so much, and I am not afraid of him now. After we came home we
all sat around the fire in our room reading over Sallie Grattan's
letters. It made me so sad to think over her sorrows—so many
bright hopes crushed by the death of Gen. Garland. I wrote her a
long letter. On Monday Cousin Betsy and children left for
Richmond. Monday night we all went to the tableaux. They were
really very beautifully gotten up. The charades were splendidly
acted, the word "novice" was acted beautifully. First, Robert
Godwin, perfectly disguised, came on the stage with crockery for
sale. He would pretend to knock at a door, and first Edmonia
Woltz came in, dressed as a maid, and looked at the ware, and
refused it promptly. Then two more maids came up, and then

---

8. Aunt Betsy was an aged slave who had cared for Lucy's mother when she was a
child. Letitia Burwell, *A Girl's Life in Virginia Before the War*, p. 86.

Mrs. John Woltz, acting an old lady, appeared. She also refused to
purchase, and all said, "No, no," very impressively, and left the
stage. Mrs. Woltz was a splendid actress, and Bob Godwin did
very well. The second syllable, "vice" was represented thus—An
old lady and gentleman (Mr. F. and Mrs. J. Woltz) came on with
two little sons. They were going to school, and their parents
parted with them with many injunctions to be good boys. No
sooner were the old folks gone than Tom and Bill threw their hats,
shouted and hurrahed, and called in 5 or 6 little companions, and
proceeded to drink from a large bottle, play cards, etc. The third
scene was beautiful. An altar was beautifully arranged, and
Edmonia Woltz, dressed in white, came in and knelt before it.
Then Mr. W., magnificently arrayed as a Roman bishop came on,
then ten nuns. In front of the stage was a piano, and Mrs.
Simmons of Alexandria played some very solemn piece. After her
hair was cut off, and the veil put on, all of the sisters and Mrs. S.
sang a hymn to the virgin. It was so solemn that old Mr. Woltz
wept, and everyone was seriously impressed. On Tuesday we
went again. The words acted were "wayward" and "stratagem."
Capt. and Mrs. Floyd came out to see us on Tuesday. On
Wednesday Mr. Bowyer came to see Uncle Wilmer. I did not go
down to see him. In the evening Cousin Kate and I rode nearly to
town to meet Cousin Robert—met him and Capt. Frank. I forgot
to mention one part of the Tuesday night entertainment—Capt.
Frank made a very good little speech. I have enjoyed Cousin Kate
so much this week. Page and I went to ride today. Little Dorrit's
side was sore so I was miserable. On Thursday the Wilmers and
dear Emma left for Pittsylvania. I miss them terribly already. Got
a funny letter from George. Miss Lelia and Page read all my letters
from dear Fan—she wrote so nicely.

Friday, Sept. 25th, 1863
This is Emma's 18th birthday. She got some presents before she
left. Miss Lelia gave her a gold button, Pa gave her two hundred
dollars, and I gave her a breast pin. Cousin Betsy and family came
today. I think Mr. Burnett likes us, he is getting so amiable and
talkative. Cousin Kate and I sat in the sitting room all morning,
she sewing, and I reading and writing. I comb her hair every day,
and have learned four plaits! Eliza was very sick today, and all of

this family have dreadful colds. I have not suffered so much for a long time. Milton Stanley came here today. He was a pretty boy, but has changed very much.

Tuesday, Sept. 29th, 1863

On Sunday some of us went to church. Cousin Kate was really sick. We girls spent a pleasant, talkative, peach-eating day. That night we sat up very late, and had alternating moods of joy and sadness. I read a good many of Fan's letters to Miss Lelia and Page, and Miss L. said they were the smartest letters she ever saw, dear Fan! So much talent and loveliness was lost in her death. Eliza wrote a very good and severe letter to Miss Letty Burwell. Monday, soon after breakfast Miss Lelia, Eliza, and Page went to Buchanan. Miss L. and Page will go from there to Lexington. I never felt sadder at parting with any friends than I did at parting with Miss Lelia, and she almost wept. Soon after they left Ma, Cousin Kate, and Cousin Betsy went to town, so I had a lonely time.

In the evening Colonel and pretty Mrs. Reynolds called. She is a little gem, so much like Sallie. About sunset Brother Lewis, Dr. Holloway, and Little Jimmy came. I did my best to entertain Dr. H. until nine o'clock when I excused myself and retired. Little Emma sleeps with me. Today I sat in the sitting room all morning talking to Dr. Holloway, and succeeded in making him *quite* miserable, accusing the poor fellow of being a flirt. He is so good and honorable. I do like him a "heap," as Cousin Kate says, but, alas, alas, alas, I *cannot* love him—My eye! How wretched it is to have to do disagreeable things. I wish I had never seen him. I got a note from Archie Oden enclosing one from Kate. I would like to see Archie. Dr. Archer is talking of coming down this week. Dr. Holloway makes me really sad. I cannot write. I must go to knitting on Rob's little shirt, and write to Emma, Annie, and Mary. We are making molasses again—it is delightful.

Wednesday, Sept. 30th, 1863

I went down early this morning to see Dr. Holloway off. My conscience has been reproaching me terribly for teasing him so much yesterday. I had a strong impulse to write to him and ask his

147

forgiveness. I wrote such a long letter to Emma and the Wilmers, and also to my dear, old Cary, bless his heart! I am the only one of Ma's children at home now. She ought to make much of me. Cousin Kate and I went to Mrs. Ninninger's today with Joshua for an escort. She, unfortunately, was away, but old Mrs. Moody and Fannie entertained us very pleasantly. I rode Fan and Cousin Kate the pony. Mrs. Ninninger was here while we were at her house. She said she had many trials and vexations, but none to equal her being away from home when we went to visit her. The ride to her house is beautiful. From the top of the mountain we had a pretty view of Fincastle and the Peaks. I enjoyed the ride, but somehow I did feel mighty sad. I had not taken that ride to Deisher's since one summer morning Lizzie Holcombe, Johnny, Capt. Houston, and I rode there—oh, I was so happy then. Whenever there is anything for me to enjoy now I do long for them to share my happiness, and the very pleasure is turned into bitterness. Johnny and I were so much together and so devoted that I cannot feel reconciled to a life without him. I feel so lonely tonight in this large, far-off room by myself, and my head aches so much.

Sunday, Oct. 4th, 1863

On Thursday, according to our promise, Cousin Kate, Jimmy Woodville, Jimmie Burnett, Robbie, and I rode up to see Mrs. Ninninger. We had a right unpleasant ride there. Jimmie B. rode behind us on Fan, and she went dreadfully. The Moody family received us with great cordiality, were all dressed in their nice cottons, and the cabin was a picture of rural comfort and plenty. Mrs. N. gave us a nice lunch of hot biscuits, cow and apple butter, honey, damsons, wild and English grapes. After sitting with them about two hours, we started home in a cold, shivering sort-of rain. We had not ridden far before Cousin Kate called out to me that my saddle girth was broken, so I dismounted hastily, found it would probably last till I got home, tried getting on my horse from the ground. She started while I was making the leap, so I had to cling to her until she chose to stop and let me make another trial. We rode on then with no other discomfiture than Jimmie B.'s groans. Halfway between Foston and home Jimmie B. said he could stand or sit the pony no longer, so I had to jump down in the road to put him on my horse. Just after I had gotten down, what was our horror to perceive coming down the road!—a *stallion* with a bridle and no rider. Cousin Kate and Jimmy put off at full speed, and there stood Fan, Jimmie and myself, defenseless. Fortunately Fan was quiet, and the creature passed us, and before long Seldon came running after it and caught it. We got home very wet, but took no colds.

I got an interesting letter from George, Ma one from Emma. She writes in fine spirits. Cousin Robert was at the Natural Bridge, so Cousin Kate slept in my room. On Friday we staid at home, it rained hard. I finished a little shirt for Rob. Ma sent for Emma and Lucy Stamps, but Lucy was sick and could not come. I wrote to George. He is so good about writing. Saturday I spent quietly knitting. Got another letter from Emma. We all went to church today. Eliza sent me a letter by Mr. McGuire. She said Miss Lelia and Page had a delightful evening at the Bank. Eddy Jones, Willie Beale, Capt. Emerson, Dr. Kean, Sue, and Sallie Jones went to meet them, and had a delightful supper. We gathered hazel nuts this evening.

Thursday, Oct. 8th, 1863
On Monday directly after breakfast Cousin Kate, Robbie, and I went to Buchanan for Eliza. We stopped at Mr. Starkie Robinson's for Miss Deborah. We spent a pleasant, cozy day, but failed in the object of our visit. Eliza could not tear herself from the Bank. We got home quite tired. I found a letter from Sister. She writes such interesting letters, tells everything. Poor Drs. Archer and Holloway are court martialed for the card they published ridiculing Dr. Hunter. On Tuesday I finished Rob's second shirt, and fixed all my old letters. It was work. I had a great mind to burn them, and try to blot out all recollection of the past. In the evening I was standing down near the front gate playing with the rabbit when I spied some ladies coming down the lane. I came into the house and told Cousin Robert who went out to see who they were. They proved to be Judge and Mrs. Dixon from Alexandria, Mrs. Gen. [Benjamin G.] Humphreys, sister of President Davis, little Lilly H., Lucy Stamps, and Capt. Frank. They staid to tea and Ma sent them home in the carriage. Lucy

Stamps is perfectly lovely. She was delighted when I told her she must come out Friday with Emma and stay until Sunday.

On Wednesday after breakfast, Cousin Kate, Betsy, and I started to Fincastle in the hack. We had not gone far when we met Jennie Miller and a Mrs. Harrison (niece of Mrs. Caroline Gwathmey), so I walked back with them. Got a letter from Cary saying he wanted Jim sent back very soon, so Ma and I went to work, made some cakes and elegant walnut candy to send the boys. We put up a bundle of candy especially for Bev. Whittle who acted gallantly in a late skirmish. I wrote to Emma, George, Cary, and Eliza. I also wrote to Sallie Grattan to get us some Shepherd's plaid dresses. I sent today for some cantharides for my hair tonic. Ma got a very kind but unsatisfactory letter from Mrs. Burwell. Got a letter from George today. He is dissatisfied at the Institute and begs Ma to let him go into the cavalry. He says pompously that he does not want to get an education at the expense of his honor. A fine boy, George is, but very funny, bless his dear, old heart! Cousin Kate, Sandy, and I took such a delightful ride this evening. Cousin Kate rode Gazelle, I the dear little pony, and Sandy Brother Gilmer's late, old bay known as "Grand-daddy Long Legs." We went to the mill. Mr. Breck Cabell is here. Evelyn Cabell was married to Russell Robertson yesterday. That is a brilliant match and will, no doubt, be a happy one.

Thursday, Oct. 15th, 1863

I have not had time for a week to write any, and must now condense as much as possible. On Friday, in the evening, Cousin Kate, Sandy, Rob, and I took a delightful ride. When we returned we found Little Emma, Coalter Logan, Lilly Humphreys, and Lucy Stamps here, so I gave myself up soul and body to amusing them. We had a candy stew and sat up until 11 o'clock. Then I brought my little brood up and put them to bed. Lucy slept with me. On Saturday Cousin Kate and I played with the little ones. Jennie and Katie Floyd joined them. I took them all to ride in the buggy when Capt. Burnett and wife returned from a visit to Mrs. Rufus Pitzer's. Lucy is a remarkable child, and Lilly is very bright and pretty. I never saw two more interesting little girls. Ma has gotten several notes from Mrs. Stamps, and from the way she writes I think she must be very lonely. All of us children sat up late telling stories, and Lucy went to sleep feeling very sad at the thought of my leaving her next morning. Dear little thing, I hope I may see her again.

Early Sunday Cousin Kate, Ma, and I went to Buchanan. We got there in time to rest before going to church and communion. In the evening Cousin Kate got so miserable about Cousin Robert that she returned with Ma. I staid to bring Eliza home on Wednesday. On Monday we sat in the house all morning playing with the dear, little children. Johnny is so lovely. I never saw as good and sweet a baby. Sister Julia was so kind, and I never felt as much at home at the Bank. Monday evening we took a delightful walk down the towpath. The river was beautiful. Tuesday directly after breakfast Eliza and I started out to visit. We went first to see the Joneses, then the Harts, then the McGuires, and finally went away up a steep hill to Mr. Andrew Boyd's. In the evening it rained. Wednesday at 12 o'clock we came home, stopped at Woltz's and brought Lilly and Lucy home with us. We sat up until late playing games with the children and telling them stories. Early Thursday morning they left. Mrs. Stamps, Mrs. Humphreys, and the children went up in our hack to Bonsack's on their way to Liberty. Late in the evening Sister and family came. Mary is lovely and Cary is a pretty boy. I sat in Cousin Kate's room talking to her until right late, then answered such a sweet, long letter from George. He sent me his likeness which is quite good. I have not answered Page's letter yet. I do not love Page much. She is mighty sweet, but we are not congenial spirits.

6

Lieutenant Bassett

Monday, Oct. 26th, 1863

For the last ten days I have been busy and troubled about many things. On Sunday, the 18th, we went to the Episcopal Church and heard the same sermon we heard in Buchanan the Sunday before. Robbie was sick with chicken pox, so Cousin Kate did not go. On Monday Ma, Eliza, and I went to tell Lulie goodbye. She went to South Carolina on Tuesday. Ma had some private conversation with her about the way the Burwells had treated us and found that Mrs. Kate Bowyer had told curious things to Lulie about Eliza and me, whereupon Lulie told her curious things; so between them they concocted more curious things, and both of them came to the conclusion that the Breckinridges were a miserable set, and not fit for them to associate with, particularly Lucy B. When we came home, Ma and I wrote to Mrs. Burwell and tried to re-establish our characters; have not heard yet with what success.

Got a sweet letter from Cousin Letty today. I received such an interesting letter from Brother James today giving an account of his narrow escapes. He is such a bold, noble fellow. All of the boys speak highly of Bev. Whittle.[1]

There is quite a large cavalry encampment on our farm now, 80

---

1. Beverly Kennon Whittle, a boyhood friend of Lucy's brother, John, served as a private in Company C of the 2nd Virginia cavalry and was highly regarded by his superiors. He was wounded at Tom's Brook, 9 September and at Millwood on 22 October 1864. Breckinridge-Preston Papers; *CMH*, p. 430.

men and 200–300 horses, sent to the country to be fattened for service. Lieut. Bassett who is in charge of them is here. He is a pleasant, gentlemanly little fellow. Mary Woodville is such a sweet, interesting child, and talks so prettily—she *is* very pretty, too. Cousin Kate has been quite sick this week. Grove Hill is too dull for her, and for her sake I am glad she is going to Oaklands soon. I have been enjoying my little rabbit this week, keeping him in the house. He is so sweet and squeezable. I have read nothing but the Bible and Butler's sermons. I am going to read *The Rambler*.[2] Mr. McGuire staid here last Sunday and was so interesting. He told me a great deal about Johnson and his writings and was very instructive. Eliza and I are staying in the little room, and have very cozy little times.

Monday, Nov. 2nd, 1863
On Tuesday we all walked down to the shop to see the encampment near the creek. Lieut. Bassett met us and we all came home together. Then Cousin Kate, Lieut. B., and I took a lunch, mounted our horses and took a delightful ride up to Mrs. Ninninger's. We bought some chestnuts, then rode down to Mrs. Bowyer's to tell Mrs. Bowyer about making some hats, and got home about sunset. Little Dorrit tried herself and went splendidly.

Brother Gilmer devotes himself to his mules. I was so much amused at him the other day—Sister Julia was eating a pear, when he came, and exclaimed that she wished she was a mule (to gain more of his attention). He replied that he wished he was a pear (pair). We were telling the Lieut. about the conversation, and he said in such a funny way, "I expect Miss Lucy's husband will wish he was a rabbit." He is so funny and smart—I am charmed with him. He has such a cute little way of saying flattering things. I got a letter from Mrs. Kate Bowyer. She and Lulie have treated us shamefully. I pray God to help me to be charitable and forgiving. All day Friday Cousin K. was packing to go to Oaklands. It was a miserable day, and she was so sweet to me that the thought of separation was unendurable. On Saturday the last day of October

2. *The Rambler* was a periodical written primarily by Samuel Johnson (1709–1784), appearing twice weekly between 1750–1752, and containing essays, character studies, allegories, and criticism.

she left. I never parted with anyone more sorrowfully. On Sunday we all went to hear Mr. McGuire preach. His sermon was the best I ever heard from him. Saw Henry Allen at church.

Monday, Nov. 9th, 1863

This week I have passed very pleasantly nursing the babies and reading Butler's ethical discourses over again, dwelling particularly on those relating to "Resentment" and "Forgiveness of Injuries." I wrote to Cousin Kate and Miss Letty Burwell. On Tuesday the Burnetts left. Wednesday Eliza, sister, and I went to town and brought Jennie Miller home with us. I made some hoarhound candy for Lieut. Bassett and in trying to get it out of the plate cut my hand terribly. It bled so profusely that I almost fainted from exhaustion. We had a molasses stew and pulled candy out in the porch until right late. A Marylander, Capt. White, and a Mr. Carter came on Thursday. Capt. White is a widower on the anxious bench, as Sister Julia says. We all amused ourselves very much at the expense of the two gentlemen. On Friday Jennie Miller, Lieut. Bassett, and I took a charming ride up to Mrs. Ninninger's, got some chestnuts and had a gay time. Jennie is a sweet girl. Saturday we spent reading and talking. I got such a sweet letter from Cousin Kate and Sallie Grattan. Sunday morning, Nov. 8th, Brother G. and Jennie Miller both went away. Rumors of Yankees kept us in a state of excitement. They have whipped our forces and are advancing in this direction.[3] I felt very low-spirited last night. Eliza slept in Sister Julia's room, so I sat up by myself and was miserable. Today I sat in the sitting room and read, *A Strange Story*.[4] I like it very much. It is, indeed, strange and mystical. I got a letter from my dear Cousin Kate. The Lieut. dined at Major Wilson's, and did not get home until right late. I like him so much. Eliza has a very bad sore throat tonight. She is so imprudent.

3. This is probably a reference to the engagement at Droop Mountain, West Virginia, on 6 November 1863 in which the Confederate forces lost 275 men and the Union forces 119. Tactically, the engagement deterred General William W. Averell from destroying a section of the Virginia and Tennessee Railroad. In another raid by General Averell in December, supply lines of the Virginia and Tennessee Railroad were destroyed. *O.R.*, I, 29, Pt. 1, pp. 921, 924, 928; *CMH*, 2, pp. 85–89.

4. *A Strange Story*, published in 1862, was written by Edward George Bulwer-Lytton (1803–1873).

Tuesday, Nov. 17th, 1863

On Tuesday, the 10th, Sister Julia and her retinue, composed of Eliza, Jane, and the babies left, so I have had a very quiet week. Jimmy and I rode on horseback twice together, and Friday evening Lieut. Bassett and I rode up to Foston to invite the ladies to spend Saturday here. We then rode to a high hill, just above Foston, and admired the view from there. There is not an inch of the landscape where you cannot see mountains.

On Saturday the three Miss C.'s [Cabells] came; Miss Marian, who is old, homely and smart, Miss Betty, who is quite pretty and intelligent, and Kate whom I like better than the others. Mrs. and Miss Meredith and Mrs. Figgat came also. We had Sergeant Watkins and the Lieut. for beaux, and had a very funny day. In the evening all the party left except Miss Marian and Kate. At twilight they were in Ma's room, and the Lieut., Emma, and Coalter Logan and I in the parlor. Lieut. B. asked the young ladies to sing some for him, and I really was surprised when they struck up and sang several songs and hymns together very sweetly. At suppertime we all adjourned to the sitting room and there the Miss C.'s and Lieut. B. discussed novels. Our little circle was agreeably added to by the arrival of Brother Lewis, though I was much disappointed not to see Dr. Archer. On Sunday Ma, Miss Marian, Kate and I went to hear Mr. McGuire. As we were coming home we were checked in our progress by a crowd of carriages by the pond near Mrs. Carper's, so we had to wait there until 12 persons were baptized. In the evening the Miss C.'s went home.

I have been busy making a "Marie Stuart" for Eliza.[5] It is the prettiest one I ever saw. Monday morning I knitted constantly and attended to my little rabbit. In the afternoon I sat in the sitting room with Lieut. B. He made himself very interesting, and tried to make me promise to be Mrs. B., but I did not quite do it, though. I do not recognize him as my *fate* though he insists upon it that Providence intended me for him. I miss Eliza and Emma so much. They certainly are the sweetest and noblest of girls.

5. The "Marie Stuart" bonnet was popular from the 1820s to ca. 1870. C. Willett Cunnington, Phyllis Cunnington and Charles Beard, *A Dictionary of English Costume 900–1900*, p. 133.

**It is eleven o'clock,
Saturday, Nov. 21st, 1863**

I am sitting by the open window. The air is mild and the rain is
falling softly and musically. The birds seem to think it is Spring—
they are singing so happily. But I feel very sad and desolate. I
want to write down the events of the last two or three days, but
my mind wanders into the far past. "How oft heart-sick and sore
I've wished I were once more a little child." This will prove a very
memorable week to me. On Wednesday directly after dinner I was
standing on the pavement prepared to mount my horse to take a
ride with Lieut. Bassett when, happening to glance up, I saw Dr.
Archer standing in the front door. I had made the engagement to
ride with Lieut. Bassett and so *had* to do so. I went in and spoke to
Dr. Archer and excused myself. We rode past Foston and then in
sight of Fincastle. When we returned just before supper I went
into the sitting room and tried to be agreeable to the Dr. He
brought me a sweet note from Cousin Kate. We all sat up talking
very pleasantly until 11 o'clock. Dr. Archer is such a perfect
gentleman, and knows so well how to be pleasant to a whole circle.
Thursday morning soon after breakfast Dr. A. and I rode down to
Buchanan to see Eliza. He has been ordered to Charlottesville,
and did not want to leave without telling her goodbye. The day
was so beautiful, and we had a delightful ride. We got there about
1½ o'clock. Sister Julia saw us gallop up to the door, and said she
did not know whether that splendid looking man was the hero of
the novel she is writing, "Earle Hastings," or some real character.
He does look magnificent on horseback, his curls flowing in the
breeze. We staid to dinner and left about 5 o'clock. Though I was
sick, I could not help enjoying the ride by moonlight. First, the
sunset and the mountains were so beautiful, then we had about
two hours of moon and stars. The Dr. discoursed beautifully
upon every subject, especially *poetry* and *love*. The first, I agreed
with him about, but took no interest in the latter subject. I
thought I should have to retire directly we got home, but I got
interested and forgot my fatigue. The Dr. gave me such a
handsome likeness of himself which I shall always prize in
remembrance of the many happy hours we have spent together. I
feel as if I should never see him again.

When we got home I found the Lieut. very much out of spirits,
and I could not do anything to comfort him. Friday at 12 o'clock
Dr. Archer bade us all a sad farewell. I sat all the morning in the
sitting room knitting. After dinner I took a walk with Lieut.
Bassett, a moonlight stroll, and made him very much happier. He
seems determined that I shall marry him and I suppose I might as
well do so. He and I have arranged a key for a cypher
correspondence.[6] After tea, he and Brother Lewis played chess
and poor Brother L. was terribly defeated in each game. I will
write the private parts of my journal now in figures. There is one
thing I must keep the date of—8 57glg5d 60254f 93 485u9
b122599 9h82 w55k & d3 43v5 h86 v5r0 6uch739 9h5 2165 w10 8
43v5d 6r h3u2937. [I engaged myself to Lieut. Bassett this week
and do love him very much—not the same way I loved Mr.
Houston.]

Monday, Nov. 23rd, 1863
I finished Eliza's "Marie Stuart" and wrote to Cousin Kate and to
Mary Wilmer. g39 1 c0ph52 45995r fr36 9h5 485u9. h5 h12 b557
23 2w559 93d10. h5 wr395 65 2uch 1 2w559, fu770 p85c5 3f
p359r0. w5 933k 1 chlr687g r8d5 9h82 5v5787g. 8 w37d5r 8f w5
2h144 5v5r b5 61rr85d. 8 w844 9r0 93 b5 f8r6 87 9h82
57glg56579. [Got a cypher letter from the Lieut. He has been so
sweet today. He wrote me such a sweet, funny piece of poetry. We
took a charming ride this evening. I wonder if we shall ever be
married. I will try to be firm in this engagement.]

Tuesday, Nov. 24th, 1863
It rained today so I spent the morning quietly and dismally until
9h5 485u9 c165. [the Lieut. came.] After dinner the mail came; I
got three letters, sweet, cheering ones from dear Cousin Kate and
Emma, and 1 6329 872u4987g & vu4g5r 375 fr36 4u485
65r8d89h, 3f wh8ch 8 2h144 91k5 73 7398c5, 610 God h54p 65 93
f3rg8v5 5v57 12 8 w3u4d b5 f3rg8v57. 61 219 w89h 65 4195
9378gh9 & 8 934d h5r 9h19 8 r51440 w822h5d 93 61rr0 485u9 B.

---

6. Lucy and Lieutenant Bassett devised the following code: A SOLEMNITY.
[1 23 4 56 7 89 0]

2h5 1dv8252 65 v5r0 pr3p5r40 739 93 61k5 up 60 687d 059, bu9 8
f51r 8 16 d5c8d5d. 8 w82h h5 d8d 739 9h87k 34485 1r73ud 23
pr5990!! 8 w844 pr1825 Dr. 1rch5r 5x9rlv8g17940 f3r h82
b575f89. [a most insulting and vulgar one from Lulie Meredith, of
which I shall take no notice, may God help me to forgive even as I
would be forgiven. Ma sat with me late tonight and I told her that
I really wished to marry Lieut. B. She advised me very properly
not to make up my mind yet, but I fear I am decided. I wish he did
not think Ollie Arnoud so pretty!! I will praise Dr. Archer
extravagantly for his benefit.]

Friday, Dec. 16th, 1863
But for Dr. Holloway's coming on Wednesday I should have had a
pleasant week of it. As it was, I had to entertain him, the most
stupid of mankind. On Wednesday Brother James came, too, with
a slight wound in the face. On Thursday, the 3rd of Dec., while we
were all at breakfast, little Fanny Burwell Woodville entered
upon "this scene of action"—a pretty, dear little thing she is. Dr.
Holloway staid until Sunday. I got my likeness from him and he
gave me a very good-looking picture of himself. Sunday evening I
spent so happily with 9h5 485u9 [the Lieut.]. 8 43v5 h86 b5995r
5v5ro d10. [I love him better every day.] I took several rides on
horseback, one yesterday with Lieut. Bassett. When I got home
Eliza brought me a very funny letter from George, which,
however, I read with some misgivings, and very quickly decided
that it was a quiz written by Lieut. B. It was a perfect imitation of
George's writing and way of expressing himself. Eliza said she
could not be easily quizzed by writing, so I was amused when I
went down this morning to find Eliza in a state of great perplexity
over a note she had just gotten from Miss Marian Cabell, which I
instantly discovered to be a quiz, as I was familiar with Miss M.'s
handwriting. The Lieut. has won all hearts, he is so smart.

Saturday, Dec. 19th, 1863
This has been a week of events. On Sunday Eliza and I went to the
Presbyterian church to attend Major Joe Anderson's funeral.[7]

7. Joseph W. Anderson had been the first captain of the Botetourt Artillery.
Promoted to major in April, 1863, he was killed the next month at the battle of
Champion's Hill, Mississippi. Apparently his body was returned to Virginia for burial.
O.R., I, 24, Pt. 1, p. 318; Breckinridge-Preston Papers.

Sue Jones and her father had come up from Buchanan and came home with us. In the evening Dr. Williams brought one of Papa's old college mates out with him, Capt. Coles of Nelson. Later the same evening Ma and Brother James returned from Avenel—so we had a merry little party. On Monday Mr. Jones left and we kept Sue.

We have had a great Yankee excitement. On Tuesday evening I had Little Dorrit for Sue to ride and Emma and I walked in sight of Fincastle to meet her. Just as we were going down Waxes' hill we met Lieut. B., so I walked home with him. Early Wednesday morning Brother James, Capt. Coles (who is the funniest, dearest old fellow!), Capt. White, and some other gentlemen went on a deer hunt over the mountain. They returned late in the night bringing the news that the Yankees had been within 8 miles of us, had captured 25 of Lieut. Bassett's men and a bridal party. We were in a state of alarm all day. That night we heard they were at Bonsack's and would be in Fincastle in a few hours. Wednesday evening, I shall never forget it—it was not very happy at the time but it is pleasant to remember. We all sat around the fire chatting and Sue read out her poem about the hunters' return which pleased Mr. Coles amazingly as he was the hero. We had several alarms—once a soldier came to see Lieut. Bassett and Brother James went to ask him in. We were certain then that [the] enemy were at the door. A second time there was a quick, suspicious knock, again we thought they had come. Ma positively refused to let any of the gentlemen go to the door. We all besought them earnestly, almost tearfully, to run, and succeeded in getting them to go into the passage where they stood peeping around the corner to see the intruder, who proved to be none other than Capt. White—a very welcome visitor. They all sat some time longer, then Brothers Lewis and James with Capt. White rode up the mountain and slept in a cabin. Lieut. Bassett and Capt. Coles staid in the office. The exiles returned to breakfast.

It rained so on Thursday that the gentlemen staid in the house all day. Brother James and the Lieut. amused themselves drawing illustrations of the night before. After dinner we had a cozy candy stew in the dining room. We sat up until late drawing and talking. Eliza laughed very much about a fish the Lieut. drew in water.

On Friday directly after dinner they all left to go to Craig to see about the Yankees and have not yet returned. So much for the movements of our gallant little army. We await their return with much anxiety.

And now to descend to trivial matters. I got a conceited letter from Rosa Burwell. One funny thing I have forgotten. On Wednesday night Sue and I tried our fortunes. We roasted two eggs, then we took the yolks out and filled the whites with salt and ate them. I know I ate at least a tablespoonful of the horrid stuff. It nauseated me terribly, and I did not dream that any gentleman handed me water. Sue did—a Mr. Richardson was so polite as to offer her some. I read *The Woman in White*;[8] it is very interesting. 8 w82h 60 485u9 w 12 h5r5. 8 6822 h86 21d40. [I wish my Lieut. was here. I miss him sadly.] Sue and I have been sitting up very late talking about matrimony and babies.

Monday, Dec. 21st, 1863

Yesterday, about day-break, Susan came in to awaken me by announcing the fact that Cary and his regiment were coming, and before we could dress there were at least 80 soldiers here—some elegant gentlemen among them. Major Wayt was one of the first and we all liked him very much. Gen. and Col. Imboden[9] and a great many officers sat here some time, and Gens. Imboden's and Fitz Lee's troops camped on the farm to feed. All day the soldiers were coming in. Cary and Brother Gilmer got here about one o'clock and staid an hour. Sue Jones thought Cary the handsomest of our brothers. We heard nothing from Brother James and Lieut. Bassett and felt a little uneasiness about them.

This morning Eliza and Sue went to Buchanan. Aunt Matilda dined here. While we were at dinner Susan came in to tell us that Mr. Tayloe, Mrs. Col. Munford, and Cousin Mattie Adams were here. Mrs. M. has almost lost her beauty. Cousin Mattie is more like me than ever. After supper Brother James and the Lieut. came. I was *so* glad to see them. They did not overtake the enemy

8. *The Woman in White* by William Wilkie Collins (1824–1889), was published in 1860 in *Household Words*.
9. Brigadier General John D. Imboden and Colonel George W. Imboden.

and fear they will get away safely, but the Yankees have lost a great many wagons and horses—that's some comfort. Gen. Imboden seemed very happy about catching them. He is such a splendid looking man.

Tuesday, Dec. 22nd, 1863
Mr. Tayloe and Mrs. Munford left. Cousin Mattie and I sat in the sitting room together all morning. About three o'clock Sister Julia, Eliza, and the babies came. After dinner I sat in the sitting room and had a happy time with Lieut. Bassett. It is the first time we have had any private chat for more than a week! How long! I do not know what I shall do when he goes.

Saturday, Dec. 26th, 1863
On Wednesday Brother Gilmer and Cary came. We are so happy to have three brothers home—I do wish George was here, too. I got such a smart, sweet letter from Sallie. She is the dearest, most charming girl in this world. I wish one of my brothers could win her. On Wednesday Mrs. Logan and Nat spent the day here. In the evening we quizzed Lieut. Bassett. Sister Julia wrote a note directed to Capt. Breckinridge and Lieut. Bassett inviting them to an egg-nog at Maj. Wilson's. He was completely taken in and had decided to go. Thursday we had an egg-nog. Mr. Utz, Nat Logan, and the 5 Cabells came. Mr. Cabell and Miss Sallie gave us some very good music. He plays so well on the violin. I was very sad, however, during all the music and gayety, sadder than I had been for a long time, thinking of the happy Xmas eves long ago when our little band was unbroken; thinking, too, of Johnny's grave over in the moonlight until I longed so to go there and stay beside him. Anything like merriment makes me yearn so intensely for him—even the thought of the joy he now feels does not comfort me. Xmas day we spent very quietly, the only happy part of it to me was the afternoon when Little Emma, Lieut. Bassett, and I walked over to Cedar Hill where I spent last Xmas all alone. How strange it seems to me now that at that time I had never heard of him [Lieut. B.]. I know I dreamed some about the future that day, and never pictured such a person to myself.

Today I played with the babies. Late in the afternoon Brother

James and Lieut. B. returned from Fincastle accompanied by Uncle William. We were so glad to see the dear old fellow. The Lieut. and I consoled ourselves tonight by writing notes to each other.

1864

1

"In Maiden Expectation"

Friday, Jan. 1st, 1864
I spent this New Year's Day very differently from last. Last night
(New Year's Eve) we all sat in the sitting room until about ten
o'clock, then all left except Lieut. B. and me. We sat there talking
until nearly one o'clock. Tonight, though I knew I ought not to, I
sat in the sitting room until very late. I am wearied, would that I
could say truly to death—yes, I want to die—I cannot sleep, and I
feel chilled and miserable. If Eliza would only wake and talk to me
some. It is so cold, that's the reason my hand trembles so. I can't
write. I will read my Bible and say my prayers and then maybe I
shall be happier.

Wednesday, Jan. 6th, 1864
I am sick of this journal. I believe I'll stop it. The—yes, I'll not
write anymore. Farewell, dear Harriet, another, a nearer and
dearer one still has usurped your place. I can think only of that
"one." Maybe when my nearer and dearer one is far away I shall
return to my Harriet, whose gentle bosom has been the recipient
of my joys and sorrows for so long.

Saturday, Jan. 9th, 1864
I must tell you, my dear H., about the manner in which I spent
Friday, the 8th, and some of the events of this day. Yesterday,
soon after breakfast, Eliza, Cousin Mattie, Lieut. B., and I went to
Fincastle. The Lieut. got out at the C. H. [Court House], and we
girls went to call on Jennies Miller and Caldwell. We sat with
them an hour and then went to the C. H. where the dinner was

165

prepared for "Company C." The meeting was opened by prayer
from Mr. Etcheson. Then Uncle Will spoke. He was right much
frightened, but made quite an amusing speech, which was
followed by an address from Mr. Corran, Mr. Radford, Cols.
Munford, Green, James, Tip Griffin and others. Mr. Etcheson
made a very funny speech, a satire upon the "Home Guard."
Brothers James and Gilmer made very concise remarks, but
Brother James' noble, handsome face spoke eloquently enough
for him. About 4 o'clock we all came home. Col. Munford, Lieut.
Walton, Tip Griffin, and Sandy White came home with the boys.
Cary, Tip, and Sandy went to a ball at Woltz's. After the others
retired, I sat some time in the sitting room with Lieut. Bassett and
had a wretched time. I'll tell him some of these days how terribly
he has worried me, sometimes, so much that I have almost sworn
to cut his acquaintance, but *that man* wiles me. If he looks at all
unhappy I can't stand it, and must ever pardon and love him.
Heigho! How I have changed, but I am afraid when his influence
is withdrawn that some miserable reminiscences will make me
dislike him. I wish I could send "Drainsville" to the H.'s
[Houstons]. I do not like to wear it now. The scene at the C. H. on
Friday made me think so sadly of Capt. H. [Houston]. This
morning Lieut. Bassett left. We all miss him right much. I wrote
to Sallie Grattan and read "Fantine."[1] After sunset Cousin Mattie
and I walked up and down the passage for a long while, both very
quiet, both thinking of our sweethearts, I expect. Tonight we
came up early. Uncle Will was very attentive to me tonight,
particularly admired the arrangement of my hair. He said it was
"a fine, flowing mane." Cary went to the dance at Woltz's again.

Saturday, Jan. 16th, 1864

I feel like returning to my old friend tonight, though I have
nothing to relate of any interest, and though I know I shall
destroy this volume very shortly. On last Sunday, Eliza, Cousin
Mattie, the boys and I went to church and heard a very good
sermon from Mr. McGuire. In the afternoon, Mr. M. and four
officials of Jenkins' Brigade came, and this addition to our large
circle so crowded the sitting room that I could not get into the
room. On Monday morning Cousin Mattie and Uncle Will left.

---

1. "Fantine," Book I of Hugo's *Les Misérables*, published in 1862.

We miss them both very much. On Tuesday, soon after breakfast, Eliza and I went to Fincastle and brought Jennies Miller and Caldwell home. They are both sweet, bright girls. They staid until Friday. We had candy stews, horseback rides, and had a very merry, happy time. Cary came out wonderfully, and he and Brother James both seemed to enjoy the girls very much. Mr. and Fanny McCue spent Thursday night here, and we had so much fun laughing about Miss Hale's *feats*. Mr. McCue had just whispered an account of them to Cary, but the girls did not know and were very innocently making allusions to them. Jennie Caldwell and I overheard the whispered conversation, and led Jennie M. on to talk about it until we got into convulsions of laughter. I never saw Cary so amused. But for a few drawbacks, the last month would have been the happiest I have spent since the war began. I have had only one trouble, and that one I hardly think I could dispense with. Let people talk as much as they choose about engagements being happy; my late experience does not increase my faith in the idea. Engagements lead too certainly to matrimony. It is happy to be "in maiden expectation fancy free." I envy girls who are free—they cannot realize the blessedness of it. I hate the idea of marrying. I saw a quotation tonight that expressed my ideas exactly, "The hour of marriage ends the female reign! And we give all we have to buy a chain; Hire men to be our lords, who were our slaves; And bribe our lovers to be perjured knaves. O, how they swear to heaven and the bride, They will be kind to her and none beside; And to themselves, the while in secret swear, They will be kind to everyone but her." Perhaps I am unjust in my opinion of man and too partial to woman. Sometimes I am wild and school-girlish enough to dream of connubial bliss. I am going to try very hard "a gude wife to be," at any rate, and I expect I shall be enabled to endure all the hardships. I feel certain, as if I had a peep into the book of fate, that I shall never marry Lieut. Bassett, not that I shall prove false, but something will prevent it. Maybe *he'll jilt me*! That would be funny. Mamma and Eliza love him so much they would make me remain faithful if I needed any compulsion. I got a letter from him a day or two ago. He had sprained his wrist. I wish he was here so I could make him well.

Brother Gilmer and family left yesterday. Just as I was going to ride yesterday I met Stafford Whittle—I was so glad to see the little fellow. He came to borrow a horse for Bev., and took a very fine colt. Little Dorrit is getting so pretty again. I think her *maiden girth* would meet on her now. She and I came very near having a sad accident when we were up in a woods above Foston. She stepped very badly on the ice, but I happened to be holding the bridle and stuck on.

Wednesday, Jan. 20th, 1864

On Sunday we all went to hear Mr. Grasty preach. He gave us a very severe sermon against dancing. Willie Lewis came and brought us a letter from George. Bob Saunders was shipped. Willie has a furlough of ten days. Mr. Miller and Beverly Whittle came. On Monday Brother James and his company left. On Tuesday Cary and Brother Gilmer went away. I never felt so sad at parting with my brothers. What dear, noble fellows they are! We spent the day very sadly. I read, "Marius"—it is not as beautifully written as "Fantine" and "Cosette."[2] Today I wrote letters and awaited the arrival of the mail, hoping to hear from Mr. Bassett, but I was bitterly disappointed. I felt that my love was freezing and wanted something to keep it alive. I do not know what to think of his not writing. This evening Eliza and I took a delightful ride—I rode Cary's fine, grey charger; Eliza, Little Dorrit. Dr. Lake overtook us as we were coming home. I did not feel very genteel, having no hat on, but did not mind the Dr. much. There is one good thing about being engaged—it makes one so indifferent. Eliza enjoyed her ride intensely and looked so innocent and funny. I have been gay today. I have laughed more than I have done for months. I cannot help thinking that something sad is going to happen.

Monday, Feb. 1st, 1864

I am 21 today! Of age! Independent! I feel right old now. This birthday is much happier than last; all of my brothers are at home. George came last night. He was so discontented at the [Virginia Military] Institute that we all thought it better for him to come home. I wish Emma was here so we could once more have

2. "Cosette," Book II of *Les Misérables.* "Marius," Book III of *Les Misérables.*

a united family. Messrs. Cobb and Watkins called this morning. I
like Mr. C. so much, but Mr. Watkins is not at all attractive. I
have gotten several letters from the Lieut. He wrote a note by Mr.
Watkins directed to Eliza, and today Mr. C. asked her very
politely if he could attend to any commission for her. Jennies
Miller and Caldwell spent last week with us. Cary is desperately
smitten with Jennie C., and I am afraid she is more pleased with
Brother James. Willie Lewis spent a day with us. He is a sweet boy
and so handsome. Jennie Caldwell and I are really in love with
each other. I wish I could love Mr. Bassett as I love her. There was
a mistake made about me by Mother Nature. She gave me a man's
heart. I fall so desperately in love with girls and do not care a
straw for gentlemen.

Wednesday, Feb. 3rd, 1864

I enjoyed today reading some in a very bad book, *Peregrine
Pickle*.[3] It is very funny and interesting, but I cannot bear to read
anything coarse, so I won't finish it. The boys have all gone and
we feel very desolate. I got a very sweet letter from "The Lieut."

Thursday, Feb. 11th, 1864

I have been so occupied all this week that I could not write any.
On last Thursday Mr. Bassett came. I was not very glad to see
him, but soon became reconciled to his presence and we spent a
very happy day. Friday Mamma, Sister, and Sister Julia spent at
Mrs. Logan's and feasted on "calves head." Mr. B. and I quarreled
all the morning but made up in the afternoon. On Sunday we all
went to hear Mr. McGuire preach. Mr. McG. came here to stay
Sunday night, and, as usual, made himself very agreeable. I sat
downstairs until one o'clock entertaining Mr. B. I did not enjoy
staying up so late and resolutely determined not to stay
downstairs anymore after the others retired. On Monday Sister
Julia left and Eliza helped me take care of Mr. B. In spite of my
feeling badly and out of spirits and Mr. B.'s numerous anecdotes
relative to hogs, dogs, cats and other animals, we spent quite a
happy day. That evening after tea we all assembled around the

---

3. *Peregrine Pickle*, a novel written by Tobias George Smollett (1721–1771), was
published in 1751.

table to draw. I was very stern about retiring when the others did, but, unfortunately, destroyed a little lemon-colored verbena "bush" that I had given Mr. B. and thereby incurred his hot displeasure, so I had to stay and appease him. We were so happy and loved each other so much that we *could* not say goodbye until 12 o'clock. I certainly have no reason to, and yet, I do love him better now than I ever did. I believe our difficulties make us love all the better. I did a good many things to worry him—burned all of his letters from me and teased him a great deal. We are so happy now that I am more opposed than ever to marring our happiness by getting married. On Tuesday he left. On Wednesday Sister, Eliza, and I called on the Cabells and had quite a pleasant visit. Our evenings are spent very soberly and sadly. We generally retire before nine. I was *so* sick all last night and have not entirely recovered yet. I read two novels today, *Rinaldo Rinaldini*, and *Darrell Markham*, both very ordinary.[4]

Tuesday, Feb. 23rd, 1864

I have forgotten all about you, dear Harriet. I always tell the truth, though it is sometimes disagreeable. I have fasted so hard that I am stupified. I actually have forgotten the events of the last 12 days. I have indistinct recollections of receiving some letters from Lieut. Bassett and of answering them on dark blue paper. Also, a faint remembrance of having spent a day and night at Mr. Miller's and having a very happy time, of meeting with Dr. Lake and Mr. Caldwell, and of liking Dr. L. very much. I have been a little more industrious and *housekeepy* this week, too. I have crocheted bridle reins and breakfast mats, hemmed some ruffles, and made some ice cream and custard. The Cabells spent a day here. Young John is quite handsome, but not the style I admire; the young ladies I like better than I ever did. Today I felt sick and out of spirits. Mrs. Ninninger came down to see us and brought me some chestnuts and sourkrout. I spent a greater portion of the day with my precious Little Dorrit—George rides her so hard. Cary has written home three times; he is still dreaming of Jennie Caldwell.

4. *Rinaldo Rinaldini*, written by Christian August Vulpius (1762–1827), was published in 1820. *Darrell Markham* or *The Captain of the Vulture* was written in 1863 by Miss Mary Elizabeth Braddon (1837–1915).

Monday, March 7th, 1864

So much has happened since I last wrote. The most startling and tragic event was the *fire*. One day Eliza and George went to Buchanan, and the night they were absent Ma slept with me. About 12 o'clock I was awakened by a terrific shriek in the hall. I started up and in my whole life never experienced such horror as I did when I saw a brilliant light pouring in at the windows. I jumped up, and my first confused thought was that it was Eliza I was sleeping with, and I felt so sorry for her. I put my hand on Ma's shoulder, in a most patronizing way and said, "Don't be frightened, child," and we both rushed violently downstairs, barefooted in our gowns. Ma stopped to awaken Papa, but I ran out on the pavement and found the wood-house a sheet of flame. The wind, blowing tremendously, carried the sparks over the office, and though it and the ice-house caught, they were easily extinguished. If the wind had shifted, the house would have been burnt. 'Twas a terrible night, and for a week I was so nervous I was afraid to look at the window I looked out at first that night.

Mr. John Cabell has been very sociable. On Saturday Eliza was sick, and I was hoping to have a quiet morning when there came a knock at the door, and Mr. C. was announced. I went down to see him very cheerfully, thinking he had come to *call*, but he staid until late Monday evening. I had a good deal of fun, however. He pays such delicate and delightful compliments. I had quite an interesting adventure the other day. I went to ride with George, but I had to get home in time to spend the day at Santilaine, and George said I would not have time to go as far as he had to go, so I had better come home through the meadows. Now, there were two gates to open. I jumped off of Little D. at the first gate and mounted again with great ease, but the next one I came to was just in front of Foston. It required all of the strength of both of my arms to hold it open while Little D. walked through, and confiding implicitly in her sweetness of disposition and good sense, I commanded her to go through. What was my horror when she set off at a full gallop. I watched her for one moment with an agony of suspense, fearing she would go home and leave me, but the dear little creature just wanted to tease me, and ran up to Mr. C.'s stable. John [Cabell] rushed to my assistance, and begged that I would wait and let him escort me home, but I was too much mortified even to be polite. I declined very quickly any assistance from him, but with my own hands led Little D. up to the fence, mounted and galloped off without saying, *"thank ye,"* or *"Good morning."* He said he admired me very much, though, and didn't know how pretty I could look until then. Ma gave me a warning with regard to the charming youth—he paid me too many compliments. He was here this evening and was very funny. Bye the bye, the fellow has unconsciously gotten me into a scrape with Mr. B. I wrote the latter a most innocent account of the day the C.'s spent here and the jealous wretch chose to take offense at it. No *Virginia* gentleman would be so ready to misunderstand or doubt a lady whom he professed to love! I was not angry about it until a second letter I got from him on the subject today. Now I am furious, and if I was not afraid to, would break off our engagement, immediately, and fix my affections upon someone who would have more respect for me. But Ma and Eliza would never forgive me if I were to prove faithless, even with good cause, and I really love the *horrid creature* too much to do anything unkind. He never will know how much sorrow and mortification he has caused me.

On last Thursday Sister and I went to Oaklands. I staid until Saturday and had a happy time with dear Cousin Kate. I saw all of the Tayloes, Cousin Patty Minor, and Cousin Mattie Adams on Friday at church. Rosa T. was very affectionate to me. On Saturday I came home bringing Cary and Mary. Sister went up to the Montgomery Springs. Mary is a dear little thing. Aunt Eliza Gilmer and her two little boys, Patton and Wirt, have been here for a week. Aunt E. is quite sick, had a miscarriage. Her little boys are so sweet and well-reared. I have been enjoying, "Festus," so much.[5] I feel as if I were hearing Dr. Archer talk when I read it. I ride every day. It is the greatest pleasure I have, now.

Oh, could we lift the future's sable shroud!!!

Wednesday, March 23, 1864
I do not feel much interest in my journal now. I have been too

5. "Festus," a poem by Philip James Bailey (1816–1863), was first published in 1839.

low-spirited to care for anything, but I will commemorate a visit from Cousin Emma Carr, Lieut. James Patton and some others. Sister came on last Saturday. She is moving to Powhatan, and has many difficulties to contend with. On last Monday, March 14th, Lieut. Bassett came and staid until Friday, March 18th. While he was here, the Misses Cabell and Mr. and Mrs. Gray spent a day here, and on Wednesday, he and I went to call on the C.'s. Mr. John C. was at home, and regarded Mr. B. with searching eyes. When Mr. C. was here, a few days after, he said his conclusion was that Mr. B. was a splendid fellow, and that I was engaged to him. On Thursday Mr. Bassett and I took such a delightful ride. Selim and Little Dorrit seem to enjoy each other's society very much. I sat up late Thursday night to tell Mr. B. goodbye. He left early Friday morning. About an hour after he left, I ordered Little Dorrit, and taking Annie before me rode beyond Foston. I enjoyed it so much. When I came home Aunt Eliza said she wished I would take her to ride, too, so she got up behind, and we rode to the mill and weighed. I weighed 142, but my riding skirt is very heavy. Mr. B. says he wants me to weigh a great deal, so I do not object to it. Well, when I brought Aunt E. home, Patton insisted upon taking a ride, so I took him nearly to Fincastle. After dinner Joshua sent word that Little D. was very sick. I flew to the stable on the wings of love, and found my darling lying down and, apparently, suffering greatly. I sent directly for Uncle Aaron, who administered asafetida and other physics, but my little one continued very sick. I feel miserable about her. Sister Julia is here, busy making feather flowers. Nannie and Johnny are both lovely. Mary does not stay with me much since Sister came. I expected a letter from Mr. B. today, but was disappointed. I feel very unhappy and sometimes wish—no, I won't say it—Mr. C. is here.

Wednesday, March 30, 1864

On last Thursday Uncle John and his family left. They are so sweet and lovable that we felt very sad at parting with them. All Thursday morning I had to entertain J. J. C. [John J. Cabell], and had a wretched time—he teases me almost to death. After dinner Eliza and I would not go into the sitting room, so he finally departed. On Friday I got a letter from Mr. B. On Saturday I read "Jeamse's Diary," *Legend of the Rhine*, and *Rebecca and Rowena*, by Thackery.[6] I enjoy his kind of wit so much, though he is very hard on women. I am sure he was disappointed in his marriage, but I am sure, if he was unhappy, it was his fault as much as his wife's. I never blame the women; they are all too good for the men. I got another letter from "the Lieut."—a very unusual thing, as the mail does not often come on Saturday. I sat up late that night to answer it. Nannie has been sleeping with me, and has been very restless and sick. She is a dear little creature. On Sunday none of us went to church. I sat in my own room reading until about 12 o'clock, then I sent Josephine to the stable to bring me Little Dorrit. I turned her loose in the yard and staid with her nearly all day. Mr. J. J. C. came in the evening, and brought me such a nice cake of maple sugar. He showed us a good many of his political productions, and Eliza and I laughed at him unmercifully. That night Nannie was too sick to sleep with me, so I felt very sad and lonely. I sat up very late and read over old letters. It made me very mournful. On Monday I knit industriously all the morning. Mrs. Grasty, Mrs. Hudson, Mrs. Spears, and her little daughter spent the day here. I got another letter from Lieut B., a very stern letter. I made him mad by something I wrote, but I like to have a few little quarrels. I agree with the Duke of Buckingham that, "The truest joys they seldom prove, Who free from quarrels live, 'Tis the most tender part of love, Each other to forgive." George is going for my precious old Emma this week. I am pretty crazy to see her. Tuesday I spent knitting and reading and arranging old letters. I got a sweet letter from Jennie Caldwell. On Monday Eliza got a letter from Brother Gilmer which produced great excitement. He said the 2nd Va. had had a skirmish, but had repulsed the enemy; that a ball had struck him just above the left ear, but mashed, and a headache was the only evil consequence; that he found himself surrounded in the enemy's lines, but walked safely through. Sister Julia's countenance frightened me, as she read the letter, and she read it out in great excitement. Papa commended Gilmer's cool bravery, and we all felt so thankful that the ball had mashed. Gilmer's narrow escape was the subject of conversation until the mail came next day. Sister Julia was just

6. "Jeamse's Diary," a short story, was published in *Punch* in 1845–46 and reprinted in *Miscellanies* in 1856. *Legend of the Rhine*, a humorous novel, was published in 1845. *Rebecca and Rowena*, a humorous sequel to Scott's *Ivanhoe*, was published in 1850.

mourning over the dangers which surrounded him when Ma came in and read an account of a snowball battle between a South Carolina Regt. and the 2nd, in which battle Cary led the Regt. and distinguished himself! I got a very long and interesting letter from Cary, and wrote to Jennie Caldwell and Lieut. B.

2

A Tragic Loss

Saturday, April 2nd, 1864
It has been raining drearily all this week. Sister Julia left on Thursday, so I have Eliza, and am almost too happy at owning the precious girl again. I read, *Moss Side*, a sweet, little, Virginia story by Mrs. Terhune.[1] On Friday I knit industriously all day and kept up my spirits with the hope of a letter from Mr. B. I always get one on Friday, but I was doomed to disappointment. I did not know how much I loved him before, and how necessary it is to my happiness to get a letter from him every Friday. Oh, dear! What shall I do when he goes to the army!

Tuesday, April 5th, 1864
Brother Gilmer came today. Sister and all of the little ones continue sick. I have little Mary at night. Poor Sister has a great deal to trouble her, but bears all bravely. She has had much difficulty in moving to Powhatan.

Sunday, April 17th, 1864
Brother Gilmer and Sister Julia have been with us. Nannie and Johnny are lovely children. On Monday, the 11th, I was very sick, fainted twice in the room by myself. Got no letter from Lieut. B., and expected him certainly. On Tuesday I was so confident that he would come that I fixed my hair bewitchingly and stood at the

---

1. *Moss Side*, published in 1857, was written by the American author, Mary Virginia Terhune, under the pseudonym of Marion Harland (1830–1922).

gate all the evening watching for him. Wednesday I got such a sweet letter, which made me still hope, but on Thursday my hopes were blighted by another saying he would wait until he heard of my return from "Sleepy Hollow, Bedford Co." 'Twas a just, but a terribly severe, punishment for a foolish jest. I was perfectly crazy to see him. On Friday Emma and George came. I was so delighted to see the dear girl. Tomorrow I hope my heart will be made happy by the arrival of my beloved. Oh, dear! I do love him so much, I am sorry for it. John Cabell courted Ella Godwin and, to use his own elegant expression, "got kicked." Sunday night Ma, Eliza, Emma, and I went to the graveyard. While I was there I had a [presentiment] that "the Lieut." was come, and was not much surprised when George met us at the stables and told me that somebody wanted to see me. I was *really* glad to see him, for the first time in my life. Brother G. came, too.

Sunday, April 24th, 1864

On last Monday nothing of importance happened. I sat in the sitting room all day, and until 12 o'clock at night talking to Mr. B. Tuesday I felt wretchedly. In the afternoon Brother Gilmer and Jordan Anthony came. In spite of a cold rain I took a ride with Mr. B., and went to Mr. Hinkle's. Wednesday passed the same way, talking all the morning, and riding in the evening. I sat up right late to tell him goodbye. On Thursday morning "Tommy" left. Eliza and Mamma thought I looked very disconsolate all day, but mistook the cause. He isn't coming anymore until Sept. Thursday I felt very sick and laid down nearly all day. I was just debating the propriety of taking a large dose of laudanum when the four Miss C.'s came. On Friday Eliza, Emma, and I went to Buchanan and staid until Saturday. Sister Julia has written such a sweet little poem for the *Southern Field*, called "Arnoldstand."[2] Ma and Eliza went back to Buchanan today. Eliza, Sister Julia, and Brother Gilmer went on to Lynchburg. Ma brought Nannie and Johnny home. I have charge of Johnny, Emma of Nannie. Johnny looks very merry in spite of the absence of his Mamma. E.E.G. and I went to Matilda's wedding last night. It made me feel very serious.

2. *Southern Field and Fireside*, published in Augusta, Georgia, during the 1860s, combined the services of a farm and home journal with those of a literary magazine. Jay B. Hubbell, *The South in American Literature 1607-1900*, p. 523.

Saturday, April 30th, 1864

I have spent this week very quietly and contentedly. Johnny has been a good consolation to me, and has given me scarcely any trouble. I thought he would be very troublesome to wean. On Tuesday Brother Lewis and Col. Norris, a distinguished lawyer of Baltimore, came.[3] Col. N. is one of the most charming men I ever met with; he teases me a great deal, but in so kind a way that I love him all the better for it. I have only gotten two little notes from Tommy since he left. He has been to Lynchburg, but is coming back to Rockbridge. Eliza writes me that she is enjoying herself dreadfully in Lynchburg. I have been riding every morning this week. Yesterday I rode by Foston to invite old Mr. C. and Misses Sallie and Marian to spend the day with us. Mr. J.J.C. met me at the door most cordially. He was ready and equipped to start to Louisiana. I sat half an hour listening to the song of his Iliad of woes, and when I started to leave, he did so, too, and rode home with me. He seems to be a very good friend of mine in spite of my rudeness to him. The 3 C.'s came, and we spent a very pleasant day. Col. Norris and Miss Marian had a very disputatious day of it.

Wednesday, May 5th, 1864

On Sunday Brother Lewis and Col. Norris left. We all went to church. I felt mournful all day, missing the dear Col. On Monday Ma, Sister, Misses Sallie and Betty Cabell spent the day at Mrs. Gray's. I rode soon after breakfast, and came back so much fatigued that I laid down and went to sleep in the parlor. When I waked up I heard a voice in the sitting room, which made me shake in my boots—'twas Dr. Archer's. I smoothed my hair and went in to see him. He looks wretchedly. He took me to task about Lieut. B., having indirectly heard from Cousin Kate the story she chooses to circulate. On Tuesday the weather was so bad we had to stay in the house all day. The Dr. and I were very cold to each other. Today directly after breakfast, we rode over to see Mrs. Gray. He continued to cross-question me about Lieut. B., but I was too cute for him. Just as we sat down to dinner, and I was very

3. Colonel William Henry Norris of Baltimore was a Judge Advocate in the Confederate army. His wife, Mary Norris, had been arrested on 2 March 1862, for disloyal correspondence with a Southern officer. William Wilkins Glenn, *Between North and South*, p. 382.

hungry after my ride of 12 miles, Miss Mary Gray, Jennie Miller, Fanny McCue, and Mary Hudson came. Hardly had I finished kissing them when Aunt Matilda and Letty came, and soon after the 4 Misses Cabell. We spent a very merry evening though my pleasure was dampened by getting no letter from Tommy. I have enjoyed my precious little Johnny so much.

Sunday, May 8th, 1864

On Thursday Sister and her three youngest went to Powhatan. Dr. Archer left for Oaklands. He evidently has designs upon Cousin Letty. I felt very lonely after they all left, but a sweet letter from Tommy consoled me. On Friday George and I took a ride. I then, with Emma's assistance, moved all of the best books out of the library into the sitting room. About 2 o'clock Sister Julia and Eliza came. Sister J. was really distressed to find that Johnny was thoroughly weaned. On Saturday I felt poorly and laid down all day reading, *Macaria*, a novel Sister J. brought me.[4] It is very pedantic and not very interesting at the beginning, but improves.

Saturday, May 21st, 1864

Poor, old journal—it doesn't like Yankee raids. It came so very near being consigned to the flames last Friday (the 13th of May) when we thought the Yanks were coming, but Ma hid it away in the folds of an old dress—and so 'twas left to tell its tale to generations yet unborn. That same Friday was quite an exciting day. Betty McGuire and I took a long walk after wild flowers and when we returned found that some soldiers had brought intelligence that the enemy were at New Castle. We went to work and hid silver and everything of value that could be put away in our room, thinking that the wretches would hold our dormitory sacred. About 30 wagons and 500 horses stopped here, running away from the Yankees, and we feared they would attract them, but Pa persisted in saying there was no danger. We all went to sleep about 12 o'clock. George and his company were ordered to Salem, and Capt. George only returned today, and has to go to Dublin next Thursday.

4. *Macaria* or *Altars of Sacrifice* was a novel published in 1864 by American author, Augusta Jane (Evans) Wilson (1835–1909).

On Sunday we heard that all danger was over and commenced to get out an occasional silver spoon. Our anxiety about our dear brothers was relieved, too, as on Monday everything was so peaceful that we began to think of future happiness, and I ruffled a chemise.

On Tuesday, the 17th, I worked very hard all day, and was right much discomfited at being interrupted by Eliza's exclaiming, "There's a white-faced horse"—and sure enough there was dear Selim and Lieut. B. He staid until Friday the 20th. I did not tell him goodbye. I enjoyed his visit somewhat—enjoyed teasing him about being bald, etc. We are D. V. [*Deo volente*] to be married next September. I do not look forward to that time with much pleasure though I do love him a great deal more than he loves me—more than any selfish, wicked man *can* love—not meaning to insinuate that he is more afflicted with those qualities than all the rest of mankind. He has some qualities that I admire very much. I always wanted to love someone upon whom I could lean, someone to protect me, to be firm for me and help me to do what is right. I am so weak and yielding with those whom I love. It is woman's nature to love in a submissive, trusting way, but it is better and safer to rely altogether upon themselves—poor creatures! God help them! I got a letter from Tommy the day he left, a very smart letter as all of his are.

Sunday, May 29th, 1864

I have been very wretched this week. I have worked a good deal and have done all I could to banish reflection or thought. I wrote to Tommy and got a letter from him. Emma and Betty wrote to him, too, Emma to "disgard" him and Betty to offer her heart in lieu of E.'s.

Yesterday, I drove Emma B. in the buggy, and Eliza rode Little Dorrit to Foston. We were caught in a rain, and I drove so rapidly that we got terribly bespattered with mud. When we got home we found Maggie Glasgow, Mary and Henry Godwin, Jennie Hudson, and Louis and Coalter Logan here. We entertained them all day and sent them home in the evening in the hack.

Mr. Godwin sent us a note by Uncle Phil saying that a Tel.

Dispatch had been sent to Mr. H. M. Bowyer that Brother Gilmer had been wounded and captured. After dark the dispatch came from Brother James. He said that Brother G. was badly wounded on the 24th and left in the enemy's lines. Mamma seems to have no hope, but I cannot help trusting that God will spare him to his poor wife. He is her all. She has no relatives, and I have never seen a more devoted couple than they are. Brother Gilmer was so sweet and gentle when he was at home that I love him better than I ever did. He is such a kind brother and son. Ma went to Buchanan early this morning to bring Sister Julia here. Mr. Bowyer came over and staid with Pa until after dinner. About 7 o'clock Mamma and Sister Julia came and soon afterwards Mr. McGuire. He offered such earnest prayer tonight for Brother G. Ma made me write to Mr. Bassett to ask him to find out something about Brother G. from his friends in Hanover. Poor Sister Julia seems completely broken-hearted and hopeless.

Monday, May 30th, 1864

We have had nothing but bad news today. Mr. and Mrs. Gray called this morning and comforted us somewhat, but after dinner Mr. Cabell brought us a letter enclosing an extract from the *Lynchburg Republican* saying that Cary was mortally wounded on the 25th. We heard no further news from Brother Gilmer, but none of us have any hope of ever seeing him again. Strother came up on the cars with a man just from Richmond who said 'twas believed there that both Brother Gilmer and Cary were killed. George and his company are in Richmond—another source of anxiety. I suppose Brother James has not had time to write.

Thursday, June 2nd, 1864

Yesterday, we got a letter from Brother James written on the 28th. He says he sent the dispatch, as we feared, to prepare us for the worst, and gives an account of the fight. He says: "Gilmer had just been promoted to a Lieutenancy and assigned to the command of Company B. The same day we received orders to go to Charles City Co. where we found the enemy at Kennon's Landing on the river, in a strongly entrenched camp with gunboats and land batteries. We dismounted and made the assault and were repulsed. Gilmer was grazed by a ball on the wrist. We then changed our position and charged again through some obstructions of fallen trees and sharpened limbs. Gilmer pushed on, working his way through these obstructions under heavy fire. He got within 50 yards of the parapet, with only a few men around him, when he was seen to fall, struck somewhere in the body. It was impossible for him to be brought off from that place, every man near him being either killed or wounded. I was told he did not speak after he fell and I have no hope that we shall ever see him again."[5]

At first, we thought we would not tell Sister Julia, but I came upstairs and told Eliza to go to Ma, and when she came back Sister Julia just looked at her face and with an agonizing shriek fell down. She told them not to tell her, that she knew what we had heard. I pray God I shall never witness such a heart-rending scene again. Today she looks as if she had had a long illness, so pale and wasted, and just lies still moaning, and takes no notice of a thing except little Johnny. Poor Mamma! She has to think so much of Sister Julia that she has but little time to think of her own loss. He was a greater comfort to her than any of her children. He was always so loving and confiding. All have given up any hope of ever seeing my dear brother again, but I cannot despair.

I wrote to Sister, Brother James, and Mr. B. today, and sent a copy of Brother J.'s letter to Mr. Gray. Cary is safe and unhurt.[6]

Sunday night, June 5th, 1864
We have no further news of Brother Gilmer. Got a letter from Col. Munford today, who writes as if he was certainly killed. I cannot realize that I shall never see my noble, kind brother again. We heard from dear George yesterday. He is camped near Richmond. Poor boy, his ambition was to be in the service so he might be able to tell his grandchildren that he fought for our

5. Peachy Gilmer Breckinridge was promoted to acting Captain of Company C of the 2nd Virginia Cavalry. He was killed at Fort Kennon on 24 May 1864, during operations on the James River, having mounted the parapet when he fell. His body was never recovered. H. B. McClellan, *Life and Campaigns of J.E.B. Stuart*, pp. 426–29; Breckinridge-Preston Papers.
6. Of the five Breckinridge brothers, only Cary and George survived the war. James Breckinridge died in the closing weeks of the war at the Battle of Five Forks on 1 April 1865.

liberties. I feel so hopeless tonight. If I could only believe, as some, that peace may be declared in a few months, there would be some light in the darkness, but I can see no prospect for it. So many hearths will be desolate when we do have peace that many a heart's bitter cry will be, "The light hath risen but shineth not on me." Dear Sister Julia, there is little left to make life desirable to her. If God should take my love! Oh, it is too terrible a thought. I have thought so constantly and so hopefully about him today. It makes me tremble to find how entirely my happiness in this life depends upon him. I got a sweet letter from Sallie this evening. She wrote very sadly, and congratulated me upon the safety of my brothers. She has lost so many friends. I will write to Tommy tomorrow and beg him to come to see us. I have such sad forebodings with regard to our marriage. I feel that it can never be, but I am despondent now—"They view life's future through a tear, who know the past too well." Miss Sallie and Miss M. Cabell, Mrs. Read, and Mr. Isaac Cocke called yesterday. I love the Cabells; they are so kind and sympathizing. Friday was the 2nd anniversary of my precious Johnny's death. I feel all the sorrow for his death afresh. I love him so dearly, my noble, gentle boy.

3

Yankees and Deserters

Thursday, June 16th, 1864
How much excitement we have had in the last few days. On last
Sunday, we heard the Yankees were in Buchanan and on Monday
that they were this side of the town.[1] So, we commenced secreting
things in servants' houses, etc. I basted all of Tommy's letters in
my flannel skirt. On Tuesday morning, Emma and I buried the
silver. I, acting as gravedigger, had a hard time. After dinner, the
Yankees were really in Fincastle. Pa wouldn't believe and rode off
to town. Some of the servants, standing on a hill near the town,
saw Pa ride up to the Yankees and soon after heard them
shooting, and ran home to tell us that they had killed him. I never
had such a shock in my life, but soon the brave Breckinridge
blood rushed to my cheeks. I stopped fainting and started to town
to see Papa when someone exclaimed, "There he comes," and,
sure enough, he had slipped off from them. I was so burdened
with letters, journal, silver, etc., that I don't think I could have
walked far.

On Wednesday, we found ten of our servant men had departed,

1. This is a reference to the forces of General David Hunter. Grant had dispatched
Hunter to the Shenandoah as a diversionary force while the Army of the Potomac
moved toward Richmond. In his march up the Valley toward Lynchburg, Hunter left a
path of destruction and desolation. His troops arrived in Buchanan from Lexington
where he had burned Virginia Military Institute and a number of private residences,
including the home of Governor Letcher. Later in the Valley campaign, General Philip
H. Sheridan completed the devastation begun by Hunter. So effective were Sheridan's
efforts that he claimed a "crow in traversing the Valley would be obliged to carry his
rations." A.L. Long, *Memoirs of Robert E. Lee*, pp. 352–68; *CMH*, pp. 476–515.

two Bookers, Mat, Peter, Willis, Jim, Jasper, Anderson, Goen, and dear little Josh—the older servants made him go. In the evening Mr. Stratton came and interrupted Nelson in the midst of his preparations for leaving by taking him off to Franklin. I shall always be grateful to Mr. S. for taking Little Dorrit away. He came again today and took some more horses, and brought the cheering news that we have whipped the enemy at Lynchburg.[2] If we could only hear from the boys. The last mail we got had a letter about Brother Gilmer. Gen. F. Lee promised to send a flag of truce to Butler to find something about him, and Mr. William Robinson said he would write to the Commissioner for the exchange of prisoners and try to find out something. Oh! dear, I want to hear from Tommy.

Sunday, June 19th, 1864

The Yankees have come at last! Yesterday we were feeling very secure, sitting at dinner, when Mr. Stratton came to tell us they were in town. He started a few horses off and rode towards Fincastle. I stood at the gate watching and presently 5 men came galloping down the road. Mr. S. was among them. He waved his handkerchief and called out, "They are coming." We all stood in the yard watching for them and soon saw some rushing down the lane. We all sat down very composedly. I had my little pet bird, feeding him when they came up. They insisted that we had rebels hid in the house, but were tolerably decent in their behavior. We got one fright. One impudent scamp rode up and took out a bottle and pointed to me and told me to fill it with brandy. I told him very calmly that we had none. Whereupon, he said, "Damn you, I'll make you fill it," and started to get off his horse. I was not at all alarmed, but Sister Julia saw my danger, and ran down the steps and just prayed the other men to defend us. They then tried to quiet the wretch, but he insisted in going upstairs, in cellar, and everywhere to find some. Three of them were fearfully insolent. Oh God! What horrible things men are. Eliza wrote to

2. This news was a bit premature. The engagement at Lynchburg took place on 17–18 June 1864. Perhaps the reference was to the arrival of the forces of General John C. Breckinridge on 15 June to organize the defense of Lynchburg against the combined forces of Generals Hunter, Crook, and Averell. Breckinridge was reinforced on 17 June by the forces of General Jubal Early. Long, *Memoirs*, pp. 352–68; *CMH*, pp. 475–515; *O.R.*, I, 37, Pt. 1, p. 98; *O.R.*, I, 40, Pt. 2, p. 658.

the officer in command, Col. Putnam of Ohio,[3] and begged his protection. He came up and proved to be as disgusting as any of the men. He said, "Are all you ladies married? I suppose you find some difficulty in getting rebel husbands. We'll send some Yankees here to marry you and that's the way to build up the Union again." He left a guard here who were kind, but Oh! so insulting in their way of talking about the South. 'Twas hard to stand. I just sat in the door and listen to them and prayed more fervently than I ever had done that our brave, noble Southerners would be successful. They talked dreadfully about the negroes and said they took no care of them whatever. There were about 300 with them, the women and children just dropped, so tired and dirty, and yet 8 more of ours joined them—Lydia and her two children, Dolly, Ferdinand, Albert, Lovelace, and Randal. They took all of our horses and cattle. Joshua took them where that horrid Capt. Frank had hidden some shells near Foston. They threatened to burn the house and scared the poor girls nearly to death. About 9 o'clock all were gone, but they said Averell's [Maj. Gen. W. W., U.S.A.] men are just the other side of Fincastle and will be here tonight. The Yankees told us that Lee had been terribly whipped by Grant, but I don't believe it. I think they are retreating now from Lynchburg, though they boast so loudly.[4] Papa behaved so beautifully. Some who staid in the house last night were looking for something to read and got Brother Gilmer's card. They admired it very much and told Ma that that was a noble son of hers, but Mamma said he had laid down his life in defense of Virginia. I feel so uneasy about Mr. Stratton, he is so rash. We fear that Strother, Nelson and Charles were either captured or killed.

Sister Julia was nearly distracted about Johnny today. Virginia

3. David Putnam was Colonel of the 152nd Ohio National Guard, a regiment of hundred-day volunteers. This short term of service may account, in part, for the lack of discipline evidenced by some of the soldiers. *O.R.*, I, 37, Pt. 1, p. 682.

4. On 17 June 1864, Lieutenant General Jubal Early arrived at Lynchburg with reinforcements to take command of the Confederate forces. He established a line of battle three miles west of Lynchburg, and on 18 June repulsed Major General David Hunter's forces. Hunter retreated later that night with Early in pursuit by the next morning. Early had saved Lynchburg, but had failed to crush Hunter's forces. Long, *Memoirs*, pp. 352–68; *CMH*, pp. 476–515.

had taken him to the Yankee camp and we were afraid she had been carried off with the little fellow. Sister Julia appealed to them to send him back and soon we saw Jesse bringing him up. When Mr. Ross and Benjy Nany went away they said to Emma and me that they hoped we would meet under happier circumstances some of these days. I hope so, too. The happy circumstances to me would be their capture, though Benjy Nany was very kind. My sakes, how Mr. Ross abused the "Nabobs" of the South. He said that they had no nobility in the North, that no man there was ashamed to use the implements of industry, and that his wife was too much of a lady ever to let a nigger enter her house. I had forgotten entirely that this was Sunday, went downstairs and picked up my knitting. Some Yankees came into the hall and asked me some questions. Sister Julia said she was thinking how admirably coolly I was acting and whispered to Eliza to get her knitting, too, but presently Ma came up and reminded me that it was Sunday and took it away. Mat and Joshua [slaves] behaved shamefully, showing where the horses and cattle were. Both started away on mules but were soon dismounted and had to walk. Poor women had to march along almost naked and starved.

Monday, June 20th, 1864

No Yankees today, on the contrary, very cheering news from all quarters. Mr. Stratton came last night and reported Strother and the others safe. I am so grateful to him. We heard firing in town today and hoped some of our Southern troops had come, but not a soul has passed since, so we can hear no intelligence. Uncle Phil told us that Amanda and family were ready and packed to go, but finding that they had to walk, determined to remain at home. She had all of our clothes, so I am glad she did not go. I guessed those brutes were retreating—from their boasting. They said Lynchburg was burnt to the ground. When some of the nasty things said they would marry Southern girls, I felt so tempted to tell them that I had heard it was their plan to marry our negroes and that they were the only Southern girls they would ever get. I'll remember Col. Putnam!

Sunday, June 26th, 1864

This has been a week of alternate fear and joy. There was some fighting near Salem on Tuesday, and on Wednesday, Mr. Stratton told us Ransom's command would pass here, but they came so late that we had given them up. We were looking from the garret window when the first detachment passed and waved our kerchiefs. I had none, and had to use my underskirt. Then we went out in the yard and waved. The soldiers cheered and some galloped down the lane. I reckon 100 came to get ice water, milk, bread and meat. Two elegant young officers came, a Lieut. Whiting who knew Brother Gilmer and Johnny at the University, and I don't remember the other's name. A great many left their broken-down horses here and some are still here. Sister Julia commenced telling the soldiers how the Yankees took all her jewelry and silver when such a dear, little fellow named Saunders, from Wood County, handed her a pair of her sugar tongs he had captured the day before. He refused to take any reward, but Mamma gave him a nice, new pair of cloth pants. Gen.'s Ransom, Jones, McCausland and Imboden passed here but we did not see any of them. After all, Hunter has escaped. Gen. Early couldn't catch him.[5]

Willis and Booker have returned, thoroughly disgusted with Yanks. A Mr. Givens has been staying here for three or four days, who is so much like Tommy. Mr. Stratton went over in the direction of the Sweet Springs to see if he could recover any of our property. Mr. Cocke who is here said he had heard that all of our negroes had gone and our house had been burned. Several persons say that the Yankees had sworn to burn Grove Hill. Miss Sallie and Kate Cabell spent Friday here. They had a right hard time. The Yanks found Capt. Frank's shells near Foston, and threatened to burn the house. Miss Marian was very spunky.

Sunday night, July 3rd, 1864

My mind has been so full of doubts of God's goodness and mercy

5. On 20 June 1864, General Early, in pursuit of General Hunter, engaged in a skirmish at Liberty (Bedford City). On 21 June Imboden's cavalry attacked Hunter's rear and left flank at Big Lick and forced his retreat through Salem. Ransom's cavalry converged by way of Buchanan and attacked Hunter's line of retreat. On the night of 21 June the Valley army encamped near Big Lick. Ramseur established headquarters at Botetourt Springs, and Ransom's cavalry marched to the vicinity of Fincastle. Hunter's forces retreated into West Virginia. *CMH*, 3, pp. 476–79.

today. I have been so sinful. I read my Bible and prayed, but the light of God's countenance was withdrawn from me. I longed so for some kind friend or pastor to guide and comfort me. Tonight I sat out here in the hall, writing all my sinful doubts, when I heard Eliza and Sister Julia talking about Jesus and the quietness and loveliness of his character until my heart was touched—and I believed. Sorrows are too apt to harden my heart against God, yet, I must reconcile myself to a life of hardship and sorrow. We are born to suffer and to die. The gloomy state of the country depresses me so terribly I cannot see the dawn of peace that I hear some people talk about. They cry, "Peace, peace, when there is no peace." But I *will* try to believe that "He doeth all things well." I had three letters from Tommy this week and wrote one to him. We have heard from George several times. No news yet from dear, Brother Gilmer. I still hope he may recover.

It is late. I must stop writing and go to bed. I have been sick in bed all day.

Tuesday, July 5, 1864

These are truly terrible times! Mr. Stratton, who has been staying with us for some time, left today. I felt very sad parting with him for we are so helpless without anybody but Papa to protect us.

This evening Dolly told Ma and us that she wanted to put us on our guard. She said that Saturday evening the children at the quarters raised a cry at seeing a man clothed in red in the woods, and she slipped out to see what it was. Sure enough, in the ravine back of the quarters she saw the man with red velvet pants braided up the sides and a blue jacket on. He beckoned to her and she went to him. He asked her to get him something to eat and to induce her to do so said he was a Yankee. He asked her all about this house—where we kept our silver and how a man could get into the house, said if there were no soldiers here he could manage for he was not afraid of the old man. Dolly told him we generally had some gentlemen at the house. He said he knew the young ladies were in the habit of walking in the graveyard woods and that if he caught them there he would do something terrible, etc., etc. As Dolly turned to go to her house and get the bread for him he looked at her very hard and told her if he was betrayed he

189

would know who did it and would kill her. The thing makes me a little uneasy. I know he is not a Yankee but a deserter. When Walker took the supper Dolly had fixed he [the deserter] whistled and four men joined him. Mr. Rudisill [Judge John G.] had heard of them, but has taken no measures to capture them. I wish we did have a man here, but we have no one to protect us and must look only to Providence.

Saturday, July 9th, 1864

This week has passed very quietly—no visitors except Mr. Olivar Bierne and three Godwins. On Monday night about 12 o'clock I was roused from sleep by a pistol shot near the house. I acknowledge I am nervous about *that man.* I jumped up and went into Sister Julia's room and found her and Eliza up, and soon Ma joined us. We talked and consulted for an hour, then the others went to bed, but I stood by the window watching all night and heard two more shots. The next day Ma wrote to Mr. Godwin about it, and Maj. Morland sent out some men to capture our enemies.

Thursday I got a letter from Sallie Grattan saying there was no longer any doubt about Brother Gilmer's death. I cannot witness poor Sister Julia's suffering, and feel resigned to his death. I also got letters from Jennie Caldwell and Mr. B. On Friday I occupied my time writing to Sallie, Page, Jennie C., Cousin Kate, Mr. B., and Cousin Letty Rives. Eliza and Nannie went to Buchanan today. Jimmy Woodville came on Wednesday—Emma is teaching him, Little Emma, and Betty regularly.

Col. and Mrs. Pendleton returned with Eliza. Mrs. Pendleton gave us very gloomy descriptions of the shelling of Buchanan and the Yankee outrages there—a captain drew his sword on her and said that he wished she was a man that he might put a bullet through her. I can't take much interest in anything. When Mrs. Pendleton was here last summer we were so happy, but now— "Joy no longer soothes or cheers—And even hope that threw a moment's sparkle o'er our tears, Is dimmed and vanished too"—

Wednesday, July 20th, 1864

Receiving the mail is the only important event of our lives now.

Until last night, we had not gotten it for a week. We sat up very late waiting for Strother, and then all went to bed except me. I was in such a state of feverish suspense and anxiety that I could not lie down, but leaned out of the window listening for him. Late in the night he came. There were letters from Cary, George, Miss Deborah, Aunt Belle, Mary Wilmer, Mrs. Yancey, Sallie Grattan, and Mr. B. Cary says he saw an extract from a Northern paper telling of some paper taken from the dead body of Major Breckinridge—so there's no longer a ray of hope left us.[6] Poor Sister Julia! Her sad face nearly breaks my heart. I never witnessed such hopeless sorrow.

George writes cheerfully—he is near Richmond. Dear boy, I wish he could come home. Miss Deborah says she and Mr. Woodbridge will select four sick soldiers to send up for us to take care of. Mary says Annie has been very sick. Mamma intends sending the hack to bring them here. Sallie's letter was so sweet and loving. She and Lizzie will be here in two or three weeks. I have to write six or seven letters today—it is sad work to me.

Saturday, July 23rd, 1864

Last night I got three letters from Tommy, one very kind, two rather harsh. It is well for me that, but no, I won't be so misanthropic. I also got a very kind note from Mr. Gray. Today Eliza and I rode early this morning to Foston. I wrote to Mr. B. and Miss Fannie Burwell, to the latter to ask her to do some shopping for me. I then hemstitched a handkerchief. I feel terribly low-spirited this evening. I have felt like crying all day. I believe it's owing partly to Tommy's being angry with me. I must

---

6. Ironically, the body of Gilmer Breckinridge was mistaken for that of his brother, Cary (both of whom were engaged in the James River operations on 24 May), as revealed in the following reports: in a report from Major General Benjamin F. Butler to Secretary of War E. M. Stanton, 25 May 1864-11 a.m., the following is noted, "Gen. Fitzhugh Lee abandoned his attack on our post on Wilson's Wharf during the night, having completely failed. He lost 20 killed, whom he left on the ground in our hands. Among these is reported Maj. Breckinridge, of the Second Virginia Cavalry." Another report of the action at Wilson's Wharf, Virginia, on 25 May 1864 from Brigadier General Edward A. Wild to Captain Solon A. Carter, Acting Assistant Adjutant General, contains the following comment, "A memorandum book in the pocket of the dead major (Cary Breckinridge, Sixth Virginia Cavalry), gives on pages 41 and 42. . . ." *O.R.*, I, 36, Pt. 2, pp. 269-71.

be harder and more indifferent, it will never do to let so slight a cause bring tears.

Things look brighter for the Confederacy, but I fear peace is very distant, yet. I shall not delude myself with any vain hopes. When "war does flap his dusky wings" and depart the God-scourged South, I shall be totally unprepared for such bliss.

4

"Brother Charlie"

Friday, July 29th, 1864

The principal event of this week was the arrival of my beloved
Tommy. The dear fellow had actually stolen away from his camp,
risking the censure of his superior officers, and ridden 80 miles in
two days to see me. I must really try to love him better. I believe I
am never out of his thoughts. He is going to return to the army as
soon as he leaves here. He is *glad* to go—I am *sorry* I must lose
him. Heigho! I wish I knew what three months more will bring
forth. The week has been a succession of morning and evening
rides, sometimes with Eliza and sometimes with Tommy; and of
"tête-à-têtes," generally with the latter. "T." and I have made
some pledges and agreements that I shall note down here to
prevent forgetting them. First, we have agreed never to quarrel
again either by letter or word of mouth. An excellent idea! There
is no pleasure to me in either receiving or inflicting pain. Second,
we agreed to marry at anytime after the 1st of September next
when the Lieut. could get leave of absence to reach Grove Hill. I
wonder if my dear, old Harriet will last 'til that time. Tommy does
not know, can never know, how dearly I love him, how terribly I
miss him; and to think that he could have staid until tomorrow if I
had begged. Oh! Tommy, that was cruel. I came upstairs, directly
after I had kissed Selim, to read, and then I felt too sad and sick to
do anything but lie down and think of my good, sweet love. We
rode together this morning. I wonder how long it will be before I
see him again. It will be more than a week before I can hear from
Tommy. How can I stand it!

193

Tuesday, August 2nd, 1864

On Saturday I did nothing but miss my darling and hemstitch handkerchiefs. On Sunday I read all of his letters, etc. Monday I read Dr. Dogget's discourse on the War. Annie, Mary, Uncle Wilmer, Breck and George came. Breck is splendid. Eliza and I continue our rides. I got a long letter from Kate tonight. She enclosed her likeness. I cannot think, cannot write about anything but Tommy, so I might as well stop this odious journal. I told Annie and Mary my secret. They are so delighted, and are such sweet, pretty girls.

Thursday, August 11th, 1864

On last Wednesday, August 3rd, Mr. Willie Wise and Mr. Charlie Kellterwell came. Mr. W. is a tolerably good-looking, agreeable young man. He lost his foot in the first battle near Petersburg and suffers very much. Mr. K. is from Baltimore. I never saw anyone who excited such kind and friendly interest. He is remarkably handsome, has very polished and delightful manners, is smart and so good. He has consumption and suffers a great deal. It makes me so sad to see one so bright and charming and know how short his life will be. Sometimes I look at him when he is unconscious of being observed, and his eyes are full of tears—he is so homesick. All the girls are desperate about him, but he does not show any preference. Willie Lewis has been here, too, so the young folks are well-provided with beaux. I have gotten two letters from Tommy and answered them immediately. They are such sweet letters. I have scarcely time to write any. Mr. W. keeps me playing chess and I have to sit downstairs with the gentlemen. On Monday Cousin Letty Rives, Cousin Alice Robertson, and Cousin Stanhope Breckinridge came. They left yesterday. Cousin Stanny reminded me of Brother Gilmer. Annie, Mr. Kellterwell, Emma, and I have taken some very pleasant evening rides. Yesterday dear, little Johnny was christened. It was a touching scene. Directly after prayers he was brought in. Pa, Ma, Sister Julia, and Cousin Letty stood for him. He is called after both of our dear brothers, John Gilmer.

Saturday, Sept. 10th, 1864
Morning

It has been so long since I wrote, and so much has transpired, that

194

I scarcely know where to begin. We have had a houseful for the last month. First, Miss Deborah and Lilly Pendleton came, then Nannie Munford, Mrs. Carrie and Willie Yancey, Capt. Henry A. Wise, and Sallie Grattan. The girls have had a gay time, flirting with the beaux, riding about, hunting squirrels and spending the days out in the woods. Nannie Munford caught Wm. Wise away from me, but his brother showed a preference for me, and that was some comfort. Henry is greatly superior to W. [William]; he is very intelligent and so respectful to ladies, a thing rarely met with now-a-days. Sallie is sweeter than ever, and so smart. I have heard quite regularly from Tommy. He writes such good, sweet letters. Mr. Kellterwell remains as fascinating as ever. Everybody who has seen him has fallen victim to his charms. I never saw such a man! I little thought when he first came what sorrow he would cause me. At first, we used to cut at each other all the time and I thought he did not like me, but for the last ten days I observed a change in him, yet he was capricious, seeming to like me one day and perfectly indifferent the next. Day before yesterday Mr. Wise (horrid wretch!) called me in the parlor and said, "Miss Lucy, I want to put you on your guard. Don't you see K. wants to flirt with you? He declared his intention of doing so and made me vow not to tell." I thought a man who would break a vow would feel no scruples in making a story, and his mean jealousy of Mr. K. has made him tell me a great many untruths. But still, I was hurt and could not help showing a little difference in my manner to Mr. K. He observed it and asked me the cause, and I could not explain for fear of implicating Mr. Wise. Something in Mr. K.'s manner convinced me he was in earnest in his love, and I rather avoided him after that interview. Yesterday all of the girls went out walking and he and I happened to be left alone. I made him read the Bible to me and determined not to have anything like a *love* talk, but somehow we got to discussing jealousy. I said I never loved anyone enough to be jealous, that in truth, I did not love any one person so entirely as to care much what they thought of me. He took my hand before I knew it and said so tenderly it nearly killed me, "Lucy, don't you love me." I answered very coolly in the negative and then he told me how very dearly he loved me and asked me if I had nothing to give in return. I told him that I could only give him my warmest friendship. He said so sadly, "Oh! Lucy, I hoped for so much and

195

must be content to receive so little. I asked for bread and you gave me a stone." We talked a long while, and he was so sweet and gentle that I felt—I can't say what I felt. I told him what Mr. Wise had said and he said, "Lucy, do you think I could look into your eyes and tell you a story," and then he declared that it was all a fabrication of Mr. W.'s. He looks so sad and is, yet, so gentle and kindly that it nearly breaks my heart. No one in the house suspects he is in love with me and I will do all I can to keep it secret. I wrote to Tommy yesterday and told him, as I thought it was my duty. I know he will be angry with me. Cary came home a week ago, wounded through the leg. He suffers a good deal, but is recovering as rapidly as we could desire.[1]

Saturday night

Today I was alone in the parlor when Mr. K. came in and renewed his conversation of yesterday. I discarded him very decidedly and he became very angry. I was terribly distressed at his accusing me of flirting, for it was unjust. I was going to explain and fix up affairs when Mr. Yancey came in and begged me to play chess, so Mr. K. rushed off to the office, very bitter in his feelings. He came around to dinner looking very pale and disconsolate. Mr. Wise called attention to it saying, "Doesn't K. look as if he had been crying." In our conversation in the morning Mr. K. in his anger said something about going away, so I felt uneasy; the thought of driving him off being very painful. After dinner my fears were confirmed by seeing Ralph saddled, standing at the office. I remembered that his hat was in the house, and so took my position by it. Presently, he came in. I said in a trembling tone, "Mr. K. come in the parlor a moment," so he came and sat down by me. Then I asked him to forgive me and feel kindly toward me. He took my hand and asked me very sweetly to pardon his harshness to me in the morning. I said, "Well, now you are my friend," and he answered very warmly, "Yes, Lucy, your true friend." Then he gave me a letter from a friend of his, a Miss Julia Hamner, to read, and got up to go to town. He wanted to tease me and said, "Goodbye, I am going to Lynchburg." I don't think a

1. Cary was wounded in an engagement at Opequon Creek, West Virginia, on 29 August 1864.

196

face could express greater agony and despair than mine until he stooped down and kissed my hand and said he was not going, sure enough. After he went Sallie and I took a drive in the buggy, and he came out to meet us. I thought he was discarded, and that he took it so sweetly, but I find he is not. He still has some hope and I avoid him carefully, and have not had another private conversation. I told Eliza about it, and she advises me not to tell Ma, but Ma suspects and makes my life perfectly wretched by her scoldings. On Sunday all went to church except me. I went over to the graveyard and sat by Johnny's grave until one o'clock, reading the prayer book and praying as I never prayed before for guidance and strength. In the afternoon I was so despairing that I took 30 or 40 drops of laudanum to make me forget my woes, but it only excited me. That night Sallie, Mr. K., and I took a long walk by moonlight. On Monday I saw Mr. K. only a few minutes, and he would not give me an opportunity to be decided, but persisted in calling me his *friend* and talking the sweetest love that ever reached a susceptible maiden's ear. Sallie and I brought the Daniels out from Fincastle. Gussie and Lottie are very sweet girls. On Tuesday Sallie and I walked home with Gussie and Lottie, and sat in the woods talking for an hour. Came home and went to bed where I remained until after tea. Wednesday, Sept. 15th, Sallie and I did not go down until 11 o'clock. Mary brought us our breakfast. When we went down Mr. K. joined us and we walked to Cedar Hill where we sat for an hour or two. The rest of the morning I spent writing to Miss Oden, in answer to a letter received yesterday telling me of dear Kate's death,[2] and to George, Lilly Pendleton, Emma Woodville, Cousin Mat Adams, and to Tommy. I asked the latter not to insist upon my being married this winter as I want to go to Pittsylvania. I walked over to see Jane and her infant. The child is very pretty and *fair*. This evening we walked to the garden. On returning we saw all of Sister's chairs on the pavement, ready to be packed. I sat down on a big rocking chair, and all followed my example, so we ate supper there and had a very merry time. Then we went into the parlor, where we sat in the dark telling ghost stories, and played a game

2. Miss Oden had been a governess at Grove Hill, 1857–1858, and her sister, Kate, had been Lucy's friend and fellow-classmate.

that amused us intensely. Sallie was sitting in my lap and a very
peculiar dream she had a week ago was, to me, sadly realized, but I
almost killed myself laughing over it. When we all got up to go
out, Mr. K. detained me a moment to beg me to talk to him some
tomorrow. When I staid upstairs yesterday, he sent me such a
sweet, little note—oh! dear, how can I help loving such a man. *No
one* could resist his charms.

Tuesday, Sept. 28th, 1864

I must write a few circumstances that have transpired in the last
two weeks. First, I must commemorate my most serious quarrel
with Tommy. I heard something that made me very miserable,
and I wrote him a right short, unloving letter, and told him I
would be absent all winter; whereupon, he wrote me that our
engagement was at an end. A day afterwards he relented and
wrote a very sweet letter to which I replied rather coolly. Now, I
must commemorate another quarrel. Mr. Kellterwell and I have
been rather distant, and the other day he said something very
unkind and rude, and made me cry, but for the last two or three
days we have been very friendly.

We have had some delightful rides. One day Mr. K., Mr. W.,
Annie, Mary, and Emma went to Mr. Gray's and spent the
morning. Sallie and I mounted Fan and L. D. [Little Dorrit] and
rode to the top of the mountain, returned by Foston and after a
little begging decided to dine there. We had a charming day, came
home after sunset, and really almost died laughing. Then we had
cold, rainy days, and sat around the fire chatting and having a
merry, gay time. One day Annie, Sallie, Charlie Utz, C.
Kellterwell, and I rode up the mountains to a Mr. Clapsaddle's
and got some damsons and apples. Mr. K. is the very best comic
actor I ever saw and just keeps us in a roar of laughter all the time.
He is one of the wittiest and most humorous persons I ever saw.
Then another amusement after we came up is to eat fruit and
dance. One night we all dressed in party dresses and sat in the
parlor until eleven and after we came up, I got a jew's-harp and
played while Annie, Mary and Sallie put on pants and danced. We
kept up the romp until one o'clock. Then the others left and Sallie
and I read our Bibles and loved each other and talked about my

darling Tommy. I have gotten to fixing my hair so beautifully with braids. Ella Godwin, Hall and Jennie Miller and the Cabells spent yesterday here and worked on my cuffs and collars. This evening the Daniels came. Annie, Mary, Emma, Charlie, and I supped in the side porch. Dear Charlie, he was so sweet. Mrs. Ninninger brought me a bowl of damson butter which Sallie and Mr. K. enjoyed extremely. Mr. K. looks so sad at leaving us all. Gussie and Lottie are such sweet girls. We had real coffee for supper, and Mr. K. enjoyed my cup very much. Annie looked so pretty tonight. I sat in my dear, old Emma's lap and could hardly make up my mind to leave her. Cary is getting so much brighter and sweeter.

Monday, Oct. 4th, 1864

On Wednesday, Sept. 29th, I got up early, fixed my hair prettily, put on my beautiful new alpaca, and went down to breakfast. Sallie and the girls were not ready. Immediately after breakfast I went to the front door to tell Uncle Phil something, and coming by the parlor saw Mr. K. alone in there. He beckoned me in and I had a sweet farewell talk. He seems to love me dearly as a *friend*. When I turned to leave the room, he took my hand and looked so sweetly at me and said, "Now, Lucy, you will think of me as a brother and write to me as such." I promised and he kissed my hand with such a fervent, "God bless you!" I then got into the buggy with Sallie. Annie, Mary, and the gentlemen rode in the hack, and Charlie on horseback. We left the sweet shades of Grove Hill in the distance. Sallie and I stopped at Mr. Godwin's to get an umbrella as it was raining. Mr. K. begged me to ride part of the way with him, so when we got to Amsterdam Mr. K. got into the buggy; we had a very sweet time, and ratified our engagement of everlasting *friendship*! He gave me some very fatherly advice— told me not to flirt any, to try to live more earnestly and more for others. When we got to the depot we found we had three hours to wait, so Sallie took us to a house of one of her friends, Mr. James Alfred James. Misses Mary and Belle James received us with the warmest cordiality, and I felt that I had known them always. They kissed and petted me so. We then got on the train. Nannie Munford met us. We had a very funny trip down. Mr. Wirt Harrison was on the cars. He is a great wag and kept us laughing.

We went through a tunnel and Sallie and I had a heap of fun!!!
Oh! dear!!!! We got to Lynchburg after dark. Mr. Yancey had a
hack and took Annie, Mary, and Mr. Wise to his house. Spot
Payne met Sallie and me and we went to Mr. David Payne's. Mr.
and Mrs. Payne were very kind and nice, but Ella—"gracious
alive," she is horrid. Sallie and I slept in a room to ourselves.

The next morning early I walked down to the depot to see Sallie
and Lizzie Grattan off. Then I took up my baggage and trodded
back to Mr. Payne's with Ella. Then I sat in their library and
longed to go to Mr. Yancey's. I got really homesick and heartsick.
At length, however, I heard a quick footstep I knew, and ran out
to welcome Mr. K. He took me up to Mr. Yancey's and I was so
delighted to get there, and they petted me so, that I made a goose
of myself and cried. I then dressed and went down in the porch
where Mr. K. was sitting. He introduced Lieut. Virginius Rhodes
to me—an elder brother of Gen. Robert R. who was killed about 2
weeks ago.[3] The Lieut. is the most interesting man I ever saw. I
really fell in love with him. Capt. Wise was there, but Charlie told
me not to encourage him, so I was very cool. He came very near to
crisis, however, and begged me to allow him to write to me.
Charlie told me not to do it, and I refused decidedly, thereby
distressing the poor fellow very much. He seemed very earnest in
his admiration. He could not tear himself away, so staid all night.
After tea Mr. K. and I sat in the porch and had a very pleasant
time until Capt. Wise, Annie, Mary, and all followed. We sat out
there until one o'clock then retired. At four in the morning we all
got up. Mr. W. and H. Wise, Charlies Utz and K. accompanied us
to the cars. Capt. Wise took advantage of an opportunity for a
tête-à-tête, and expressed great surprise at my course. Then they
all told us goodbye. Mr. K. lingered after the others. My heart was
almost breaking, but I am unfortunate enough to see something
ludicrous in everything. His eyes were full of tears (so were
mine); he shook hands with me, then putting my hand in his left
one and containing it all the while, shook Mary's, then Annie's,

---

3. Virginius H. Rodes served on his brother's staff. Robert Emmett Rodes, a former
professor at Virginia Military Institute, was promoted to Major-General on 7 May
1863. He was killed in the battle of Winchester on 19 Sept. 1864. *O.R.*, I, 43, Pt. 1,
p. 574; Jon L. Wakelyn, *Biographical Dictionary of the Confederacy*, p. 372.

and stood holding Annie's and mine as if he could not tear himself away. Mary was the most wretched mortal I ever saw and said in the most agonized manner, "Oh! Give me one hand," and took a piece of Annie's. And so we stood until the car commenced to move and I told him to go. He looked at us all, his eyes running over, and in a choking voice, and so fervently said, "God bless you!," and tore himself away. That's the last we saw of our "Brother Charlie."

The cars were deserted with very few on. The conductor was very attentive, and we really had a merry time, and talked of nothing but Charlie. We got to Lovingston [Nelson County, Virginia] where Uncle Harmer's carriage met us. We had a rough but rather pleasant ride. We got to Soldier's Joy to dinner. Aunt B. [Belle] and Uncle H. were very kind, but we missed Charlie, and felt sad at first. On Sunday Annie, Mary, and I wrote letters. I wrote to Ma, Eliza, Sister, Nannie Munford, Carrie, and Sallie. Annie and Mary wrote to Charlie. We spent the evening sitting around the fire in our beautiful bedroom recalling everything *he* ever did or said. But *I think* of my old Tommy and long so to hear from him. Tonight I got so wretched thinking of him that I could not refrain from writing him a note. My love for Charlie does not interfere with what I feel for Tommy—they are so different. Charlie is so bright and beautiful, no one can resist his charms. "He is a light that never can shine but once on life's dull stream!"

5

Soldier's Joy

We have been having a really pleasant time. On last Wednesday
Annie, Mary and I went down to the canal and got into a little
boat. We were just going to push off when an old Mr. Jake advised
us to get someone to go with us, so we sent for Tommy and Sam
and rowed down a mile or two. We returned in gay spirits and
after tea Aunt Belle played for us and we danced until we were
completely exhausted. On the 4th Lewis Walker came home. He
is a very handsome boy and I think a good deal like dear John was.
He is so affectionate and bright. On the 8th Aunt Eliza, Uncle
John and old Mrs. Patton came. They had heard of Col. George
P.'s death, and Mrs. Patton is going to Goochland.[1] Aunt Eliza
and Uncle John left for Pittsylvania today. On the 8th the
convocation commenced. We went over to New Market to
church, and heard a fine sermon from Mr. Phil Slaughter. Miss
Deborah was there and I was introduced to about 50 Cabells!
They all begged me to go home with them and I was almost torn to
pieces, but we dined at Mr. Mayo Cabell's. The bride, Mrs. Alice
Cabell, was there. She is beautiful. I like Mrs. Caroline C. so
much, and her daughters are quite pleasant. Mr. Wm. Cabell, a
young widower, is charming. They all want me to catch him, but I

1. Colonel George S. Patton, of the Twenty-second Virginia Regiment, and a
graduate of the Virginia Military Institute, was left in the hands of the enemy, mortally
wounded in the Battle of Winchester on 19 Sept. 1864. *O.R.*, I, 43, Pt. 1, p. 597.
Colonel Patton, whose commission as a Brigadier General arrived several days after his
death, was the grandfather of General George Smith Patton, Jr., of World War II fame.

am satisfied with Tommy. I got a letter from Tommy, very sweet and loving, asking me to renew our engagement, but I declined doing so yet awhile. On Sunday I was aroused early to get a letter from dear Mr. Kellterwell. He wrote six pages, and so affectionately. I really believe he is a good friend. Annie says he loves me more than I deserve; if he loves me *at all* it is more than I deserve! We are expecting him here every day. He said he would come to see us before going to Maryland. Dear, little fellow, I do love him as much as it is possible to love a friend. We went to church and heard two fine sermons from Mr. Slaughter. Mr. Washington Cabell seemed crazy with delight at seeing me. All his family overwhelmed me with caresses and took me to Annie Cabell's to dine. Mary Cabell was at church—she is beautiful. Her mother, Mrs. Margaret, wrote me a very cordial invitation to pay her a visit, which I, as affectionately, declined. I got a long letter from Sallie today. She is so sweet! I got such a nice letter from Little Emma, also one from Sister. On Monday I wrote to Tommy, Charlie, Sallie, Ma, Sister, and Sister Julia. Aunt Belle and all are so sweet and affectionate to us. Cousin Mag Pryor came on Saturday. I love her very much.

Tuesday, Oct. 18th, 1864

I got such a sweet, scolding letter from my dear Charlie today, which I replied to, immediately. I took it to the P. O. myself. The Cabells have been very attentive and we have had a nice time. I feel that Charlie is coming tomorrow.

Wednesday, Oct. 19th, 1864

Aunt Belle gave a dinner party for Alice Cabell. We were wishing so earnestly that Mr. Kellterwell would come to enjoy the magnificent dinner. About two o'clock Sam came up to me and whispered, "Mr. K. has come." I just flew out to the door and there he was, looking so handsome in his new uniform—dear, little scamp! After dinner they all danced until after dark.

Friday, Oct. 21st, 1864

Yesterday Mary, Annie, Mr. K., Lewis and I went to Union Hill and had a very gay time. We danced until one that night and played all sorts of games. They are tiresome people to me, though we staid all night and all today. We were so glad to get back to Soldier's Joy!! I got a letter from T.

Tuesday, Oct. 25th, 1864

Today I mounted Aunt Isabel's old, gray mare and rode with Tommy and Uncle Harmer to Union Hill. I felt very miserable for I knew Charlie was going the next day, but I had promised Alice C. to go with her and spend the day at Mr. Wash Cabell's. We spent a cold, wretched day. I found Tommy and the gray mare awaiting me at Union Hill, and had a pleasant ride home by starlight. They all seemed delighted to see me. I never had so much hugging and kissing in my life! We four Annie, Mary, Charlie, and Lucy sat in the sitting room by ourselves until 2 o'clock and were so happy. I made Mr. K. promise to stay and go with us to Sister's.

Thursday, Oct. 27th, 1864

Yesterday I wrote to Tommy. Bless his dear heart. Aunt Belle says I must marry him this winter. I think I shall. Mrs. Pink Bolling Cabell came to invite us to dine with her today. At three o'clock through a heavy rain we four went to Liberty Hall. I never saw such an elegant dinner. All of the Union Hill C's were there and the widower and Lieut. Richard Bolling.[2] We came home after dark and had such a nice time all together in the carriage. Charlie seems to love me more than ever. Tomorrow is our last day at Soldier's Joy. They all seem sorry to give us up.

Friday, Oct. 28th, 1864

The Mayo Cabells came to tell us goodbye. I wrote a great many letters and got a long one from Sallie. I must pack up now to leave at 12 tonight.

Monday, Oct. 31st, 1864

We left S. J. Friday night and took the boat about 1 o'clock. We were so happy and had such a delightful trip. Dear Charlie was so sweet and kind. A Mrs. Diamond, on the boat, asked me if he was

2. Richard M. Bolling was a Second Lieutenant in Company G of the 24th Virginia Cavalry regiment. He was on furlough recuperating from wounds received on 7 Oct. 1864. *CSR-Va.*, Roll 174.

my brother, he was so much like me. Aunt Belle put up a most delicious repast for us and we ate cakes and apples all the way. We got to the landing about 9 o'clock, a very dark night. We had to wait there on the bank of the canal, feeling right helpless, until Mr. K. succeeded in getting four or five servants to carry our trunks. We walked a mile and then were ferried across the river. We were terribly put out at finding that Sister had not sent for us, but one of the servants showed us the way to a Mrs. Whitlock's. After waiting in the cold an hour, she let us stay all night. Her daughters, Alice and Addie, very sentimental young ladies, were very kind and attentive, especially to Mr. K. He is so smart. It really astonished me to see how perfectly he knew how to get on with everyone. We sent a note to Sister to let her know of our arrival, and about 2 o'clock Sunday, Seldon came for us. We had a very sweet ride and got here to dinner. Everything looked so sweet and pretty in Sister's parlor, and she was very sweet and cordial. Mary is beautiful and Fanny is the loveliest, gentlest little thing I ever saw. When Sister took the girls in the chamber I lingered a moment in the parlor to say some sweet words of welcome to Charlie. He seemed to feel uneasy and de trop. I could not help being affectionate to him.

6

"The Days That Are No More!"

Woodside-Wednesday, Nov. 9th, 1864
I have been too busy writing letters, talking to Charlie and playing
with the children to write any. I have gotten two sweet, smart
letters from Tommy, one from Sallie, and some from home; I
have written a dozen. Annie and Mary seem to enjoy Woodside
very much and so did Charlie, for he intended leaving on
Wednesday and staid until the following Tuesday. Oh! dear, we
four were so happy together. I used to have such sweet talks with
Charlie in the front porch at night, and we took such sweet walks.
It almost killed me to part with him. The last day he was here we
were alone all day nearly, and that night we had a long
conversation in the porch and both of us wept. We walked up and
down the pavement for a long while reviewing the past and
trembling for the future. If I had not been engaged to Tommy I
should have married Charlie. He loves me with such a pure, holy
love. I think he is the purest man I ever saw, and his character has
made me feel more kindly toward the male sex than I did some
time ago. God bless him! We all four sat around the parlor fire
holding hands until 2 o'clock, and then went into the porch to say
goodbye. He kissed Mary and held Annie's and my hands for ten
minutes. I saw that he *could* not leave *us*, so led him out to his
horse. He held my hand in both of his and with a trembling voice
said, "God only knows, Lucy, how I love you. Remember my
love!" and I did—oh! me—I felt a great deal. Yesterday we all
wrote him a poem called, "A Feller in Distress," and sent it to
him.

One night my hair was down, so I took a lock and fixed it like a moustache, and commenced talking like a young gentleman and courting Miss Charlotte, as I called Mr. K. Annie was so taken with the thing that she joined in and we burlesqued the gents, and Mr. K., the ladies, and really were very smart and funny. The picture represents A. thrown back in a chair with a very mournful expression, a pipe turned upside down in one hand, a cigar in her mouth, a broken bottle, a goblet and tobacco bag on the table, and her foot on a book, *The Reveries of a Bachelor*. It was splendidly done! I must commemorate one of Annie's and my fast doings while at S. J. It makes Mr. K. sick to smoke at night, and yet he will do it, so one night I took his pipe of tobacco in my room, and to make the girls laugh I smoked two pipes. I smoked until I dropped out of the chair unconscious. One day Annie and I took a strong toddy and were so *drunk* that we could not walk. Annie became very much flushed and excited, but I was as pale as a ghost and could scarcely open my eyes. Mr. K. said he was ashamed of us. It was the day that Cousin Mattie Duke came, and she looked perfectly horrified. I did not sew much after Charlie came. I knit some socks for him and for Walker and stitched a few collars and cuffs. I have missed him so much that I have been really sick. It nearly breaks my heart to go into the parlor and see the mirrors that have reflected so often his dear face. They reflect nothing but sorrow when I look at them now, and the rocking chair that he and I used to have such races for every day, and the pavement he used to promenade, and his seat at table—oh! dear, I thought Tommy had all of my heart, but Charlie has a very large portion and I scarcely know sometimes which piece to follow! I wish Tommy loved me as Charlie does. Tommy's is such a—I don't know what sort of love, but, to tell the truth, I never could love anyone as much as I do my own, dear, old Tommy.

Annie is very sick with diphtheria, poor darling! She has to suffer a great deal for so young a person. How good and merciful God is to me in everything, and I make such a poor return! On Sunday we had such a sweet walk to church. The church is situated in a beautiful forest. I never saw such a refined, elegant-looking congregation, and they have delightful music. Mr. Powell, the preacher, is a charming man. His wife called to see us yesterday.

207

As we were walking home on Sunday, Annie riding Pet, Mr. Dabney's carriage overtook us, and he insisted on sending us home. I would much rather have walked with Charlie.

Friday, Nov. 11th, 1864

Mary and I cleaned up our room. I read the Bible to Annie, made a collar, stitched a pair of cuffs, and then walked to Emanuel Church to meet Sallie. I was disappointed, though, and returned to the house, ate dinner, took my sewing down in the front porch, and waited for the mail boy. He came and brought me three letters; a long one from Eliza, who is the purest and sweetest of mortals, one from Sallie saying she could not come and expressing her distress at my engaging myself to Mr. K. (which I never even dreamed of), and one from my own, dear Tommy. His letter was a very short, disconsolate affair, and he enclosed five nice envelopes. Poor dear! I think he is jealous and worried at my having a nice time. I shall write him a long, sweet letter tomorrow. Annie is much better. I have been so bad and funny tonight, taking off married ladies and saying all sorts of wild things until I made the poor little thing shake her feeble sides laughing. I'll make Tommy laugh next winter. How I do want to see him! I cannot help having some misgivings about my marriage. We won't be happy—he is too jealous and suspicious, and I too prone to play upon such feelings. Fanny McCue has a daughter. How funny it is for *her* to be a mother. If Gen. Young doesn't let Tommy come to my wedding I'll, I'll "tap him a nugget!!!!" It is so much more pleasant to stay engaged. "Hard is the lot of man, to be lured by the meteor of romance; only to be snared and to sink in the turbid mudpool of [reality]."

Woodside, Wednesday, Nov. 16th, 1864

This is the day appointed for fasting and prayer. Mary, little Emma and I walked to Emanuel and heard a very good sermon from Mr. Powell. As we were coming home we met Charlie going to the C. H. [Court House] for the mail, and, being confident that we should hear from Mr. K., we went with him. But after our walk of six miles we were destined to be bitterly disappointed—there was not a single letter for any member of our household. We could scarcely drag ourselves home—got here just before sunset.

Annie seems much worse today. I feel anxious about Mr. K.—am so afraid some Provost Marshall has taken him up. I wrote yesterday to Eliza, Nannie Munford, Bob Saunders, Mamma, Sallie Grattan, and then Little E. and I wrote to Tommy telling him to come to see us. I made a pretty, little collar for Annie.

Saturday, Nov. 19th, 1864

Yesterday I made two collars, fixed a corsette and washed a good many things, and was proceeding to iron when Charlie came and told me that a lady said I must meet her at the church. I put on my hat and flew the mile and a half in ten minutes, and was rewarded by seeing my own, dear Sallie there. We came home and I have done nothing since but enjoy her and knit corsette laces and write long letters to my own Tommy and to Emma. Mary got a letter from Mr. K. He is still at S. J. [Soldier's Joy]. Ma wrote me a very severe note about my being engaged to Mr. K. I do love the little fellow very much, no one could help it, but I have never faltered in my allegiance to Tommy.

Woodside-Saturday, Dec. 3rd, 1864

On Tuesday, the 22nd, Tommy came. About an hour after his arrival Sallie left. Wednesday Mr. Wm. Dabney, the Miles Hobsons, and Miss Jane Willis called. On Thursday I burned all my letters to Mr. Bassett. On Friday Selim threw me and Mr. Bassett left. Soon after he departed Annie, Mary and I started to Richmond. We had a pleasant trip, but met no one at the depot. Fortunately I saw Mr. Woodbridge who escorted us to Cousin Peachy Grattan's, and after they rested he took Annie and Mary to Col. Munford's. On Saturday I called to see Miss Deborah, saw Walker G. there—took him to see the girls. Sunday I went to St. Paul's and spent the day at Col. Munford's. Monday I went all over the town shopping, etc. In the evening the Munfords, Wilmers, Mr. George [illegible], (a friend of Mr. K.'s), Mr. Polk, Col. Whitehead and Mr. Pollard paid a visit. On Tuesday, the same party with some additions met at Col. Munford's. We acted charades and had a pleasant time. On Tuesday in the morning we went to Dr. Blackman's and Minis', and I dined at Col. M.'s. Lewis Walker and Bob Saunders came to see us. Thursday George came—we all had our "cartes visites" taken. Sallie got a letter from Mr. Bassett. I wrote to Mr. K., a letter of six pages which I hope he will appreciate. Early Friday morning A., M., and I started from R. [Richmond]; we had a delightful ride. There was an elegant *full surgeon* who was so polite to me, offered me a seat two or three times—I had given mine to a lady who had a little child—and when I got to the station he helped me off. I felt very sad at parting with Annie and Mary. I told the conductor to take the best possible care of them, and I know that the charming surgeon will help them. I came to the C. H. in Mr. Hague's little wagon with Claude and Mary Willis, there B [illegible] met me with Pet and I flew home, and was delighted to get back. I was so pleased with Miss Charlotte and Mag Lee and Maria and Sallie and Nannie Munford, all lovely and cordial to me. Mary Cabell came to see me and was very sweet. When I got here I found 8 letters for me, three from home—four of our servant men had gone to the Yankees.

Monday, Dec. 12th, 1864

I have spent this week receiving and writing letters. I have written 14 and received 12—two from and to Mr. Bassett and two to Annie and Mary. I fixed all of my dresses, mended my clothes, made a pretty cravat and knit a shirt for Emma. Mrs. Harvey and Miss Helen Blair came to see me. I communed last Sunday at Emanuel. I read a book by John Angell James called, *The Family Monitor*, a very good book in which the duties of husbands and wives are forcibly set-forth.[1] I know I am totally unable to perform my part—for I fear I shall fail in the first requisite. I hope and pray though that my marriage will prove a happier one than I now picture for myself. I *will* strive to do my duty at any rate.

Boiscote-Friday, Dec. 16th, 1864

Yesterday Sister and I went to see Miss Judy Mayo and Mrs. Wash—they are plain people but so kind and good. Old Miss Margaret Mayo gave me a lecture on the subject of matrimony— everybody does—as if *I* won't know how to be a good wife; and all the old folks say so solemnly, "Be sure you *love* the man you

1. John Angell James, a minister and popular writer, published the ninth edition of *Family Monitor* in 1848. Samuel Allibone, *Allibone's Dictionary of Authors*, V. 1, p. 951.

marry with your whole heart, or you will be wretched." Why are they always telling me that. Miss Margaret gave me one very good piece of advice—viz: "To make more effort to keep my husband's love than I ever did to win my lover's."

I find I am a true abolitionist in heart—here I have been crying like a foolish child for the last half hour because I saw Jimmy chasing poor, little Preston all over the yard beating him with a great stick, and Sister not making him stop but actually encouraging him. I never shall forget Viola's expression of suppressed rage—how I felt for her! My blood boiled with indignation. I never saw such a cruel-tempered and wicked child as Jimmy. I guess *my* sons had better not beat a little servant where I am! I am so thankful that all of us have been properly raised and never allowed, when we were children, to scold or strike a servant.

Boiscote-Wednesday, Dec. 21st, 1864

I have been at Grove Hill for the last hour! I was sitting in the large, old chair in the hall—my eyes closed—I was in a sort of trance. I had summoned around me from the depths of the past, the far-scattered members of our dear "World." Again it was seemed we were all in the hall—our "omnibus" as we were wont to call it. Near the door in the rocking chair sat Mr. K., the *bien cheri* of the whole "World"—Mary stood on one side, handing him a yellow pear, on the other side was Annie proffering a bunch of grapes, and looking up I saw Emma "warbling" down the hall with a mint julep, and on the sofa was Lilly Pendleton plaiting him a straw hat, on the step near him was little Nannie showing him her doll babies—and on the purple lounge, work-bag in her lap, sat Sallie G., intent on the stitching of a linen collar *for him also*, and Nannie Munford bringing him "What will he do with it." And I with my *assumed* indifference was filling his pipe from that little purple *Ratcliff* tobacco bag, of which we were all so jealous. And there, too, was "Wisey," with girls all around him, and his "limb" stuck up on the sofa making peach-stone baskets and telling of the many poor victims to his charms—and there was grave, sedate-looking Capt. Wise fixing the chessmen, and insisting on my playing "just one game." Yes, I saw them all. I heard their dear voices, their merry laughs—and looking up to find myself *alone*, and in a low tone and with streaming eyes, I murmur, "Oh! death in life, the days that are no more!"—My life is like a plain, little novel, written by a silly, but practical schoolgirl. I sometimes, of a windy night, pick up this brown-backed novel, which is now somewhat old and worn out, and sit down on the floor near the hearth and read it by firelight. I glance carelessly over some portions—they fail to interest me. Some chapters I scarcely ever read, they are gloomy and filled with accounts of my enemies—those who feigned love and friendship only to deceive and wound me. Others, though they are sad, very sad, are yet sweet to remember, and I read them often and always with a softened, penitent heart. But one of my favorite portions is near the end of the book (God grant it may be!). It is the heroes and heroines of that chapter whom I have had in my heart all day—whose faces and forms I have been recalling with such sadness and regret. That chapter of the last four months is the one I shall read with most pleasure, which makes me happiest to recall and, yet, which puts me into the saddest, most melting mood—the tears will come when I think of it for I fear that this last, beautiful episode, so full of love and joy and poetry to me, will be the last bright one throughout this old volume. Henceforth, for me there will be written only the bitter disappointments, the stern realities, the sore trials of life—for my lot must be the common lot of all. I am shamefully sad today, but this was the day I expected to be at home and the lameness of Sister's horse prevented our going. I wrote to Mr. B., Mamma and Cary, and Little E. and I walked over to the Church to see Mr. Hague and ask him to mail them for me. I have been reading and playing with the little ones and am very contented at Woodside.

Sunday, Dec. 25th, 1864

How different this Xmas from last—and, strange as it may seem, last evening was far more happy than last Xmas eve. I was busy all day fixing a doll for Mary and Sister and I sat up late to fulfill the duties of Santa Claus for him. Today the little ones are so merry and happy—it recalls my young days very vividly. This is the first Xmas I ever spent away from my precious Mamma and Grove Hill, may it be the last! Tonight a trunk of presents came for Sister and the children from home. There never was such a sweet mother as ours. I wish Sister felt it as much as I do, but she did seem very grateful and pleased at Mamma's taking so much trouble for her and the children. It suits me to be here—I am too self-indulgent and spoiled at home. Here I do make a little exertion to make myself agreeable to others and do not spend quite as much idle time. I wonder when I shall go home. I feel right hopeless about it, but I always feel that "whatever is, is right" and so never allow any train of events to trouble me much. I wonder what they are all doing at home today. My philosophy breaks down when I think of them, and with all my heart I wish I were one of the little circle. Last Xmas we were *all* at home except George and Emma. Tommy was there!

Epilogue

Lucy, in spite of her apprehensions, married her Tommy on 28 January 1865, in a quiet ceremony at Grove Hill. The young couple's life together was poignantly brief. On 16 June 1865, five months after their marriage, and just three weeks after the cruel war had departed the "God-scourged South" with the surrender of the last Confederate troops, Lucy died of typhoid fever. Tragically denied the peace and happiness she had longed for, Lucy was buried at the age of twenty-two at Grove Hill beside her beloved brother, John.

After the war, Thomas Jefferson Bassett returned to his home in Brenham, Washington County, Texas, where he later remarried and reared a family. He maintained close ties with his Virginia family for many years.

In a letter to Eliza, dated 22 January 1868, Tommy mentioned that he was having a portrait made of Lucy from a small photograph. Efforts to locate Lucy's portrait, thus far, have been fruitless. In the course of the search, however, some interesting facts have come to light regarding Jefferson Bassett's life after Lucy's death.

Upon his return to Brenham, Tommy and his older brother, Ben, established the Bank of Bassett and Bassett in 1866. The bank operated successfully for almost twenty years, and was finally dissolved in 1881, shortly before Tommy's death.

Tommy and his second wife, Jodie Roberson, had four daughters, one of whom he named after Lucy's mother. His esteem for the Breckinridges was such that he later sent his daughters

215

and nieces to Grove Hill for their education in literature, art, and music.

The surrender of the Confederate forces ended the "cruel war" and also ended life at Grove Hill as Lucy had known it. The longed-for peace brought with it the hardship and struggle of reconstruction as families attempted to restore a degree of normalcy to their lives. The Breckinridge family circle, decimated during the war years, was further diminished by the death of "Papa" Cary Breckinridge in 1867.

Eliza and "Big" Emma remained at home and, with "Mamma," Julia, and Nannie, undertook the education of a number of young ladies in the Grove Hill tradition. Emma Walker maintained her home at Grove Hill until her death in 1893 at the age of eighty-six, having survived all but three of her nine children (Eliza, Cary, and George).

By the turn of the century, the Breckinridge estate, consisting of Grove Hill, Catawba, and some few hundred acres of land, passed into the hands of George's son, Hunter Breckinridge. Grove Hill, in the possession of the Breckinridge family for over one hundred years, was tragically destroyed by fire on 24 October 1909.

Bibliography

Manuscript Sources

Botetourt County Court House Records
    Records of births, marriages, deaths, and wills
        Tax Records, Deed Books, Common Law Order Book, County Court
        Order Book, 1857–1867; Surveyors Record, 1799–1822
    List of Taxable Property within the district of James McClanahan,
        Commissioner of the Revenue of Botetourt for the Years: 1827, 1829,
        1834, 1835, 1840
Duke University, Durham, North Carolina
    Confederate Veteran Papers:
        Papers: 1861–1929, Biography: 1786–1932, Military Campaigns:
        1864–1925, Battles: 1861–1932
    Diary of Major J. D. Ferguson, Adjutant General, General Fitzhugh Lee's
        Division (4 May to 15 October 1864) Thomas T. Munford Division
    Munford-Ellis Family Collection (Thomas T. Munford Division)
        1770–1942
    Thomas T. Munford Papers
    George Newton Wise Papers, 1861–1863
Roanoke Valley Historical Society, Roanoke, Virginia
    Breckinridge-Preston Papers
The University of Virginia, Charlottesville, Virginia
    Francis Walker Gilmer Papers
    Woodville-Breckinridge Papers, 1821–1879

Other Primary Sources

Alexander, Edward Porter. *Military Memoirs of a Confederate.* Bloomington:
    Indiana University Press, 1962.
Anderson, John Q., ed. *Brockenburn, The Journal of Kate Stone, 1861–1868.*
    Baton Rouge: Louisiana State University Press, 1955, 1972.

217

Blackford, L. Minor, ed. *Mine Eyes Have Seen the Glory, The Story of a Virginia Lady, Mary Berkeley Minor Blackford, 1802-1896.* Cambridge: Harvard University Press, 1954.

Booth, Andrew B., comp. *Records of Louisiana Confederate Soldiers and Louisiana Confederate Commands.* New Orleans: Commissioner Louisville Military Records, 1920.

Brown, John Mason, comp. *Memoranda of the Preston Family 1870.* Printed for Private Distribution, Frankfort, Ky., 1870.

Burwell, Letitia. *A Girl's Life in Virginia Before the War.* New York: F.A. Stokes, 1895.

Chesnut, Mary Boykin. *A Diary From Dixie.* Edited by Ben Ames Williams. Boston: Houghton Mifflin, 1905, 1949.

Dawson, Sarah Morgan. *A Confederate Girl's Diary.* Boston and New York: Houghton Mifflin, 1913.

Deming, Henry C. *The Life of Ulysses S. Grant.* Hartford: S.S. Scranton, 1868.

DuPont, Henry A. *The Campaign of 1864 in the Valley of Virginia and the Expedition to Lynchburg.* New York: National Americana Society, 1925.

"Early Days in Fincastle," A Speech Given by Thomas D. Houston, June 20, 1783, from an undated clipping, Fincastle Herald (1869-1879), in a scrapbook of Ann Anthony Robertson owned by James Robertson of Adelphi, Maryland.

Evans, Clement A., ed. *Confederate Military History.* Atlanta: Confederate Publishing, 1899; New York: Thomas Yoseloff, 1962.

Freeman, Douglas Southall, ed. *Lee's Dispatches.* New York and London: G.P. Putnam's, 1915.

Humphreys, A. A. *The Virginia Campaign of 1864-1865.* New York: Scribner's, 1890.

Jackson, Mary Anna Morrison, ed. *Memoirs of Stonewall Jackson.* Louisville: Prentice, 1895.

Johnson, John Lipscomb. *The University Memorial Biographical Sketches of Alumni of the University of Virginia Who Fell in the Confederate War.* Baltimore: Turnbull Brothers, 1871.

Johnson, Robert U. and Buel, Clarence C. *Battles and Leaders of the Civil War.* New York: Century, 1884-1887.

Kelly, James, ed. *The American Catalogue of Books Published in the United States from Jan. 1861 to Jan. 1866.* New York, 1866, 1938.

King, Spencer Bidwell, Jr., ed. *Ebb Tide as Seen Through the Diary of Josephine Clay Habersham, 1863.* Athens: University of Georgia Press, 1958.

————. *The War-Time Journal of a Georgia Girl, Eliza Frances Andrews.* Atlanta: Cherokee Pub. Co., 1976.

Long, A. L. *Memoirs of Robert E. Lee, His Military and Personal History.* New York: J.M. Stoddart, 1887.

McClellan, H. B. *The Life and Campaigns of Major-General J. E. B. Stuart, Commander of the Army of Northern Virginia.* Richmond: Randolph and English, 1885.

McIlwaine, Richard. *Memories of Three Score Years and Ten.* New York: Neale, 1908.

Mosby, John Singleton. *Stuart's Cavalry in the Gettysburg Campaign.* New York: Moffat, Yard, 1908.

New York Times, 15 September 1862, 17 December 1862.

Page, Thomas Nelson. *The Old South, Essays Social and Political.* New York: Scribner's, 1894.

Peck, R. H. *Reminiscences of a Confederate Soldier of Co. C. 2nd Virginia Cavalry.* Fincastle, Va., privately printed, 1913.

Pember, Phoebe Yates. *A Southern Woman's Story, Life in Confederate Richmond.* Edited by Bell I. Wiley. New York: McCowat-Mercer, 1959.

Richmond Enquirer, 11 January 1861; 25 January 1861; 8 February 1861; 16 March 1861.

Robertson, James I., Jr., ed., *James Longstreet, From Manassas to Appomattox.* Bloomington: Indiana University Press, 1960.

Roorback, Orville A., ed. *The Bibliotheca Americana, A Catalogue of American Publications, Oct. 1852 to May 1855.* New York: 1855; O.A. Roorback, Peter Smith, 1938.

Smith, General Francis Henney. *The History of the Virginia Military Institute.* Lynchburg: J.P. Bell, 1912.

U. S. National Archives, comp. *Compiled Service Records of Confederate Soldiers Who Served in Organizations from the State of Virginia.* Microfilm.

United States Slave Census 1850, 1860.

U. S. War Department, comp. *The War of the Rebellion: A Compilation of the Official Records of the Union and Confederate Armies,* Washington: Government Printing Office, 1880–1901.

Von Borcke, Heros. *Memoirs of the Confederate War for Independence.* New York: Lippincott, 1866; Peter Smith, 1938.

Walker, Charles D. *Memorial, Virginia Military Institute. Biographical Sketches of Graduates and Élèves of the Virginia Military Institute who Fell During the War Between the States.* Philadelphia: Lippincott, 1875.

Wallace, Lee A., Jr., comp. *A Guide to Virginia Military Organizations 1861–1865.* Richmond: Virginia Civil War Commission, 1964.

Wise, Barton H. *The Life of Henry A. Wise of Virginia.* New York: Macmillan, 1899.

Secondary Sources

Ahlstrom, Sydney E. *A Religious History of the American People.* New Haven: Yale University Press, 1972.

Alderman, Edwin A.; Harris, Joel Chandler; Kent, Charles W., eds. *Library of Southern Literature.* New Orleans and Atlanta: Martin and Hoyt, 1909–1913.

Allibone, Samuel. *Allibone's Dictionary of Authors.* Philadelphia: Lippincott, 1859.

Ambler, C. H. "The Cleavage Between Eastern and Western Virginia." *American Historical Review* 15 (1910): 762–80.

Baker, Liva. "George Wythe: First Professor of Law and Police at the College of William and Mary." *Virginia Cavalcade* 22 (1973): 31–35.

Ballagh, James C., *A History of Slavery in Virginia*. Baltimore: Johns Hopkins, 1902.

Bergman, Peter M. *The Chronological History of the Negro in America*. New York: Harper and Row, 1969.

Biographical Dictionary of the American Congress 1774–1961. Washington: U. S. Government Printing Office, 1961.

Blanton, Wyndham B. *Medicine in Virginia in the Nineteenth Century*. Richmond: Garrett and Massie, 1933.

Burke, W. J. and Howe, Will D. *American Authors and Books 1640–1940*. New York: Gramercy, 1943.

Cappon, Lester J. *Virginia Newspapers 1821–1935*. New York and London: D. Appleton-Century, 1936.

Cunnington, C. Willett; Cunnington, Phyllis; Beard, Charles, eds. *A Dictionary of English Costume 900–1900*. New York: Barnes & Noble, 1960.

Davis, Burke. *They Called Him Stonewall*. New York: Rinehart, 1954.

Davis, William C. *Breckinridge, Statesman, Soldier, Symbol*. Baton Rouge: Louisiana State University Press, 1974.

Douglas, Henry Kyd. *I Rode With Stonewall*. Chapel Hill: University of North Carolina Press, 1940.

Dunstan, William Edward, III. "The Episcopal Church in the Confederacy." *Virginia Cavalcade* 19 (1970): 5–15.

Dyer, Frederick H. *A Compendium of the War of the Rebellion*. New York: Thomas Yoseleff, 1959.

Forrest, Mary. *Women of the South Distinguished in Literature*. New York: Charles B. Richardson, 1865.

Freeman, Douglas Southall. *Lee's Lieutenants*. New York: Scribner's, 1946.

————. *R. E. Lee, A Biography*. New York: Scribner's, 1962.

Gerrish, Theodore. *The Blue and the Gray*. Portland: Hoyt, Fogg, and Donham, 1883.

Glenn, William Wilkins. *Between North and South*. Rutherford, N.J.: Fairleigh Dickinson University Press, 1976.

Guild, June Purcell. *Black Laws of Virginia, A Summary of the Legislative Acts of Virginia Concerning Negroes from Earliest Times to the Present*. New York: Whittet and Shepperson, 1936, 1969.

Harrison, Lowell. *John Breckinridge, Jeffersonian Republican*. Louisville: Filson Club, 1969.

Hubbell, Jay B. *The South in American Literature, 1607–1900*. Durham: Duke University Press, 1954.

Johnson, Allen, ed. *Dictionary of American Biography*, New York: Scribner's, 1929.

Kegley, F. B. *Kegley's Virginia Frontier*. Roanoke: The Southwest Virginia Historical Society, 1938.

Lyle, Royster, Jr. and Paxton, Matthew W. Jr. "The V.M.I. Barracks." *Virginia Cavalcade* 23 (1974): 14–29.

Munford, Beverley B. *Virginia's Attitude Toward Slavery and Secession*. New York: Longmans, Green, 1909, 1969.

Bibliography

Nevins, Allan; Robertson, James I., Jr.; Wiley, Bell I.; Hubbell, John T., eds. *Civil War Books, A Critical Bibliography.* Baton Rouge: Louisiana State University Press, 1969.

New Catholic Encyclopedia. New York: McGraw-Hill, 1967.

Niederer, Frances J. *The Town of Fincastle, Virginia.* Charlottesville: University Press of Virginia, 1965.

Papashvily, Helen. *All the Happy Endings.* New York: Harper, 1956.

Peterson, Helen Stone. "Francis Gilmer's Mission." *Virginia Cavalcade* 14 (1964): 5-11.

Pond, George E. *The Shenandoah Valley in 1864.* New York: Scribner's, 1883.

Pugh, Anne Reese. *Michelet and His Ideas on Social Reform.* New York: Columbia University Press, 1923.

Reniers, Perceval. *The Springs of Virginia.* Chapel Hill: University of North Carolina Press, 1941.

Ross, Margaret. *Arkansas Gazette, The Early Years 1819-1866.* Little Rock: Arkansas Gazette Foundation, 1969.

Sadleir, Michael. *XIX Century Fiction, A Bibliographical Record.* Vols. I & II, New York: Cooper Square, 1969.

Stephens, Sir Leslie and Lee, Sir Sidney, eds. *Dictionary of National Biography.* London: Humphrey Milford, 1921-1922.

Stevenson, Lionel, *The English Novel,* Boston, 1960.

Stickles, Arndt M. *Simon Bolivar Buckner: Borderland Knight.* Chapel Hill: University of North Carolina Press, 1949.

Stoner, Robert Douthat. *A Seed-Bed of the Republic.* Kingsport: Roanoke Historical Society, 1962.

Stribling, Robert M. *Gettysburg Campaign and Campaigns of 1864 and 1865 in Virginia.* Petersburg, Va.: Franklin, 1905.

Swem, E. G., comp. *Virginia Historical Index,* Roanoke: Virginia Historical Society, 1934-1936.

Turner, Edward Raymond. *The New Market Campaign, May 1864.* Richmond: Whittet and Shepperson, 1912.

Wakelyn, Jon L. *Biographical Dictionary of the Confederacy.* Westport, Conn.: Greenwood, 1977.

Walmsley, James E. "The Change of Secession Sentiment in Virginia in 1861." *American Historical Review* 31 (1925): 82-101.

Walsh, William S. *Heroes and Heroines of Fiction.* Vol. 1. Philadelphia and London: Lippincott, 1914.

Warner, Ezra J. *Generals in Gray: Lives of the Confederate Commanders.* Baton Rouge: Louisiana State University Press, 1959.

_____. *Lives of the Union Commanders.* Baton Rouge: Louisiana State University Press, 1964.

Wentworth, Harold, ed. *American Dialect Dictionary.* New York: Crowell, 1944.

Wiley, Bell I. *Embattled Confederates.* New York: Harper, 1964.

Wise, Jennings C. *The Long Arm of Lee.* New York: Oxford, 1959.

_____. *The Military History of the Virginia Military Institute from 1839–1865.* Lynchburg: J.P. Bell, 1915.

Wooster, Ralph A. *The Secession Conventions of the South.* Princeton: Princeton University Press, 1962.

Wright, Lyle H. *American Fiction, 1851–1875.* San Marino, Calif.: Huntington Library, 1965.

Index

223

Buckner, Cousin Kate, 113

Buckner, Lt. Gen. Simon Bolivar, C.S.A., 123 and n

"Buena Vista," 81

Bullock, Rev. Dr. J. J., 113n

Bullock, Mrs. J. J., 113 and n

Bulwer-Lytton, Edward George, 154n

Burnett, family, 137, 145–46, 154

Burnett, Mrs. Betsy, 137–40, 144, 147, 150

Burnett, Jimmie, 138–39, 148–49

Burnett, Mr. 138, 150

Burnside, Maj. Gen. Ambrose E., U.S.A., 82n

Burwell, family, 103, 144, 152

Burwell, Catherine, 10

Burwell, Miss Fannie, 9, 20–21, 24–27, 30, 32–33, 35–41, 46, 50, 81, 191

Burwell, Letitia (Cousin Letty), 5 and n, 10, 25, 42, 70–76, 79–81, 100, 104, 108, 112, 115, 117–18, 121, 127, 130–31, 147, 152, 154, 179

Burwell, Lucy, 133

Burwell, Mr. Nathaniel, 85

Burwell, Rosa, 10, 55, 70–74, 76–77, 79–83, 87, 93, 96, 98, 100, 102–9, 112, 118–19, 121–22, 124, 133, 160

Burwell, Mr. William of Franklin, 106

Burwell, Mr. and Mrs. William M., 10

Burwell, Mr., 106–7, 109, 111, 132

Burwell, Mrs. 70, 106, 144, 150, 152

"Bushnell's Mountain," 87

Butler, Gen. Benjamin F., U.S.A., 185, 191n

Butler, Bishop Joseph, 54 and n (*see also* Religion, sermons by)

Cabell family, 161, 170, 172–73, 177, 179, 183, 199

Cabell, Mrs. Alice, 202–4

Cabell, Annie, 203

Cabell, Betty, 10, 155, 178

Cabell, Mr. Breckinridge, 10, 133, 139, 150, 161, 178, 181

Cabell, Mrs. Caroline, 202

Cabell, Evelyn, 150

Cabell, John J., 10, 170–71, 173–74, 177–78

Cabell, Kate, 10, 155, 188

Cabell, Mrs. Margaret, 203

Cabell, Marian, 10, 155, 158, 178, 183, 188

Cabell, Mary, 203, 210

Cabell, Mr. Mayo, 202, 204

Cabell, Mrs., 204

Cabell, Mrs. Pink Bolling, 204

Cabell, Sallie, 10, 161, 178, 183, 188

Cabell, Samuel Jordan, 76n

Cabell, Mr. Washington, 203–4

Cabell, Mr. William, 202

Caldwell, Ella, 120

Caldwell, Mr., 170

Caldwell, Sallie, 120

Caldwell, Virginia (Jennie), 8, 165, 167, 169–70, 174–75, 190

Calhoun, John C., 25

Campbell, Bettie, 68, 74

Campbell, Mrs., 80

Caperton, Mr. Allen, 108

Caperton, Dr. and Mrs., 119

The Capitol (prison), 112–13

Carey, Miss Connie, 122

Caroline, Queen, 54n

Carper, Mr., 53

Carper, Mrs., 155

Carr, Cousin Emma, 173

Carr, Col. George, 20, 81

Carrington, Col. Henry A., C.S.A., 127 and n

Carrington, Mrs., 80

Carter, Mr., 154

Carter, Mrs., 113, 138–39, 144

Carter, Capt. Solon A., U.S.A., 191n

Castle Richmond, 37

"Catawba," 4, 114, 121, 127, 133, 216

Catawba Creek, 3

Catawba Mill, 3

Catawba Mountain, 4–5

Catlett family, 141

Catlett, Cousin Bettie, 141–42

"Cato," 94

"Cedar Hill," 197

Cedar Run, Va., 20n

Chambersburg, Pa., 46n; Gen. Stuart's raid, 64n

Charles City County, Va., 181

Charlottesville, Va., 156

Chesnut, Mary Boykin, 6

Chickasaw Bayou, Miss., 94n

Churchman's, 36

Cincinnati, Oh., 42 and n

Clapsaddle, Mr., 198

Clark, Capt. Frank, C.S.A., 70 and n, 72, 76, 79–82, 86, 121, 123, 125, 129–30, 140, 146, 149

Clarke, Johnny, 124

Clothing: tarleton Van Dyke, 30; blue merino, 66; sewing for soldiers, 75–76; bombazine, 93; worsted hoods, 102; "Marie Stuart" bonnet, 155 and n, 157

Index

Cobb, Mr., 169

Cobb, Brig. Gen. Thomas R. R., C.S.A., 82 and n

Cochran, family, 144

Cochran, Cousins Hovie and Nannie, 135

Cochran, Jimmy, 141

Cochran, Cousin Linn, 141

Cochran, Mittie, 141

Cochran, Cousin Willie, 120, 135–37

Cocke, Mr. Isaac, 133, 183, 188

Coles, Miss Agnes, 94

Coles, Capt., 159

Collins, William Wilkie, 160n

Confessions of an English Opium Eater, 122 and n, 123

The Confessions of a Pretty Woman, 60–61, 64, 122

Copeland, family, 115

Copeland, Mr., 132

Corinth, Miss., 59 and n

Corran, Mr., 166

"Cosette," 168 and n

Costume (*see* Clothing)

Couch, Miss Deborah, 9, 37, 39, 41, 43–45, 101, 105, 139–40, 142, 149, 191, 195, 202, 209

Covington, Ky., 42n

Covington, Va., 25, 31

Cowley, Abraham, 93 and n

Craig County, Va., 6, 110n, 126n, 160

Cralle, Mr., 25

Crank, Capt. William H., C.S.A., 111, 117–18 and n, 119

Crenshaw, Dr., 40

Crenshaw, Mr., 135

Crook, Brig. Gen. George, U.S.A., 185n

Cross, Miss, 143

Cullum, Brig. Gen. G. W., U.S.A., 20n

Culpeper, Va., fight at, 107, 143 and n

Cynthiana, Ky., 42n

Dabney, Mr. William, 208–9

Daniels, family, 197, 199

Daniels, Gussie, 197, 199

Darrell Markham or *The Captain of the Vulture*, 170 and n

Davies, family, 104

Davies, Mr. D., 87

Davis, President Jefferson, C.S.A., 110n, 111, 131, 149

Deisher's, 148

Denton, Cpl. James W., C.S.A., 104 and n

DeQuincey, Thomas, 122 and n. 123n

Diamond, Mrs., 204

Diarists (*see* Chesnut, Mary Boykin; Stone, Kate; Andrews, Eliza Frances)

Dickens, Charles, 139n

Dixon, Judge and Mrs., 149

Dogget, Dr., 194

Douglas, 112 and n

Droop Mountain, W. Va., 154n

Dublin, Va., 179

Duffié, Col. Alfred Napoleon Alexander, U.S.A., 113 and n

Duke, Cousin Mattie, 207

Duke of Buckingham, 174

Dunmore, Gov. (John Murray, Earl of), 1

Earle Hastings, 156

Early, Maj. Gen. Jubal Anderson, C.S.A., 125n, 185n, 186n, 188 and n

Edmundson, Mr. William, 41

Education, 2–5, 18, 60–61, 65, 190

Edwards, Jonathan, 10

Eliot, George (pen name of Mary Ann Evans), 37n

Elizabeth City County, Va., 3

Ellett, Dr., 120

Emanuel Church, 208, 210

Emerson, Capt., C.S.A., 149

The English Theater, 93

Episcopal Church, 18, 47, 120, 152

Etcheson, Mr., 166

Ewell, Maj. Gen. Richard S., C.S.A., 36 and n

Fales, Lieut. James M., U.S.A., 109n

Falls, Mr. Robert, 108

The Family Monitor, 210 and n

"Fantine," 166 and n, 168

Federalist Party, 2

"A Feller in Distress," 206

La Femme, 25n

"Festus," 172 and n

Fickett, Nannie, 130

Figgat, Mrs., 155

Fincastle County, Va., 1

Fincastle Express, 125

Fincastle Rifles, 40 and n, 99, 126n

Fincastle, town of, 1–2 and n, 3, 10, 24, 30–31, 35, 45, 67–68, 79–80, 93, 102, 104, 106, 112–13, 116, 127, 130, 136, 148, 150, 156, 159, 162, 165, 167, 173, 185–86, 188n, 197

Fincastle, Viscount, 1

Floyd, Capt., 146

227

Index

Index